MW01670964

Marketplace Disciples

Spiritual Prescriptions for Businesspeople

By Dick Woodward

A Companion Leaders Guide to Marketplace Disciples will be available in the near future, as a tool for discussion around each of the chapters. Please check the MBC page through www.icm.org for this downloadable tool for small group leaders.

icm

Marketplace Disciples:
Spiritual Prescriptions for Businesspeople
is a special publication of
International Cooperating Ministries

Marketplace Disciples

Requests for information should be addressed to:

icm

International Cooperating Ministries
1901 North Armistead Ave.
Hampton, Virginia 23666-4311
www.icm.org

Library of Congress Cataloging-in-Publication Data

Woodward, Dick.
Marketplace Disciples: Spiritual Prescriptions / Dick Woodward

ISBN 978-0-9726606-9-3
1. Religion
2. Christianity

Printed in the United States of America
10 9 8 7 6 5 4

TABLE OF CONTENTS

Foreword

When I first heard Dick's teachings in the late 1970s, I was captivated and immediately knew they would be life-changing … for me and for many others. But what I did not initially realize was the critical connection these teachings had to the *marketplace.* As I experienced Dick's teaching of his Mini Bible College (MBC) to businessmen in a Thursday morning breakfast setting, I saw the transformation that was possible for these businessmen … in terms of their roles and how they could impact other people in the *marketplace.*

After completing the four-year Bible study, I saw an opportunity and wanted others to have access to this life-changing material. Partnering with Trans World Radio, I funded the translation and native language radio broadcasts of MBC in Latin America, China and India. In 1986, while traveling from Hampton, Virginia, to India to evaluate the impact of the radio broadcasts, I realized the desperate need for church buildings, particularly for those who had come to Christ through the study of MBC. Clearly, God had presented me with an opportunity, one He had been grooming me for through many years as a businessman.

I share my experience to point out that God wants us to use our gifts, in whatever form we have received them, including those we apply in the *marketplace.* My wife (We've *now* been married for 70 years!) helped me understand at age 65 this important concept when I was trying to decide whether to direct my energies to the *marketplace* or to ministry. Wisely she told me there were not really two choices, but actually only one, since *it* was *all God's business*!

Dick's book, *Marketplace Disciples*, is his crowning achievement, in that it goes where Dick has never been (the *marketplace*) to teach what God has given him: messages on how we are to conduct our lives. As you read this jewel, ask yourself the three questions Dick tells us to ask whenever reading God's Word: *What does it say*? *What does it mean*? *What does it mean to me*? The answer to the last question will make this book a transforming one in your life as a *marketplace disciple.*

It is our belief that in any business, what you want to achieve should be supported by goals that will lead to that achievement. And as this certainly applies in a business, it also applies in a ministry, or in your *marketplace* situation. In all cases, once goals have been set, they are to be broken down into pieces, with responsibility assigned to determine *who* and *what* it will take to meet each goal. Dick speaks of the biblical importance of many of these applications in this book.

As a fellow *marketplace disciple*, I challenge you to consider what God has been preparing you for through your professional life—and to find a way to put those principles to work for His Kingdom as you witness in the *marketplace.*

I pray Dick's insight into the Word of God and his *marketplace* applications in the following pages will be as much a blessing on your life as it has been on mine.

Dois I. Rosser, Jr.
Founder and Chair Emeritus – ICM

Foreword by Dick Woodward

As a pastor I was called to the marketplace for several reasons. The first reason is that one of the most important things that ever happened to me was a man leading my father to Christ in the trenches and *the shot and shell* of World War I. The impact that had on my life is immeasurable in terms of spiritual perspective and values. I wanted to reach out to other people's fathers the way that man reached out and brought salvation to my father.

Secondly, I was given the extraordinary opportunity for ten years to reach women by having Bible studies on a talk show for women, which were telecast on a large secular TV station. Through those women I was able to reach their husbands by having Bible study breakfasts for men. The women told their husbands about the breakfasts and the men told their wives about the TV Bible studies. Those ten years of ministry to women led to 20 years of breakfast studies for men and convinced me that women reach men and men reach women.

A third reason is that most evangelism takes place today in the marketplace rather than in evangelistic meetings. Nearly everybody has to earn a living and that places them in the marketplace. These realities motivated me to invest 20 years in having breakfast Bible studies for men.

For ten years I had a breakfast in Norfolk, Virginia in the Metropolitan Baseball Park restaurant called *The Diamond Club*. So many attended that breakfast that even very secular men who did not attend church called it "The Thursday Morning Happening," and they attended regularly. I formed relationships with many of them who have become lifelong friends.

In 1979, I was called to another church, which relocated me to Williamsburg, Virginia. After two years, I started two more men's breakfasts, one in Newport News, and one in Williamsburg. At those breakfasts I did not even consider telling businessmen how to run their businesses. I simply shared with them devotional and practical biblical truths that apply in the marketplace. If you read this book as a businessperson, do not expect to hear an experienced businessman telling you how to run your business. Read this book expecting to hear from a pastor who has taught and met with hundreds of businessmen over many decades, sharing biblical truth that applies to the business and personal life of every authentic Marketplace Disciple.

The most important man in my life, alive today, is my partner in ministry, Dois Rosser. He made it possible for me to realize my dream of teaching the whole Word to the whole world. When we met at a breakfast in the late seventies, I never dreamed of telling him how to run his many businesses. The dynamic of our relationship was, and has continued to be, that he found my teaching of the Scripture to be relevant and helpful. In fact, he felt a strong call of God to give my teaching wider circulation. That was the beginning of what we now call *International Cooperating Ministries* and *The Mini Bible College.*

The development of the phenomenal ministry God has given Dois all over the world is written in his book, *The God Who Hung on the Cross.* It tells of a panorama of miracles that have occurred worldwide because a successful, Christ-like business man learned the meaning of the word stewardship. When he was sixty-five years old, Dois experienced a life crisis that led him to do something meaningful with the rest of his life. He has now become an example for so many of how to bring meaning to your life when the culture tells you it is time to retire, play golf and sail your sailboat, or drive your yacht.

Dois brings the principles that made him successful in business into the ministries God gives him. An MBA professor named Ralph Miller told me those business principles have made ICM the best leveraged ministry he has ever seen. As a businessperson you will find Dois' story of how that miracle came together compelling reading. More than 4,500 churches, schools and orphanages have been built or are under construction and a 4-year Bible study curriculum has been translated into over thirty languages. In these two ways his ministry nurtures believers and contributes to the growth of the Church of Jesus Christ all over the world.

I have told the story of this miracle from my perspective in a book entitled *4 Spiritual Secrets*. That book describes how God brought Dois into my life and ministry in answer to the cry of my heart; I was learning some spiritual secrets that both define me and the miracle of our relationship and ministry together.

I now look forward to visiting with you as a pastor, relating some very powerful Scriptures to your life and labors in the marketplace, where God has placed you. Have your Bible with you as you read. Think about having a weekend retreat, a day off or regular quiet times in the early morning that you might read through the chapters of this book with some continuity.

Dick Woodward
Founder and Teacher of Mini Bible College

Chapter One
Called to the Marketplace

In the seventies I attended a meeting where business executives of a major city asked the vice president of a large shipyard to speak to them about why his shipyard was continuously awarded contracts to build aircraft carriers. His company had just been awarded a contract to build a large carrier and the next highest bidder was $38 million above them.

The shipyard vice president informed them that he could answer their question with one word: *apprenticeship*. He explained that a student in a university absorbs information for many weeks and then is asked to show they remember and understand that information. After doing that for four years they are given a degree and declared *educated*. But unless they specialize in something that equips them for a job, they are often educated fools who can't do anything. In the shipyard, however, a person is placed in the classroom for two weeks and then in the shipyard for two weeks, alternating back and forth for the duration of the apprenticeship. After doing that for five years they can build aircraft carriers. That practical application makes *all* the difference!

SO, WHAT IS A DISCIPLE?

Here at the starting gate, I believe it is necessary to define what I mean by marketplace *disciples*. A synonym for discipleship is that word *apprenticeship*. The definition of a *disciple* is "a person who is learning what they are doing and doing what they are learning." Thus, apprenticeship and discipleship are basically the same concept. In this book I address every authentic disciple who works in the marketplace as a business owner and employer, or as an employee.

In chapter 7 of the Gospel of John, Jesus made the claim that His teaching was the teaching of God and not merely the teaching of another Rabbi coming down the pike. He also taught we can prove His is the teaching of God. "If any man will <u>do</u>, he will <u>know</u>" was the heart of what He prescribed. Intellectuals often take the position "When I <u>know</u> I will <u>do</u>." Jesus threw down a gantlet and said to people with that approach to learning, "Oh no! When you <u>do</u> you <u>know</u>!" If you think about it, this is the core meaning of apprenticeship and discipleship.

It is the application of every teaching that sets the apprentice apart from the university student. It is while the apprentice does what is being taught that they really come to know. We see that clearly in medicine and engineering programs, where students spend time in the classroom, followed by practicing medicine and working on actual projects. We see it in science courses where students must demonstrate in the laboratory what they heard in their lectures. Jesus gave us a definition of apprenticeship in one verse of Scripture: John 7:17.

SO, WHAT IS YOUR MARKETPLACE?

Your marketplace is any situation that puts you in contact with secular people. It could be your workplace where you earn a living. It could be your business or the business that employs you. If you are in the military it could be the base where you are stationed or the ship on which you serve. It could be the school or the college where you study, teach or coach. It is anything or anyplace that brings you in contact with the secular or unspiritual people of this world, who are loved by God but unaware of that beautiful reality. In the sense in which I am using the term, that is your marketplace.

THE COMMITMENT OF A DISCIPLE

A disciple is not a casual follower of Jesus giving a nod of approval or tip of their hat to the beliefs and values of Jesus as they live for Christ in the marketplace. This, then, presents an intriguing challenge for us to consider. What is it like when a serious disciple of Jesus is called to serve Him in the marketplace? *Called to the marketplace?* It may be you never even considered being called to the marketplace. Perhaps you thought people were called to be a pastor or a missionary, but not to the marketplace.

In chapter 14 of the Gospel of Luke, Jesus gave us a definition of a disciple of His we might call *The Cost of Discipleship*. A German Lutheran pastor, Dietrich Bonheoffer, who died for his faith in the last days of World War II in a Nazi prison camp, gave that title to his excellent book (which I highly recommend). He reminded us that according to the Gospel of Luke, Jesus preached:

"If you want to be my disciple, you must hate everyone else by comparison—your father and mother, wife and children, brothers and sisters—yes, even your own life. Otherwise, you cannot be my disciple. And if you do not carry your own cross and follow me, you cannot be my disciple... What king would go to war against another king without first sitting down with his counselors to discuss whether his army of 10,000 could defeat the 20,000 soldiers marching

against him? And if he can't, he will send a delegation to discuss terms of peace while the enemy is still far away. So you cannot become my disciple without giving up everything you own. Salt is good for seasoning. But if it loses its flavor, how do you make it salty again? Flavorless salt is good neither for the soil nor for the manure pile. It is thrown away. Anyone with ears to hear should listen and understand!" (Luke 14:26-35 NLT)

This is considered by scholars to be one of the *hard sayings* of Jesus. We pastors spend much time and effort trying to increase the number of our hearers. Here Jesus modeled the need to sift down to a committed minority rather than work with an apathetic majority. When He speaks of the king doing reconnaissance and evaluating the quality of his army to defeat the enemy coming against Him, He speaks of Himself. He is the King, who knows what He will face. He cannot afford to have a disciple of inadequate quality in His army.

In the same way, in another part of this passage He describes counting the cost before starting to build something and not being able to finish. He is the One counting the cost. Jesus does not say we should literally hate those we cannot put first when we put Him first in our life. He's saying we are to love Him so much that our feelings for them, compared to our feelings for Him, would seem more like hate.

When He speaks of carrying our cross to follow Him, Jesus uses a metaphor that strikes fear into the hearts of those who hear Him. Many of them had probably been in Jerusalem or some other city and witnessed some poor victim of crucifixion carrying their cross to the place of execution. It was unforgettable and horrific to see. The essence of this metaphor was that they must love Him more than they love their own life. And when you put it all together, Jesus teaches that a disciple of His must love Him more than their own life, more than the people nearest and dearest to them and more than all their possessions … or they cannot be His disciple. He concludes His message on the cost of discipleship with the observation that when salt loses its salt quality it is good for nothing. It is not even useful as fertilizer in the soil or fit for the manure pile. It is good for *nothing*!

When He uses this metaphor, Jesus makes a statement about His disciples as well as the people of this world. Scholars interpret this metaphor in many different ways. One interpretation is that salt makes people thirsty for what the disciple is and has to offer. Another interpretation is that salt burns when it gets into the open moral sores of those who are encountered by a disciple of Jesus. That is why they are so often persecuted.

Still another interpretation and application is that salt preserves from corruption. There was no refrigeration when Jesus used this metaphor, so the only way people could preserve meat or fish was to rub salt into them. Jesus teaches that the world is corrupting and His disciples are preservatives that can have an influence that works against that corruption.

A LIFE GIVING PRINCIPLE

My favorite interpretation and application of this "salty" teaching of Jesus can be traced through the fact that our word "salary" comes from the two root words *salt* and *money*. This is because more than twenty centuries ago the Roman Empire knew that no human being could live without salt. Since they wanted to control the people of the world and the people of the world wanted to live, the Empire controlled the salt and often paid their slaves in cubes of salt. This is where we get the expression, "a person is not worth their salt."

The original language shows us Jesus taught His disciples: "*You and you alone are the salt of the earth.*" This means Jesus was teaching that people do not have real life and His disciples are the only hope people have of finding this quality of life. In the Gospel of John, Jesus called this quality *eternal life* (John 3:16).

A PRINCIPLE OF APPLICATION

No matter how you interpret and apply this metaphor, one principle is always true. A missionary statesman named Kenneth Strachan describes the principle this way: "If a large group of missionaries live together in a foreign country in a compound with a fortress mentality, they are like manure. They stink! But if you spread those missionaries around, they do a lot of good." The same metaphor can be said of disciples of Jesus when they gather in churches to worship, hear the Word of God taught and fellowship with Christ and each other. They are like salt in a saltshaker unless they spread themselves around.

All these interpretations and applications are legitimate. But no matter how you may interpret this salty teaching of Jesus you cannot deny the principle described by Kenneth Strachan. The salt influence of the disciples of Jesus cannot have an impact as long as the salt remains in the salt shaker.

One way our Lord gets the salt out of the saltshaker is through our need to make a living. This moves us out of our comfort zone with other believers into the marketplace, where we interact with secular people, establish relationships with them and have the opportunity to share the Gospel of Jesus Christ with them. A recent book, *Marketplace Evangelism*, emphatically makes the point that the marketplace is where evangelism is taking place today.

Every disciple of Jesus Christ is called by Jesus to fit into His plans for reaching the lost and secular people of this world. I'm convinced the risen, living Christ would love to call millions of disciples to the marketplace to reach the millions of those lost people He loves so very much.

I heard a businessman say, "There are two things to be gained in a business deal. One is money. The other is experience. When you do business, be sure you always get the money and give that other person the experience." The risen, living Christ is not calling His disciples to the marketplace so they can get the money and give people the experience. God wants to call disciples to the marketplace and energize them as they form relationships with secular people, possibly leading them to a life changing encounter with Jesus Christ.

SO WHAT IS A CALL?

What do we mean when we say we believe God is calling us to be a pastor, a missionary, make a career change, go to seminary or do something special for the Lord? We hear stories of people who have had dramatic experiences, which they interpreted to be a "call" to ministry of one kind or another. What is a call and how do we know when God calls us?

My personal call to ministry was eloquently and simply expressed when the Apostle Paul wrote in one of his letters, "*Woe is me if I preach not...*" (1 Corinthians 9:16). I seriously considered becoming a lawyer, a doctor, or a professor. But as I grew closer to what those choices really were, I had the strong conviction that, at least for me, those professions were not worth the investment of my entire life. I believe the essence of a call is related to the conviction that for you this is what is worth the investment of your life.

I have been deeply moved by the God story of a medical missionary to Africa. Her call to be a medical missionary parallels my experience of a call to the ministry. Her name is Dr. Helen Roseveare and for twenty years she poured out her life, building a hospital in Africa.

All her life she had the unique spiritual discipline of asking herself, "Is it worth it, Helen?" She did this at every juncture, like her decision to go to medical school in her native United Kingdom where she prepared to become a medical missionary.

After twenty years in Africa, during a Mau-Mau uprising she was raped repeatedly and then tied naked to a tree while her hospital went up in flames and burned to the ground. While that was happening, the thought occurred to her, "Was it worth it, Helen?"

The Holy Spirit welled up in her with the response, "Yes it was worth it, Helen, because He is worth it!" She had not done her great work in Africa for herself but for her Lord Jesus Christ. Her entire ministry in Africa had been an expression of what she now calls "costly worship."

I have also been impressed with people in various professions who did not believe the way they invested their life had been worth it. Consider the swan songs of Solomon in the book of Ecclesiastes and in Psalm 127. As a secular example, consider these words found written in the diary of an elderly British statesman by the name of Sir Leonard Wolfe:

"Looking back at the age of eighty-eight, over the fifty-seven years of my political life in England, knowing what I deem best of results, and meditating on the history of Britain and the world since 1914, I now see clearly that I achieved practically nothing. The world today, and the history of the human anthill during the last fifty-seven years, would be exactly the same as it is if I had played Ping-Pong instead of sitting on committees and writing books and memoranda. I have, therefore, to make the rather ignominious confession to myself, and to anyone who may read this that I must have in a long life, ground through around two hundred thousand hours of perfectly meaningless work."

His negative example challenges me to see to it that I do not have an epitaph like his written across the way I have spent my life.

May I ask you a couple of questions? Are you doing meaningless work? If you are, my next question is "Why?" You have the freedom to decide how you are going to spend your life. Meaningless work is an epitaph that should never be written across the life of a disciple of Jesus Christ. If we truly understand the many Scriptures I am sharing with you, we simply will not spend our lives doing meaningless work. Realizing that the workplace is where our Lord calls us to have a salt influence on secular people should bring great meaning to our workplace lives.

A WORTHY CALL

I discovered a worthy call when I found something that was worth the investment of my entire life. When I realized I was between the love of Christ and the pain of hurting people, I found out where the risen Christ is and where I wanted to be for the rest of my life. I wanted to be a vehicle, a conduit of the love of Christ, passing on His love and channeling it to address the pain of hurting people. When I was in that position, I had the strong conviction that this was where God was calling me.

That reality is not only intended for pastors like me. That is to be the experience of every believer. And that reality can make every day in the marketplace an adventure filled with meaningful work. Even though I am a bed-fast quadriplegic, I still have regular meetings with many people. A refrain I hear consistently is that people are not finding meaning in what they do. I personally know a half a dozen men who are about 60 and have made great financial sacrifices because they want to work in the nonprofit sector. They have realized that finding meaning in what they do is more important than the bottom line of their annual income.

I'm convinced it will bring you great meaning to realize you are called to the marketplace to be a conduit of the love of Jesus Christ to hurting people. No matter where you work, you will find many people you work with, work for or who work for you, are hurting; often, to the extent they are what we might call isolated hurting people. They may have absolutely no one, like a pastor or professional counselor, with whom they can share their pain. If you are there because you have been called to be "Christ with skin on" to those you encounter, you will discover you are surrounded by a mission field of hurt and need. Brief conversations in the rest room can lead to a coffee, lunch or dinner appointment if you are available.

As a doctor, if you realize you are not there to get rich but to be Christ to your patients, prioritizing the time to listen to them, you may be a critically-needed conduit of the love of Christ. The same can be said for a lawyer who is a disciple of Jesus Christ. Whether you are with clients who can afford to pay many hundreds of dollars an hour or those who are not even billable, realizing you are not there to get rich but to be *Christ with skin on* can bring great meaning to your professional life. If you are an entrepreneurial business owner and you consider your business place an opportunity to be a witness for Christ, then you also know Christ brings greater meaning to your workplace than can ever be found in the bottom line of your profits and losses.

SOME PERSONAL EXAMPLES

I have been greatly blessed to know a godly man who installed telephones and led scores of people to Christ in that role. I have also known a mailman who carried the same mail route for 42 years and was like a pastor to those he served as a mail carrier.

Bob Miles and Jerry Johnson were two of the youngest Navy captains I ever met. They came to faith at a Bible teaching breakfast I taught for men. We often met for lunch. One morning Jerry called me and told me we needed to meet because Bob was depressed.

At lunch, I asked Bob why he was feeling heavy. He told me and Jerry that ever since he graduated from the Naval Academy he had wanted to be an admiral. However, since he had come to faith he no longer had that ambition. The absence of that goal left a vacuum in his life. In pursuit of that goal, he had sacrificed one marriage to the Navy. He was subsequently happily married to a wonderful woman who had two young sons.

When I asked him what he would like to do, his response was that he wanted to teach ROTC to high school kids in his home state of Washington. I asked if that was doable and he assured me it was. Discussing the meaning of a call, I encouraged him to respond to what he was sure God was calling him to be and do.

Many years later my wife and I visited Bob in Washington State. He had established relationships with so many high school young people he was like a Young Life Area Director in that community. He was a pied piper to high school kids and was supremely happy and fulfilled in what he was doing. I previously felt sorry for him because I thought he was receiving the salary of a schoolteacher while he was in that role. I was surprised and relieved to later learn that all the years he was doing youth work, he retained the rank and the remuneration of a Captain in the United States Navy. And the two teenagers he inherited by way of his second marriage were both missionaries.

At that same lunch, I asked Jerry how he felt about being an admiral. He was sure he wanted to be an admiral. When he was given his fourth star he came to visit me to tell me about his promotion. He also told me that when he came to that breakfast as a Navy captain he was doing very well professionally. He was winning all the awards the Navy had to offer for the work he was doing, but He and his men were known as the biggest hell-raisers in the Navy. Even though he was successful professionally, His personal, private life was suffering terribly.

He shared with me that from the time he came to faith, his career had taken a meteoric rise to four-star Admiral. He was convinced that the amazing rise he had experienced in his career could only be attributed to the Christ Who came into his life. He was extremely happy and fulfilled being who God wanted him to be and doing what God wanted him to do as a four star Admiral.

Another example of a man whose life was changed through the Word of God is Frank Brock, who was in line to become the president of his family's well known candy business. Because Frank was restless about who and what he would be in that role, we spent the better part of a Saturday discussing these questions. After much soul searching, he later decided to become the president of an extraordinary Christ-centered college which had the motto "In all things...Christ preeminent."

As a college president Frank was fruitful, fulfilled and brought forth what Jesus described as "*the fruit that remains*" or continues (John 15:16). While he did not feel he did anything noble, Frank had the satisfaction of knowing he was leading an institution that invested in the young lives of thousands of gifted students. He believes all those graduated students are ministers for Christ, whether their place of witness is vocational church work or in the marketplaces of the secular world. He is grateful for the career change he made when he gave God what was, for him, the right response to His call.

I have already mentioned my favorite example of a businessman who responded to the call of God for his life. Dois Rosser, my partner in ministry, is the greatest example I've ever met of what God can do with a man who takes his faith seriously, responding whole-heartedly to the call of God on his life.

THE LIGHT OF THE WORLD

Jesus used another metaphor when He taught His disciples that they and they alone were the light of the world. He was teaching that the people of this world are in darkness. One of the things that moved Jesus every time He saw the multitudes was that they were like sheep without a shepherd. They did not know their right hand from their left. Before His disciples met Him, they were like unlighted candles. Once they learned Jesus' way of living life, it was as if they became lighted candles. For every candle He lighted, He had a candlestick on which to place that candle. It is His plan to strategically place every one of His disciples like candles on a candlestick. As candles, the only way they can give off light is to burn up and be expendable as the light of the world He has called them and strategically placed them to be.

A TURTLE ON A FENCE POST

Several decades ago, Allan Emery and Mary Crowley wrote a book in which they explained that any time you find a turtle on a fence post you know one thing for certain about that turtle: somebody had to put it there because turtles cannot climb fence posts. Their claim was that every disciple of Jesus should feel similarly about where they are placed as they serve Jesus. As I consider what I have been doing and am now doing for Christ as a bedfast quadriplegic, I know I am a turtle on a fence post.

Somebody had to place me where I am because I could never be where I am and do what I'm doing through my own efforts.

CHOSEN TO BE FRUITFUL

After three years spent 24/7 with the apostles He chose, and just hours before He was arrested by the Romans to face clandestine trials and execution by crucifixion, Jesus dropped a bombshell on these men with whom He had invested so much. He said to them: *"You did not choose me, but I chose you and appointed you to go and bear fruit—fruit that will last. Then the Father will give you whatever you ask in my name"* (John 15:16).

These men had made many choices. For three years they left their families, their businesses, and everything that had been important to them before they met Jesus. But they now learn He was the One making those choices. He had chosen them and He was going to strategically place them where they could bring forth fruit for Him. This will be fruit that lasts. This fruit will be a legacy that will be here on earth long after they are in heaven. He then added the comment that when they understood this, God would start answering their prayers.

When He used the word "appointed," He used a Greek word that is only found three times in the New Testament. It means to be strategically placed like a candle on a candlestick. Like the metaphor of the candle on a candlestick and the turtle on a fence post, the personal application of this truth should make the day-to-day life of every disciple in the marketplace an adventure. Wherever a disciple is placed, they can know with exciting conviction that it is God's doing. If they are the only believer they know of in their workplace, rather than be overwhelmed, they should be challenged and excited to think they have been chosen to live out the eight attitudes Jesus teaches, which we call the "Beatitudes," or the *blessed attitudes*, at the beginning of His Sermon on the Mount. He followed that teaching with four metaphors.

"You are the salt of the earth; but if the salt loses its flavor, how shall it be seasoned? It is then good for nothing but to be thrown out and trampled underfoot by men… You are the light of the world. A city that is set on a hill cannot be hidden. Nor do they light a lamp and put it under a basket, but on a candlestick, and it gives light to all who are in the house. Let your light so shine before men, that they may see your good works and glorify your Father in heaven" (Matthew 5: 13-16).

In summary, Jesus taught they were the salt of the earth, the light of the world, a city set on a hill that cannot be hidden and a candle strategically placed on a candlestick. He taught them to look in and make eight attitude adjustments. He then taught them to look around and relate His teaching to all those secular people they encountered. They critically needed to look up and receive from God the power to be and do what He was training them to be and do for Him.

WAKING THE SLEEPING GIANT

"I am the true vine, and My Father is the vinedresser. Every branch in Me that does not bear fruit He takes away; and every branch that bears fruit He prunes, that it may bear more fruit. You are already clean because of the word which I have spoken to you.

Abide in Me, and I in you. As the branch cannot bear fruit of itself, unless it abides in the vine, neither can you, unless you abide in Me. I am the vine, you are the branches. He who abides in Me, and I in him, bears much fruit; for without Me you can do nothing. If anyone does not abide in Me, he is cast out as a branch and is withered; and they gather them and throw them into the fire, and they are burned.

"If you abide in Me, and My words abide in you, you will ask what you desire, and it shall be done for you. By this My Father is glorified, that you bear much fruit; so you will be My disciples. As the Father loved Me, I also have loved you; abide in My love. If you keep My commandments, you will abide in My love, just as I have kept My Father's commandments and abide in His love. These things I have spoken to you, that My joy may remain in you, and that your joy may be full. This is My commandment, that you love one another as I have loved you.

"Greater love has no one than this, than to lay down one's life for his friends. You are My friends if you do whatever I command you. No longer do I call you servants, for a servant does not know what his master is doing; but I have called you friends, for all things that I heard from My Father I have made known to you. You did not choose Me, but I chose you and appointed you that you should go and bear fruit, and that your fruit should remain, that whatever you ask the Father in My name He may give you" (John 15:1-16).

When Jesus gave this teaching about the disciples having been chosen to be fruitful, He followed that with a great exhortation in which He gave six reasons why they must be fruitful where He placed them (John 15:1-16). It is imperative we understand that this teaching is not only addressed to apostles but also to every serious disciple of Jesus Christ. If every devout disciple of Jesus would make this application, that would wake the "sleeping giant" of the Church into an awesome force for Jesus.

I have had a marvelous and wonderful experience as a pastor/teacher of the Word of God, and I know of no greater joy than to be called to that ministry. I feel the same way about being called to be a cross-cultural, cross-lingual foreign missionary. I think the call to be a medical missionary is one of the greatest callings in the world. However, I am convinced what the Church of Jesus Christ needs most in the world today is not so much more pastors and missionaries, but disciples who will take their faith as seriously as these vocational fulltime servants of the Lord. When *laymen* realize they are called and placed by Christ on a candlestick, somewhere like the marketplace, that will wake the sleeping giant of the Church.

To state it very simply, if you were Christ and you wanted to reach all the people in a city, would you not place those who know You and love You in all the professions and business organizations of that city? As much as we need pastors and missionaries, we desperately need serious disciples of Jesus in all the professions, including in the military, in politics, as judges in court rooms and on the front lines of justice issues fighting for the rights of those who have no advocate.

A MESSAGE AND A MINISTRY

The Apostle Paul wrote a passage of Scripture which shows us clearly that the Great Commission was not merely for the apostles but, rather, for every believer. Paul wrote: *"All this is from God, who reconciled us to himself through Christ and gave us the ministry of reconciliation: that God was reconciling the world to himself in Christ, not counting men's sins against them. And he has committed to us the message of reconciliation*" (2 Corinthians 5:18-19).

This passage of Scripture teaches that every believer who has been reconciled to God through Christ has had committed to him or her the ministry and the message of reconciliation. A devout theologian has summarized the meaning of this Scripture in this way: "It is the will of the Reconciler that the reconciled are to be the vehicles of reconciliation in the lives of the un-reconciled." I want to emphasize the word every in what I have just written. This is true for *every* believer.

In many ways the concept of laity and clergy has done great damage to the function of the Church in this world. The result of making this distinction has excused millions of believers for hundreds of years from applying Scriptures to their own personal faith and ministry. When many have read verses like these I am referencing, they believe the applications are not for them but for the clergy. It is vitally important for us to realize that these verses and their applications are for *every* believer.

So many believe God means these teachings only for people set aside to be pastors, missionaries and other kinds of vocational Christ-like spiritual leaders. The truth is our God delights in doing extraordinary things through ordinary people. The Old and New Testaments give us scores of examples of that truth. If every member of a local church realized these Scriptures were for them, the Church of Jesus Christ would be a dynamic power within communities.

THE JOB DESCRIPTION OF EVERY PASTOR

In his letter to the Ephesians the Apostle Paul gave every pastor their job description when he wrote: *"He Himself gave some to be... pastors and teachers, for the equipping of the saints for the work of the ministry...."* (Ephesians 4: 11-12).

In many churches congregations are convinced that the *work of the ministry* has been concluded when the pastor pronounces the benediction. According to Paul, the work of the ministry is then only beginning. This work of the ministry, noted in Paul's inspired job description, is not committed solely to the pastor or the professional staff of a church. This work of ministry is also assigned to the congregation as they move out into the marketplace to earn their livings. It continues where they relate to the secular people who cross their path in the neighborhoods where they live, shop, eat in restaurants and attend events at the schools where their children study. They have contact with secular people who many of the vocational ministers in their churches will never meet.

If a pastor in an evangelical church gives an invitation at the conclusion of a church service and ten or twelve people respond to his invitation, the congregation is greatly blessed and pleased. However, if there are five hundred people in that congregation and each one reaches just one person that week, - go do the numbers. It is not only because of the numbers that we who are pastors should apply this job description. We should implement this into our congregations because it is the Holy Spirit's inspired job description for His people, given by Almighty God and the risen, living Christ.

MOBILIZING THE MEMBERSHIP

Can you see how Paul's job description for pastors and his strategy for the purpose of a church service fit together with the plan of God? He calls every believer into the ministry of getting next to the secular people of this world, that Christ might be shared with them. It can make your day-to-day work place an adventure when you realize why you have been called and strategically placed there by the risen, living Christ. It should also motivate people who are bored to death with early retirement to pray about a call to come out of the saltshaker, not to supplement their incomes, but to be with secular people. At the very least this can motivate believers to circulate with people on some level for the purpose of being a witness for Christ.

Being a witness does not necessarily mean having the gift of evangelism or disciple-making. Being a witness really is a matter of being who you are in Christ *with secular people.* You must build a relationship with such people to have a salt impact.

WHEN OUR LORD PRAYS FOR HIS CHURCH

When Jesus prayed His high-priestly prayer, recorded for us in the seventeenth chapter of the Gospel of John, He prayed for His apostles and those who would become His disciples through those apostles. So we might say He was praying for His Church. Observe how much He loves the world. As He prays that prayer He uses the word "world" nineteen times! The peak of His passion for the world is when He prays: *"O righteous Father! The world has not known You"* (John 17:25). Yet He tells His Father that He is not praying for the world but for His Church because the world does not know Him. His Church knows Him, His Word and many other things. He prays His Father will not take His Church out of the world but will send the Church into the world. Also observe His love for the world when He prays His Church will live in such a way in this world: *"That the world may know and believe that You have sent Me,* ***and have loved them as You have loved Me****"* (John 17:23).

This is a wonderful commentary on the familiar verse from the same Gospel which tells us God *so* loved the world that He gave His One and only Son for our salvation (John 3:16). If you can grasp the perspective of Jesus Christ in this prayer, I have some questions for you: If God loves the lost secular people of this world as much as He loves His only begotten Son, would He not call many people to the marketplace where those people are? Are you willing to consider the possibility that if you are already placed on a candlestick in the marketplace, you are strategically placed and called to be there by God Himself? Are you open to the reality that God may want you to serve Him in these ways and with these motivations in the marketplace?

Chapter Two
Equipped for the Marketplace

Since most evangelism takes place today in the marketplace it is imperative that believers be trained to articulate the Gospel with those they meet there. How are the spiritual leaders of the church to do that? A first step in that direction is this: every believer should realize the Holy Spirit is the Evangelist and we are merely conduits through whom He works. Additionally, any of our efforts in evangelism should be done in the context of what we might label *friendship evangelism.*

When Jesus stayed up late with the Rabbi Nicodemus, the first words Nicodemus said were: *"Rabbi, we know that You are a teacher come from God; for no one can do the works that You do unless God is with him"* (John 3:2). Jesus earned His hearing with the outstanding Rabbi by what the Rabbi had seen Him do. Likewise, we must also earn our hearing with people. This begins with our understanding that what we do demonstrates what we believe. All the rest is just religious talk. People are not interested in our religious talk unless they are impressed by what they see us do and are favorably impacted by what we are. It's as if Nicodemus were saying he was impressed with what he had seen Jesus do, so he had come to hear the religious talk of Jesus. We are deceiving ourselves if we think it is not that way with us today.

What I'm calling *religious talk* is our theological explanation of what we believe and why we believe it. This can be a negative if we overwhelm people with our theology and use what Paul Little called "Protestant Latin." Many secular people do not understand even the simplest theological terms, which we think everybody understands. At any rate, whether positive or negative, people will not be interested in our religious talk if they are not impressed with who and what we are and the things we do.

When we earn our hearing by the grace of God, secular people will often give their own invitation. Just as the jailor in Philippi asked the Apostle Paul and Silas, "*Sirs, what must I do to be saved?*" (Acts 16:30), people will often ask us that kind of question. When they do, they are telling us they want to hear our religious talk. At that point we need to be prepared to tell them what they need to know and what they need to do to be saved and to become authentic disciples of Jesus Christ.

A friend of mine and I once had lunch with a man we both wanted to see come to Christ and salvation. He made it easy for us because he opened our conversation by telling us he was made Chairman of the Board of Stewards at his church the night before and he was not even a Christian. My friend told him that would never happen in my church because you could not even be a member of my church if you were not a believer. So you certainly would not be Chairman of the Board if you were not a disciple of Jesus Christ. He then turned to me and said, "Then you're the guy I've been waiting to meet for a long time. What the hell <u>is</u> a Christian?"

After I had talked for about five minutes he interrupted me and said, "Hey buddy, I asked you for the time and you're telling me how to make a watch! Can't you answer my question more clearly than this?" At that point I made the commitment to myself that the next time someone asked me that kind of question I would have a clear and precise answer. I then went to my study and wrote out my answer.

I will share with you some of the ways I have answered that question over many decades as a pastor. However, I want to emphasize strongly that it would be better for you to think about how you would answer that question, considering how you would, in your own words, naturally and conversationally, touch the necessary bases in providing the answer. The Apostle Peter instructs us to always be ready to give an answer to those who ask us about the hope we have of salvation (1 Peter 3:15).

When you have earned your hearing, since they have been impressed with what you are and do, things can break down if you merely take someone else's answer out of your wallet or purse. Remember, I am a pastor. I preach. That is what pastors do. They will accept that from me since I am a pastor. But it will be much more effective for you to write out and memorize your own presentation of what they need to know and do to experience salvation. Having formed your own answer then, naturally and conversationally, present your well thought-out answer.

Everything I do is in the public domain. That is because I am honored when someone teaches something I have presented and my passion is to get the Word out. If you like my presentations I would be honored if you used them. But I believe it would be more effective if you did not have your Gospel presentation in writing but, rather, were familiar enough with the Gospel to share your faith naturally and conversationally. You don't have to say your presentation came from me or some other author. In fact, it would be more effective if they thought it was coming from you. You could say something like "I heard it expressed this way." And then give the presentation without reading it or using notes. Familiarize yourself with yours or mine enough that you can present them from memory. And present them naturally and in dialogue with your inquirer.

So that you will understand the bases that must be covered, I will now share with you several ways I have presented the Gospel to people. I have shared these presentations one-on-one at lunch, in my study or anywhere we could have some privacy. I have also shared them with twenty-five hundred people at a time or at high school commencements in football stadiums. I call my first presentation *The Seven Spiritual Wonders of the World.* At the end of my presentation of each of these spiritual wonders I share several Scripture references so people who read them will know these are not merely my ideas. These wonders I present are based on the Word of God.

THE SEVEN SPIRITUAL WONDERS OF THE WORLD

A police officer on a motorcycle noticed a large enclosed truck that was being driven down Sixth Street in Los Angeles, California. The driver stopped every few blocks, got out of the truck, and beat all the way around the sides of the truck with a large baseball bat. After observing this for some time, the officer finally turned on his siren, flashed his lights and with strong hand signals ordered the driver to pull over. The policeman then said to the driver, "Mister, as far as I can tell, you're not breaking the law. But I just gotta know. What are you doing?"

The truck driver explained, "Officer, this truck here has a capacity of five thousand pounds. But, you see, I've got six thousand pounds of canaries in this truck. So, I gotta keep a thousand pounds of canaries up in the air all the time!"

Perhaps you are "up in the air" about the answer to these questions: "What is a Christian? What do you have to know and what must you do to become a Christian? How do you become an authentic disciple of Jesus Christ? What does it mean to be born again? How can we know we have been born again? How can a person be born again? How can I be born again?" I want to answer those questions. I call my answers, *The Seven Spiritual Wonders of the World.*

A good encyclopedia will tell you about the seven ancient wonders of the world, the seven modern wonders of the world and the seven natural wonders of the world. The Bible will tell you that God is a Spirit and the true wonders of the world are therefore the *Seven Spiritual Wonders of the World.*

THE GREATEST DESIGN IN THE WORLD

The ***first Spiritual Wonder of the World*** is *the greatest design in the world.* People who study this world through a telescope or a microscope are intrigued by its amazing design and order. The design and order we see in the big and little things of the world is majestic, beautiful and complex. When you consider the phenomenal design in the macrocosm and the microcosm of the world, it takes more faith to believe it all just happened (like an accident), than it does to believe in an Architect and Creator of the universe and the earth. People of faith believe that the spectacular design we observe in the world is the signature of God, written on the canvas of His creation.

There are now seven billion people on earth and every one of them has unique fingerprints. They also have unique voiceprints. What we know today about DNA proves that in the physical realm there never has been anyone exactly like you. There is no one now living and no one ever will live who is exactly like you because our God has made every single person on the face of the earth to be an original. The dictionaries define the word *self* as "the uniqueness, the individuality of any given person that makes them distinct from every other living person." In addition to our physical being, the Scriptures tell us that God has designed a plan for our life that will make us different from every other living person. For you and me, that is the greatest design in the world.

At the end of each section, I am going to list some Scripture references so you will know these are not just my ideas. These spiritual wonders I am telling you about are taught in the Bible.

Mark 8:36-37 NEB; Psalm 139:16; Jeremiah 1:5; Romans 12:1-2

THE GREATEST DIVORCE IN THE WORLD

You may be wondering, "How can there possibly be a God, or order and design behind a world like ours that is filled with alienation, divorce, fractured families, crime, murder, nuclear and biological weapons of mass destruction, wars, ethnic cleansing, genocide, refugees, riots and perplexing, Rubik's Cube problems that completely baffle and overwhelm us? If God has a design for everything and everybody, why is our world so filled with the kind of suffering that appears to have been assigned by some kind of random chaos? Why are so very many people in this world hurting, depressed, confused, alienated, lonely and unhappy? And why is my life so messed up?"

The Bible addresses those questions. You will not find a more realistic view of this life or better answers to those questions anywhere else. The Bible tells us God wants us to live our lives in alignment with His design for our lives, but God has also given us the freedom to either accept or reject a relationship with our God and His design for the way we live our lives. We can use this freedom to go our own selfish ways, do our own ego-driven things, and declare our independence from God. We can divorce ourselves from God and from His design for our lives. When we divorce ourselves from God and His plan for our life, God calls that sin.

The hard reality that God creates us with the freedom to make the wrong choices and then permits us to divorce ourselves from Him, makes this epidemic divorce between ourselves and our God *the greatest divorce in the world* – ***the second Spiritual Wonder of the World***. The reconciliation of that divorce is what the Bible is really all about.

Genesis 3; Isaiah 53:6; John 3:19; Romans 1:24, 26, 28; 3:23

THE GREATEST DILEMMA IN THE WORLD

The God revealed in the Bible, Who is the definition of perfect love, earnestly desires a love relationship with His children. However, He is also holy, the personification of perfect justice.

Biblical descriptions of the character of God give us an absolute standard by which we can measure right and wrong in our lives and in this world. This means there is no way that a loving and holy God can ignore the greatest divorce in the world.

While He is the perfect heavenly Father, there is a sense in which God faces a dilemma. In some ways, the dilemma God faces is quite similar to that faced by many parents. When we as parents want to have a love relationship with our rebellious children, how do we show them godly, unconditional love and acceptance, without violating what we believe and have taught our children to be right?

Similarly, how can our God, Whose character can be described as perfect love and perfect justice, respond to our serving Him with divorce papers in a way that is consistent with His character? That is *the greatest dilemma in the world* – ***the third Spiritual Wonder of the World.***

Genesis 3:8-13; Luke 15:11-24; Hebrews 12:5-11; Revelation 3:19-20

THE GREATEST DECLARATION OF THE WORLD

The greatest declaration in the world is not the American Declaration of Independence. The greatest declaration in the world is the Good News that God has resolved the greatest dilemma and reconciled the greatest divorce. At the heart of the Bible you will find the great declaration of Jesus, that when He died on His cross He was God's only Son. As He died on the cross, He offered God's only solution to this alienated, hurting world in general, and God's only salvation to human beings, individually and personally.

When Jesus died on the cross, God did something entirely consistent with His perfect love and His perfect justice. God laid on His only beloved Son all the chastisement we rebellious human beings rightly deserved for our sins. In this way, God exercised and satisfied His perfect justice. God certainly expressed His perfect love but most importantly, when Jesus died on the cross He gave all of us access to the only way we can reconcile our divorce from God.

This is the way Jesus communicated the heart of His great declaration: *"For God so loved the world that He gave His one and only Son, that whoever believes in Him shall not perish, but have eternal life"* (John 3:16). This statement makes the cross of Jesus Christ *the greatest declaration in the world,* and the ***fourth*** and most important ***Spiritual Wonder of the World.***

John 3:14-21; Matthew 20:28; Isaiah 53:5; 1 Peter 2:24;
2 Corinthians 5:18-21

THE GREATEST DECISION IN THE WORLD

Jesus put the greatest decision in the world in perspective when He told us that each one of us must personally believe the greatest declaration. Immediately after proclaiming He was God's only Savior, speaking of Himself, Jesus said, *"He who believes in Him is not condemned, but he who does not believe is condemned already, because he does not believe ... And this is the condemnation"* (John 3:18-19).

That is the most dogmatic statement Jesus ever made. The decision to believe the great declaration of Jesus has to be the greatest decision in the world, because according to Jesus, if we believe His declaration, we have solved our sin problem. Because we believe, God will forgive us and give us eternal life. However, if we do not believe Jesus, we are condemned. We are not condemned because of our sins. We are condemned precisely because we do not believe the Good News proclaimed by Jesus. This *is* the condemnation according to Jesus.

If a decision we make to believe the great declaration of Jesus is the difference between our eternal condemnation and our eternal salvation, then that decision is *the greatest decision in the world* - ***the fifth of the Spiritual Wonders of the World.***

John 3:16-19; 1:12; Acts 16:30-32; Romans 10:9-10

THE GREATEST DIRECTION IN THE WORLD

If you are tracking with me, you may very well be asking yourself the question: "How can I know when I have made the greatest decision in the world?" Jesus answered that question for you and me when He spoke these two words: "*Follow Me.*"

The spirit of a covenant Jesus made with those who professed to believe in Him was, *Follow Me and I will make you.* Jesus was saying,

You follow Me. That is your part.
I will make you. That is My part.
You follow Me. That is your responsibility.
I will make you. That is My responsibility.
You follow Me. That is your business.
I will make you. That is My business (Matthew 4:19).

Those short sentences are my paraphrase of the verbal contract with which Jesus began the spiritual faith journeys of those who believed and followed Him.

After you make the decision to believe and commit to follow Jesus, if someone could show you the future twenty years later, you would be filled with awe. What may be incredible for you at the starting gate of your faith journey is really very credible when you realize He promises to *make you.* There is hope that life can be beautiful for you, because Jesus will always do His part when you believe and make the commitment to become a true follower of Jesus and do your part.

When the people who told Jesus they believed in Him heard those two words, "*Follow me*" and considered the covenant with which Jesus challenged them, they soon discovered that following Jesus meant they had to turn away from their sins, offer an unconditional surrender of their lives, and then follow Jesus. Many of the people who told Jesus they believed in Him were not willing to validate their faith by surrendering unconditionally to Him. They were not willing to follow Jesus on His terms.

However, the committed minority who did make the commitment to believe and follow also made a discovery: following Jesus gave meaning, definition, direction, purpose and value to their lives. The apostles were ordinary men from all walks of life. Sixty years after making that covenant/commitment to Jesus, the Apostle John wrote that Jesus had made him and his fellow apostles "*kings and priests*" (Revelation 1:6). Those who profess to believe in Jesus and who are willing to make the commitment to follow Him will always discover that following Jesus is the greatest direction in the world.

If you will carefully examine the dramatic changes in the lives of professing believers who truly follow Jesus, and, conversely, the lack of change in the lives of professing believers who do not truly follow Jesus, it will be obvious to you that following Jesus is t*he greatest direction in the world*, the direction you want to travel – and another (***the sixth***) vital ***Spiritual Wonder of the World.***

Matthew 4:19; Revelation 1:5-6; John 8:30-35; Luke 5:1-11

THE GREATEST DYNAMIC OF THE WORLD

Although the greatest declaration in the world is the most important spiritual wonder of the world, the most exciting truth about Jesus Christ in the New Testament is this Good News which, according to the book of Acts, was preached by all the apostles: Jesus Christ was raised from the dead!

The risen Christ lives in His true disciples. He is responsible for all the changes in their lives. The risen, living Christ is also the *power source* who is responsible for the impact and influence of His disciples, now and in every generation. The risen Christ – living His life in and through His true disciples – is the greatest Dynamic in the world. The same risen Christ, living His life in and through you and me today, is t*he greatest dynamic in the world* and the most miraculous *Spiritual Wonder of the World!*

According to Jesus, those who receive this great dynamic have been "born again." If you have not been born again, I challenge you to make the decision to believe in Jesus Christ. Make the commitment to move in the direction of following Jesus. When you take those two critically important steps, you will discover that the risen, living Christ will then empower your life. Surrender your life to His control and direction. In His time, in His way, and for His glory, you will be born again. For clarification, I recommend you read this book's chapter 13, where I describe the new birth in greater detail.

Now to return to the *first spiritual wonder;* when you are born again, you will recover the design God has always willed for your life, which for you is the greatest design in the world! The life you then live as a follower of Jesus Christ will be distinguished by a beautiful diversity. Your new life in Christ will far surpass the beautiful diversity of your fingerprints, voiceprints and DNA.

A wealthy young man decided to spend a winter in Bermuda. He had his Mercedes convertible shipped there in advance of his visit. But when he arrived on the island, he discovered, to his dismay, that the speed limit in Bermuda was twenty miles an hour.

For several weeks he cruised at that speed all over Bermuda in his powerful sports car. One morning, while driving behind an old man on a moped, he just lost it, hit the passing gear and at a speed of 45 miles per hour passed the old man. To his surprise the old man shot by him on his moped. Instinctively, he hit the passing gear and went up to a speed of 55 miles per hour. Again the old man shot by him. He accelerated and at an enormously reckless speed for Bermuda passed the moped. For a third time the old man shot right by him on his moped.

When the young man realized what he was doing, he took his foot off the accelerator and coasted to a stop on the shoulder of the road. The old man pulled in behind him and just sat on the moped, twitching a little.

The Mercedes driver approached the moped man. He was amazed at the speed the old guy had had. "Hey," he said, "what kind of power plant have you got in that bike man?"

The old man couldn't speak for a while. When he could finally get a word out, he said, "It's not the power plant in this moped, son. My suspenders were caught on your bumper!"

A lot of people today don't seem to have their own spiritual power plant. So they attach themselves to the bumper of those who do. They experience spasmodic bursts of spiritual acceleration as they try to ride the energy of those they admire, without ever having found a spiritual power source of their own. This *greatest dynamic in the world*, the ***seventh Spiritual Wonder of the World***, comes to us by way of the new birth. It is intended for *every* believer and it is a critical factor in following Jesus Christ as one of His disciples.

PERSONAL APPLICATIONS

When a seminar for baseball umpires was concluding, one of the umpires stood and summarized the seminar by saying to the other umpires, "The way I see it, some are balls and some are strikes, and we ought to call them the way we see 'em." Another umpire stood and said, "The way I see it, some are balls and some are strikes, and we ought to call 'em the way they are." Then an old veteran umpire stood and said, "The way I see it, some are balls and some are strikes, but they ain't nothin' 'til we call 'em!"

I have just thrown you my seven best pitches. I call these pitches "strikes." I call them *The Seven Spiritual Wonders of the World*. But like the old umpire said, these spiritual wonders are nothing to you until you call them something. Carefully consider what you've read and decide for yourself what you call them.

Do you want to be born again? Are you ready to make the momentous decision to believe the great declaration of Jesus Christ? Are you willing to offer an unconditional surrender of your life to Jesus? Have you decided that you now want to make the commitment to begin moving in the direction of following Jesus? You can do that right now. If you sincerely want to begin your spiritual faith journey with Jesus, from your heart, pray this prayer with me:

"Loving heavenly Father, I confess that I have divorced myself from You and Your plan for my life. I confess that I am a sinner and I trust Your Son, Jesus Christ, to be my Savior. I place my complete trust in His death on the cross for the forgiveness of every one of my sins. I now forsake and turn away from all my sins. I want to reconcile my divorce from You. Right here and right now, I also crown Jesus Christ as my Lord. I surrender my life, unconditionally, to His control and direction. As I follow Your Son, Jesus Christ, in the name of Jesus, and for Your glory, bring my life into perfect alignment with that great design you always have willed for my life. In the glorious and victorious name of Jesus Christ, Amen!"

John 3:3-8; 1:12-13; I Peter 1:22-3:3; Philippians 1:6; 2:13; Ephesians 2:10

I want to emphasize again that this is one of the ways I have shared the Gospel as a pastor. It will be so much more effective if you share the Gospel your own way. The important thing is to touch all the Gospel bases. For example, consider what the Apostle Paul wrote in these verses to the Corinthians:

"Now let me remind you, brothers, of what the gospel really is, for it has not changed – it is the same Good News I preached to you before. That Christ died for our sins just as the Scriptures said He would and that He was buried and that three days afterward He arose from the grave just as the prophets foretold" (1 Corinthians 15:1, 3-4 LB).

In these verses the Apostle Paul gives us a very clear and precise statement about what the Gospel truly is. The Gospel is simply two facts about Jesus Christ: He died for our sins and He rose again from the dead, just as the Old Testament Scriptures said He would and the New Testament Scriptures tell us He did. Believing in the death of Jesus Christ on the cross is the basis on which God forgives our sins. Believing in the second Gospel fact about Jesus, His resurrection, then becomes the basis on which we can experience fellowship with a risen, living Christ. Those are two bases your Gospel presentation should cover. There is something to believe and Someone to receive.

It is because of His death and resurrection that we have a reality presented in one of the most familiar of the New Testament Scriptures. In Revelation 3:20, Jesus tells us He stands at the door of our life knocking. That door must be opened from the inside. When we open that door we have His promise that He will come in to our life and fellowship with us. This verse is often quoted without the preceding one, where He tells us that as many of us as He loves, He chastens.

Since the context of this verse is a letter written to a lukewarm apathetic church, we realize that the knocking on the door of our heart is chastening. The metaphor is actually directed to uncommitted believers. The hard reality is that chastening is the way He gets many of us to open the door of our life and ask Him to come in, to be our Lord as well as our Savior, and experience intimate relationship with Him.

HOW TO MAKE A DISCIPLE

There is another passage of Scripture I would like to reference that is relevant to personal evangelism and disciple-making. In Acts chapter 8, we read a beautiful account of how to make a disciple for Jesus Christ. Philip the Evangelist is having a fruitful evangelistic crusade among the Samaritans when the Spirit clearly directs him to leave his fruitful ministry and travel down a desert road into the wilderness known as Gaza. You would think an evangelist would argue with the Spirit and explain that he needed to be in a population center. But Philip knew it was only because of the Holy Spirit that he was having such a fruitful crusade in Samaria. He therefore obeyed and traveled into the wilderness of Gaza.

When he entered that wilderness area he saw a caravan of chariots crossing the desert. The Spirit led him to join himself to one particular chariot. The Greek words refer to that particular chariot in contrast to the many others, and that's how we know it was a caravan of chariots. In that particular chariot, the treasurer of Ethiopia was traveling, reading from the scroll of Isaiah. Apparently spiritual hunger had brought him all the way from

Ethiopia to Jerusalem, but all he found there were God's *frozen chosen* people. He did manage to procure the scroll of Isaiah. As Philip came alongside, he heard the Ethiopian reading from chapter 53, the greatest Gospel chapter among the sixty-six chapters of that book and one of the greatest chapters in the whole Bible on the meaning of the death of Jesus Christ on the cross.

Phillip asked him if he understood what he was reading. His response was, *"How can I, unless someone instructs me?"* (Acts 8:31 NLT). He invited Philip into the chariot with him and as they road along together, the Ethiopian asked Philip if this man was writing about himself or some other man. Philip began at that great chapter and presented Christ to him. He apparently brought his presentation of Christ and the Gospel to a verdict by informing him that he was to go public with his faith through water baptism. When the man assured the evangelist that he believed, Philip baptized him.

THE THREE LINK CHAIN

This great story recorded by Luke tells us that a three-link chain exists between God and a lost person. The first link in that chain is the Holy Spirit. The second link is the Word of God and the third link is the available disciple-maker. The agent of God in the world today is the Holy Spirit. The vehicles of the Holy Spirit are the Word of God and an available disciple-maker. The Spirit obviously led Philip out into that desert and drew that Ethiopian all the way to Jerusalem from Africa. The Word of God was central in the presentation of Philip, so when Philip got up into the chariot with the Ethiopian Eunuch, God was in business. The three link chain was now in place!

From this example, which is not only descriptive but prescriptive, I believe we should present the Gospel one-on-one when the Spirit prompts us or leads us to do so. This story illustrates that we should see evidence that the Spirit is already working in the life of the person to whom we are to present the Gospel. And, the Word of God should be central in our presentation. God uses His Word. Our personal God story is important but we should always be sure to use the Scripture when we present the Gospel to another person. This is why I listed those Scriptures at the end of each part of my Gospel presentation. It can sometimes be a good idea to get the person to read the Scripture with us as we move along from one point to another.

It is critically important for us to be available as the third link in that chain. We may be the weakest link in this chain but it is the greatest privilege in the world for us to be there as part of this process. Even though you feel you are the weakest link in this chain, the other two links are so incredibly strong we must believe they can work through us and our weakness. In many ways, our greatest ability is our *availability*.

In the beginning of my experience in presenting the Gospel in a one-on-one context, I was so terribly shy I would just about have a stroke. But when I realized how strong those other two links were it gave me great confidence to enter into a presentation of the Gospel. I have become so confident in those other two links that when I am certain the Holy Spirit is prompting me and actively working in their life, I feel as if someone should read them their rights.

A CHALLENGE AND A COMMITMENT

When I first discovered that God could use me as I applied the devotional and practical applications of this great story, I made the commitment to the Lord that when I was led by the Spirit and saw the evidences of spiritual activity in a person, I would be faithful and available. When I made that commitment, I did not think I would find many opportunities. However, I soon found myself staying up late with people, going without meals and frequently changing my schedule.

I challenge you to make that kind of commitment to the Lord. When you do, you may discover that spending time with someone might be the most important encounter in that person's spiritual journey on this planet.

I would like to close this *equipping chapter* with a verse of Scripture that has helped many people come to closure regarding the forgiveness of their sins. It was this verse the Ethiopian was reading in the chariot when he asked Philip that question. This verse, and the way I like to apply it, has aided many to see how to place their faith in the death of Jesus on the cross for the forgiveness of their sins.

Isaiah wrote: *"All we like sheep have gone astray; we have turned, every one, to his own way; and the Lord has laid on Him the iniquity of us all"* (Isaiah 53:6).

This verse begins and ends with the same word, the word "all." The first "all" of this verse is the bad news: every single one of us has gone astray and turned to his, or her, own way. As you consider that first "all" of this verse, do you believe that includes you? I don't know about you but personally I do not need a verse of Scripture to convince me that I am a sinner.

The last "all" of this verse proclaims the Good News that God laid on Jesus Christ the sins or iniquities of us all. Do you believe you are included in the last "all" of this verse? When you, by faith, include yourself in both "alls" of this great verse of Isaiah, you are confessing that Jesus Christ died for your sins.

We know this verse refers to Jesus Christ, because in the story of Philip and the Eunuch in the book of Acts chapter 8, the Ethiopian asked Philip if the writer was speaking of himself or some other person as they discussed this chapter. Philip began at this chapter and preached Christ to the Ethiopian. The Apostle Peter also confirms that this chapter refers to Jesus Christ (1 Peter 2:21-25).

In connection with the forgiveness of sins, I would like to share another teaching that has helped many people. There are times when the sins people have committed are so great and the consequences so horrible that have hurt many people. They, therefore, cannot forget their sins even when you emphasize the promises of God regarding their forgiveness. Promises such as: *"For I will forgive their wickedness and will remember their sins no more"* (Jeremiah 31:34).

I have found two basic truths to be helpful when I share with these people. I challenge them to remember what God remembers and to forget what God forgets. God remembers that we are sinners but when we confess our sins God forgets them. We forget that we are sinners. That is one reason why we fall into sin so often. And when we confess our sins we cannot forget them. We drag our guilt baggage with us long after the confession of our sins. We, therefore, need to remember what God remembers and forget what God forgets.

We forget we are sinners when we fail to have a defensive strategy against the power of sin. Jesus and the entire Bible take the position that even though our spirit is willing, our flesh is so very weak. We must therefore pray we will not face the confrontations of temptation. We are not to be ignorant of the stratagems of the evil one, and are to put on the whole armor of God that we might stand and fight a good spiritual warfare. When we do not apply this teaching of the Apostle Paul in the sixth chapter of Ephesians, we are forgetting that we are sinners.

Chapter Three

Commissioned to the Marketplace

For twenty-three years I served as the pastor of a church three miles from a large naval jet base. I often felt as if I were a navy chaplain. One thing I learned from knowing so many military people was how very seriously they took their orders. They read them like a love letter and obeyed them right down to the smallest detail.

Two thousand years ago Jesus gave those of us who profess to be His disciples our orders. How I wish we would take them as seriously as our military people take their orders today. Dr. Dallas Willard wrote an excellent book which he entitled *The Great Omission*. This was his satirical way of making the statement, which is the thesis of his book, that we are not taking the Great Commission seriously today. According to him the Church is doing many good things today, but we are not making disciples.

An extraordinary missionary statesman of another generation, Dr. Robert S. Glover, made this statement in his book *The Bible Basis of Missions*: "The Great Commission is the charter of the Church and like any other organization, the Church must fulfill the terms of its charter or it should cease and desist."

If we take the Great Commission seriously we should look at it closely and read it as military people read their orders:

"All authority has been given to Me in heaven and on earth. Go therefore and make disciples of all the nations, baptizing them in the name of the Father and of the Son and of the Holy Spirit, teaching

them to observe all things that I have commanded you; and lo, I am with you always, even to the end of the age. Amen" (Matthew 28:18-20).

In the original language there is one imperative: *make disciples.* That imperative, or commandment, is followed by three participles: *going, baptizing* and *teaching.* The argument of Dr. Willard is that we are simply not obeying the imperative commandment of making disciples today.

DO YOU KNOW WHAT YOU'RE TRYING TO DO?

I often find myself with a take-away one-liner as a result of reading a book or seeing a movie. In the movie *Patton*, my take-away came from the scene early in the movie where the general arrived just before daybreak at a North African station when he was not expected. Everything was in terrible disarray. He found a GI asleep on the floor so he kicked him in the pants. Upon seeing who it was, the young soldier jumped to his feet, saluted and said "I'm sorry sir. I was just trying to get some sleep." The general responded, "That's okay son. You're the only bleep-of-a-bleep around here who knows what he's trying to do!"

I sometimes cannot help but allow the thought that as the Church of Jesus Christ, we don't know what we're trying to do. When I hear Dr. Willard make the charge that we are not making disciples today, I believe there is plenty of evidence to convict many of us of that charge. I also agree with Dr. Glover that the Great Commission should be considered the charter of the church and we must fulfill its terms. To understand what he meant, all we have to do is read the book of Acts. The Great Commission is given at the end of each Gospel and at the beginning of the book of Acts, the only Holy Spirit inspired history book of the Church.

PENTECOST AND THE GREAT COMMISSION

It was the Great Commission that made Pentecost necessary. The Day of Pentecost was the spiritual anointing upon the Church that enabled them to obey the Great Commission. When they did not immediately spread the Gospel, hostile persecution drove them from Jerusalem to Judea, Samaria and the uttermost parts of the earth. Using Bible dictionaries and whatever resources you have available to you, do some research on the Twelve Apostles chosen by Jesus. Try to determine where they died, what they were doing when they died and how they died. If you do that, you will see what the Great Commission meant to them.

There is a difference between proclaiming the Gospel and making disciples. Paul and Silas proclaimed the Gospel to the jailor at Philippi. However, we read that after the jailor professed faith, they spoke the Word of God to him and his family. Paul's favorite church was established in Philippi because he believed in making disciples of those who professed faith in Jesus Christ. Paul proclaimed the Gospel everywhere he traveled. Because he believed in making disciples, he planted churches everywhere he preached and taught. He also wrote his inspired letters to the churches because his letters were part of the disciple-making process.

Immediately after the glorious Day of Pentecost, when three thousand were converted, the converts continued steadfastly in the teaching and fellowship of the apostles. Where did the apostles get the idea they were to teach those who were converted? Return again with me to our marching orders in the Great Commission. The Old King James Version says the apostles were commissioned to teach new disciples everything Jesus commanded them to observe.

According to the first chapter of the Gospel of John, when Jesus met some of these apostles, they were literally following Him down a road and He asked them what they wanted. They asked Him where He lived and His response was for them to come and see where He lived. The rest of the Gospel of John tells us they not only lived with Him but they lived for Him and died for Him because of what they experienced when they made the decision to come and see where and how Jesus lived.

For three years the apostles lived with Jesus 24/7. It was like a three-year seminary with no days off or weekends or holidays or summers. Just three years with Jesus. In those three years, how many things do you think He gave them to observe? Think about that and then read the Old King James Version of the Great Commission where Jesus commissioned them to teach new disciples everything He had commanded these apostles to observe. How long would it take them to do that? Would that not give them a relationship with the person or persons they were making disciples? That's why we read that those who were made disciples on the Day of Pentecost continued steadfastly in the apostles teaching and fellowship. Those new converts had fellowship with their disciple makers. The apostles learned they were to do that by considering their orders: the Great Commission.

When you realize God has <u>called</u> you to the marketplace and equipped you for the marketplace, add to those two realities that He has also commissioned you to be in the marketplace. I challenge you to memorize the Great Commission and meditate on every word of our orders as you find them there. If you do that, I promise you that you will know what you are trying to do as you intersect with secular people and establish relationships with them in the business world.

MENTORING AND BEING MENTORED

In 1953, an extraordinary pastor named Ray Stedman met with me for four hours every Thursday afternoon for an entire year. When I later profusely thanked him and asked how I could show my gratitude in a tangible way he responded, "Don't thank me. Thank the Lord and pass it on." For nearly sixty years as a pastor I have had the privilege of passing it on in a one-on-one relationship with hundreds of men. I showed my gratitude to the Lord for what that time with Ray Stedman meant to me.

I realize that many believers do not share the Gospel with secular people because they do not know how. They may not even know what the Gospel is. Likewise, many do not make disciples because they do not know how to disciple somebody. I would now like to share some *how to* information about making a disciple.

When I began meeting with a man to disciple him, I made sure he understood the Gospel. If we already shared a relationship, he was usually familiar with the Gospel as I describe it in my *Seven Spiritual Wonders of the World.* To make sure he understood the Gospel, and as a refresher, I usually began my disciple-making with him by expressing the Gospel another way. When it comes to understanding and believing the Gospel of salvation, one of the important factors is assurance. So, for review and assurance, I studied with him the first 16 verses of the first letter of the Apostle John:

"That which was from the beginning, which we have heard, which we have seen with our eyes, which we have looked upon, and our hands have handled, concerning the Word of life – the life was manifested, and we have seen, and bear witness, and declare to you that eternal life which was with the Father and was manifested to us – that which we have seen and heard we declare to you, that you also may have fellowship with us; and truly our fellowship is with the Father and with His Son Jesus Christ. And these things we write to you that your joy may be full.

"This is the message which we have heard from Him and declare to you, that God is light and in Him is no darkness at all. If we say that we have fellowship with Him, and walk in darkness, we lie and do not practice the truth. But if we walk in the light as He is in the light, we have fellowship with one another, and the blood of Jesus Christ His Son cleanses us from all sin. If we say that we have no sin, we deceive ourselves, and the truth is not in us. If we confess our sins, He is faithful and just to forgive us our sins and to cleanse us from all unrighteousness. If we say that we have not sinned, we make Him a liar, and His word is not in us.

"My little children, these things I write to you, so that you may not sin. And if anyone sins, we have an Advocate with the Father, Jesus Christ the righteous. And He Himself is the propitiation for our sins, and not for ours only but also for the whole world. Now by this we know that we know Him, if we keep His commandments. He who

says, "I know Him," and does not keep His commandments, is a liar, and the truth is not in him. But whoever keeps His word, truly the love of God is perfected in him. By this we know that we are in Him. He who says he abides in Him ought himself also to walk just as he walked" (1 John 1:1-2:6).

To gain perspective on this short letter, it is helpful to compare the way the Apostle John states his purpose for writing his Gospel and this short letter, which is found at the end of the New Testament:.

"And truly Jesus did many other signs [miracles] in the presence of His disciples which are not written in this book; but these are written that you may believe that Jesus is the Christ, the Son of God, and that believing you may have eternal life in His name… These things I have written to you who believe in the name of the Son of God, that you may know that you have eternal life, and that you may believe in the name of the Son of God" (John 20:30-31; 1 John 5:13).

This author, who also wrote the book of Revelation and two other short inspired letters in the New Testament named for him, always tells us why he is writing. He wrote the Gospel of John that we might believe and have eternal life. When we read his Gospel, we should underline all the things he tells us to believe.

He writes this short letter to those who believe (perhaps because they have read his Gospel), that they might know and then really believe. When we read 1 John, we should underline all the places he tells us, "*Hereby we know*," or, *This is how we can know*. In other words he is writing to those who are looking for the assurance of their salvation. If you do not have the absolute assurance of your salvation, the Apostle John is actually writing, "I wrote this letter for you!"

Assurance is the theme of this entire letter. Do you have the absolute assurance that your sins are forgiven and that if you died today, you would be in heaven? If you lack that assurance, then you must study this letter.

DEFINITION OF A LEADER

Someone has written: "If a man knows not, and knows not that he knows not, he is a fool. Shun him. If a man knows not, and he knows that he knows not, he is a child. Teach him. If a man knows and he knows not that he knows, he is asleep. Wake him. But if a man knows, and he knows that he knows, he is a leader. Follow him!" There are different levels of faith. John writes this letter to people who believe, that they might know they know they have salvation and then really believe and move to a more mature level of faith.

THE ASSURANCE COMPASS

I call the first sixteen verses of 1 John *The Assurance Compass.* These verses also present to us, just as the first 18 verses of the Gospel of John did, a kind of overview of what John is going to tell us. As in his Gospel, first he tells us what he is going to tell us. Then he tells us. Then he tells us what he has told us.

We all need a spiritual compass. For collateral reading, I recommend my booklet titled *A Spiritual Compass.* We will find a great compass of assurance in this inspired letter of the Apostle John. Just as there are eight points on a compass, here are the eight points I find on the assurance compass of John.

*The first point on this Assurance Compass is **facts**.* John tells us faith is based on facts. Faith is not a step in the dark or a leap in the light. As we learned in the faith chapter of the Bible, faith is based on evidence: *"Now faith is the substance of things hoped for, the evidence of things not seen"* (Hebrews 11:1 NKJV).

Faith gives substance to our hopes. That is the difference between hope and faith. Without evidence that gives us a basis for our hope, all we can do is hope. But faith always has a foundation of evidence on which it is founded. Since faith is a gift from God (Ephesians 2:8-10), faith in a person's life is itself the evidence of an unseen God, The Giver of faith.

John writes about the risen Christ when he emphatically tells his readers, "Listen, we are eye witnesses and we have actually seen Him up-close and personal. We put our fingers in the nail prints in His hands; we put our hand in His side. Our faith in a risen Christ is based on facts."

THE TWO GOSPEL FACTS

Two Gospel facts emerge in the books of the New Testament: the death of Jesus Christ and the resurrection of Jesus Christ. Again, observe how Paul emphasizes the death and the resurrection of Jesus Christ in what he wrote the Corinthians:

"Let me now remind you, dear brothers and sisters, of the Good News I preached to you before. You welcomed it then, and you still stand firm in it. It is this Good News that saves you if you continue to believe the message I told you—unless, of course, you believed something that was never true in the first place. I passed on to you what was most important and what had also been passed on to

me. Christ died for our sins, just as the Scriptures said. He was buried, and he was raised from the dead on the third day, just as the Scriptures said" (1 Corinthians 15:1-4 NLT).

The next point on the Assurance Compass is ***faith***. You must put faith in those two Gospel facts. It is not enough to simply know these facts. We must believe what we know and then grow to ever deeper levels of faith in these saving Gospel facts.

The third point is the result of putting faith in the death of Jesus, which makes all the difference in the world! Your sins are forgiven! What John builds for us is simply this: If you really have faith in the fact of the death of Jesus Christ on the cross, then you have ***forgiveness***, *the third point on the Assurance Compass.* And by this, I mean the *absolute assurance* of forgiveness.

In the Greek language, present tense represents continuous time. Therefore, anytime you have present tense in the Greek you can inject the concept of "continuously" in your understanding of the verse. For example, you could translate 1 John 1:9 this way: "If we continuously confess our sins, the blood of Christ continuously keeps on cleansing us from all unrighteousness." The result of believing in the death of Jesus Christ is a *continuous forgiveness.* Our assurance of forgiveness should be a continuous assurance of forgiveness.

The *fourth point on this Assurance Compass* is the result of believing in the resurrection of Jesus Christ –we can know Him and have ***fellowship*** with the risen, living Christ.

The word *fellowship* gives us the picture of a partnership or "two fellows in the same ship". I once shared some spiritual counsel with a man named Charlie who was on the periphery of coming to faith. He was having tremendous problems in his family. His wife was having a mental breakdown. One of his children was born with a tumor in her lower spine and she had been through seven operations. I told him he needed to learn a new word: *fellowship*.

I told him the word could be paraphrased as "two fellows in the same ship." Then I said to him "I want you to know that I'm in the ship with you." He took a long drag on his cigarette and with tears in his eyes he blew smoke in my face and said, "Well, row, damn it!"

What he was saying to me was something like, "I don't know exactly what that means, but I do want to know, what difference it is going to make? I mean, what are you going to do in my ship? Are you just going to take up room? Are you going to rock the boat or are you going grab an oar and row?" I often said these same words to people who were going through great trials. But after my conversation with Charlie, I could hear his words about rowing ringing in my ears each time I said that phrase. I found myself asking what it would mean for me to get in their ship and row.

Just as Jesus got in Peter's little ship and filled the ship with fish, Jesus Christ can get in your ship – your life – with you. Like a business partnership, everything He has in the way of resources is yours. If you are in fellowship with Him, then everything you have is His too. ***Fellowship** is the fourth point on the Assurance Compass.*

I call *the fifth point on the Assurance Compass **followship*** because the fifth point is following Christ. (I realize I have invented a new word.) When people told Jesus they believed in Him, He always said, "*Follow Me.*" John will write more than once, "*Hereby we know, because we keep His commandments and do the things that He commanded us to do*" (1 John 2:6 paraphrase). That is how we know that we know we have authentic faith and eternal life.

The sixth point on the compass is ***freedom***. Jesus taught in John 8:31, *"If you believe in Me, then continue in My word and become My disciples indeed."* Following Jesus validates and grows faith. But then Jesus described the result of following Him. He prescribed, *"If you continue in My word* [He did not say how long], *you will know* [He uses a word that means to know by relationship] *the Truth and the Truth will make you free."* He then repeated this thought and stated, *"When the Son makes you free, you will be free indeed"* (John 8:30-36 paraphrase). So the Truth we can know by relationship is Jesus Christ Himself.

John writes, *"I am writing these things to you that you sin not." In effect, he writes, If you do sin, the good news is you have an Advocate with the Father, and there is forgiveness through Him. But I am writing these things to you that you sin not* (1 John 2:1). You see, it is possible to be set free from sin.

I call *the seventh point on the Assurance Compass* ***fruitfulness***. Jesus gave the apostles six reasons why they must be fruitful. One of them was that He wanted their joy to be full (John 15:11). John believes some fruit for God in our experience of Christ will bring joy and assurance to us on our journey of faith. Paul actually writes the same thing in his letter to the Galatians:

"But let each one examine his own work, and then he will have rejoicing in himself alone, and not in another" (Galatians 6:4 NKJV). Great joy along with assurance can come into our faith journey when we realize that God is using us.

The eighth point on the Assurance Compass is what we call ***fullness***. As John writes this letter, he writes, *"And these things we* *write to you that your joy might be full"* (1 John 1:4). What we have is real and what we have is good, but there is more. John wants us to have the full experience. There is fullness of joy in moving through each point on this spiritual compass. John does not want us to merely experience a fragment of the spiritual life God intends for every believer. If we will use these points on the assurance compass as building blocks of faith, we will experience all the things God wants us to receive and experience.

We come to our spiritual journey the way we come to everything else, with a self-centered way of asking, "What's in it for me?" But as we saw in the conversion of Saul of Tarsus, we are really mature when we ask this question: *"Lord, what do You want me to do?"* (Acts 9:6). As the Lord answers that question for us, the Bible calls that being fruitful.

A SUMMARY OF THE ASSURANCE COMPASS

The eight points on the Assurance Compass are: facts, faith, forgiveness, fellowship, followship, freedom, fruitfulness and fullness. If you find that you are not fruitful, or that you do not have joy or fullness, go back to the beginning and check all eight points on your compass again. You will find these points on your spiritual compass effective as a formula for a personal spiritual revival.

THE NINE FRUITS OF THE SPIRIT

Another important step in the making of a disciple is to be sure they understand the ministry of the Holy Spirit as He works in the life of a believer. The work of the Holy Spirit is in two dimensions.

First, there is the work of the Holy Spirit in us. This is evidenced by what the Apostle Paul calls "*the fruit of the Spirit*" (Galatians 5:22-23). Paul lists nine of these fruits of the Spirit: love, joy, peace, patience, kindness, goodness, faithfulness, meekness, and self-control. I like to divide them into three sections: the fruit of the Spirit we discover when we ***look in, look around and look up***, when God demonstrates for us and proves to us, His miracle work in and through us.

There are three perspectives in life we must experience correctly if we're going to be the men and women of God our Lord wants us to be. First, we must *look in* and see the things God wants us to know about ourselves. We must confess them or agree with God until we are able to glorify Him by the way we live out our life for Him. There is a danger here that has been labeled as "a paralysis of analysis." Too much introspection can paralyze us. We can become like the man who sent his psychiatrist a card from where he was vacationing. The card read, "Having a wonderful time! Why?" However, if the Spirit of God through the Word of God is guiding us to *look in*, we can grow spiritually and serve God more effectively because God led us to *look in*.

When we *look in* we will discover a <u>love</u> that is not coming from us but from the Holy Spirit. This is like the love Paul profiles in chapter 13 of his first letter to the Corinthians. In the middle of that love chapter, he profiles fifteen virtues that will come out of our life because the Holy Spirit of Christ is in our life.

In the same way, when we *look in* we will find a <u>joy</u> that is not coming from us. We could paraphrase this word joy as "happiness that doesn't make good sense." This happiness does not depend on our circumstances. For example, when he writes a letter to the Church in Philippi, Paul uses the word *joy* seventeen times, even though he is chained between two Roman soldiers 24/7 while dictating that letter.

They tell us those soldiers were chained to Paul in four hour shifts and Paul never had a minute of privacy. In that setting Paul led many of the Palace Guard of Caesar to Christ. When they were chained to Paul for four hours, they heard the Gospel and many of them became believers and disciples of Jesus Christ.

Paul also writes that when the Holy Spirit is in our life, when we *look in* we will find a peace that doesn't make good sense because it isn't coming from us. It comes from the Holy Spirit and His presence in our life. This fruit of the Spirit makes it possible for us to have peace when the circumstances of our life are adversarial. As he dictates that letter while chained between two Roman soldiers, he not only *has* peace, but he tells us how *we can have peace.* In the fourth chapter of that letter, he gives us twelve ways we can nurture and cultivate that peace. In chapter 8, I give an in-depth prescription of those twelve conditions for personal peace.

After looking in, we must *look around* and relate to the people under our roof in our marriage and family, and in all our relationships in the marketplace. We simply must learn to relate well to all the people in our lives. To that end, God gives us the divine presence of His Holy Spirit.

As Paul teaches about the fruit of the Spirit, he writes that when we *look around* we will find patience, kindness and a goodness that are not coming from us but from the presence of the Holy Spirit in our life. This is not because we have inherited a laid-back disposition from our genetic heritage. This is a supernatural and miraculous kind of patience, kindness and goodness.

All of this begins when we *look up*. It is impossible for our *look in* and our *look around* to be what they are to be until we *look up*. It is only when we *look up* and invite God's Holy Spirit into our life that we can *look in* and *around* in the right ways. Only God can anoint our *in-look* and our *outlook* in a way that will get these critical perspectives on life together for us and make us human beings created, and recreated, in the image and likeness of God. It is only when God anoints our *in-look* and our *outlook* that we will get these critical perspectives on life together in a way that will make us a human being created, and recreated, in the image and likeness of God. The evidence of the fruit of the Spirit is revealed to us, and proven to us, as we consider how the presence of God's Spirit relates to these three perspectives on life.

When we *look up*, this patience can be described as *faith-waiting*. When we *look around*, it can be called *love-waiting*. I did not realize how selfish I was until I got married, and I did not realize how impatient I was until I found myself waiting for teenage children to grow up. The patience I needed had to come from the fruit of the Holy Spirit in me, that I might have the kind of patience that is *love-waiting*.

The kindness listed as the fruit of the Spirit comes from the word kin. It simply means we should treat everyone as if they were our kin. I frequently ate in restaurants where my daughters were working as waitresses, and I always left them a generous tip. When I researched the meaning of the Greek word for kindness I realized that I should always consider my waitress or waiter as if they were one of my daughters or one of my sons. That is the literal meaning of the word kindness. However, we must emphasize that it is a supernatural kindness that comes from the presence of the Holy Spirit in our life.

The same is true of the goodness that is the fruit of the Spirit in me giving me and all those in whom the Holy Spirit lives the capacity to be good and to do good things. When the Spirit is having His way in our lives, we demonstrate a powerful salt influence when we *look around*. Remember, when people are impressed with what we are and what we do, they will come to us the way Nicodemus came to Jesus to hear our religious talk.

When we *look up*, the fruit of the Spirit will be faithfulness, meekness and self-control. Paul addressed his letter to the Ephesians "*to the faithful in Ephesus.*" In every church you will find a committed minority of people who are "the faithful." Again, this fruit of the Spirit when we look up is not coming from us but from the presence of the Holy Spirit in our life. It is He who is giving us the capacity for this faithfulness. He gives us a supernatural quality of faithfulness that perseveres with a stick-ability that does not come from us. It comes from the Holy Spirit when we *look up.*

When we *look up*, we also find a meekness that is not coming from us. This is that Holy Spirit quality Jesus described that can give us a supernatural quality of rest:

"*Come to Me, all you who labor and are heavy laden, and I will give you rest. Take My yoke upon you and learn from Me, for I am gentle* (meek) *and lowly in heart, and you will find rest for your souls. For My yoke is easy and My burden is light*" (Matthew 11:28-30).

He invited all those who are loaded down with problems and are working themselves to a point of exhaustion trying to solve those problems by themselves, to learn from Him about meekness. He promised them that if they would learn about His meekness, they would find rest for their souls. And He also challenged them to learn about His heart, His burden and His yoke. That is the supernatural quality of meekness the Holy Spirit will supply us with when we *look up*.

The ninth fruit of the Spirit He will supply us with when we *look up* is <u>self control</u>. This is not self *in control* but rather, self *under control*. The expression "Spirit filled" is used improperly by many believers today. When someone asks me if I am a Spirit filled pastor my response is, "Not always. Are you?" We are given the impression that Spirit filled believers are always Spirit filled and all other believers are never Spirit filled.

In Ephesians 5:18, the Apostle Paul wrote that we should be filled with the Spirit the way a drunken person is under the influence of alcohol. It is to be an ongoing continuous surrender of our will to the will of the Spirit. The Holy Spirit is not a liquid and we are not a glass. It's not so much a case of the amount of the Spirit we have but how much of us the Spirit has. According to the Greek translation we are to be continuously filled or controlled by the Holy Spirit. That should be the goal of every believer, but can we honestly say we are yielding the control of our lives continuously to the Spirit?

The essential meaning of being filled with the Spirit is to be controlled by the Spirit. When we *look up*, the self control described here is synonymous with being filled with the Holy Spirit.

We have been focusing the dimension of the work of the Holy Spirit within us. There is a second dimension of His supernatural work in our lives described in chapter 12 of the first letter of Paul to the Corinthians. Paul writes that the Holy Spirit has a ministry when He comes upon us. The evidence of that work of the Holy Spirit is what he calls "gifts" of the Spirit. The spiritual gifts give a believer the capacity for ministries of various kinds.

DIVERSITY AND ONENESS

As Paul describes these gifts and ministries, he uses the words "diversity" and "oneness" several times. He brings these two opposite concepts together in a marvelous and inspired metaphor, writing that these gifts and ministries function like a human body. A human body is remarkable for its diversity. There is a great difference between a hand, an eye and an ear. All the diverse members of a body function with a oneness because they are under the control of one head. The Church is like a body where all the diversely gifted members are under the control of the risen Christ, the Head of this body. The Church should then function with a oneness while celebrating its diversity because it is under the control of Christ.

A SPIRITUAL GIFT INVENTORY

Ray Stedman wrote in his book *Body Life* that this acrostic might be called, "How to Take Your Own Spiritual Gift Inventory." Here's what Ray assigned to each of the A – H letters of the alphabet.

Acquaint yourself with the biblical descriptions of spiritual gifts. There are twenty-one of these spiritual gifts mentioned in the New Testament. I personally do not believe the list of spiritual gifts compiled from various Scriptures is intended to be exhaustive. My sense is that they are simply saying, "for example" when the authors list and describe the various spiritual gifts in their inspired letters.

Believe you are gifted. When you study a chapter like 1 Corinthians 12, observe how the word *every* is emphasized. When you summarize this great chapter, you must conclude that all born-again believers are spirituality gifted.

Consult your areas of effectiveness and fruitfulness in your spiritual community. All the gifts of the Spirit are given to edify, bless, challenge, instruct, equip, encourage and inspire other members of the spiritual community. Therefore, your spiritual community is the place to discover, identify, measure, exercise and develop your cluster of spiritual gifts.

Distinguish between natural gifts and spiritual gifts. Your natural gifts are the pattern of gifts and abilities you inherited by virtue of your physical birth and your genetic heritage. There is a sense in which these gifts become spiritual gifts when you consecrate them to God. You inherited your spiritual gift pattern, or cluster of spiritual gifts, by virtue of your spiritual birth. The Apostle Paul tells us that when the Holy Spirit comes to dwell in us, He brings with Him a cluster of spiritual gifts that were not present in our lives before we were born again (1 Corinthians 12:4-11).

Expect other members of the body or spiritual community to help you identify, acknowledge, exercise and develop your spiritual gifts. If people come to faith and become members of the body when you share the Gospel with them, you have the gift of evangelism. If people understand when you teach, you have the gift of teaching. The first person who told me I have the gift of teaching was the janitor of the church. I discovered my spiritual gift pattern by the way my teaching impacted that devout custodian. One of the most important roles of the local church is to help believers identify, acknowledge, exercise and develop their spiritual gifts.

Find opportunities to experiment with suspected gifts and ministry patterns. How do you know you do or do not have the gift of teaching if you do not have the faith and courage to try a Sunday school class or small group Bible study?

Give yourself time to develop the spiritual gifts you think the Holy Spirit has given to you. One negative experience with an attempted Bible study does not mean you do not have the gift of teaching.

Hold a consecration service and sincerely dedicate your spiritual gifts to your God Who is the Source of these gifts, the Power behind these gifts and whose glory is the purpose for all these gifts.

Your natural and spiritual gifts inventory may show you that you are gifted to serve the Lord in the marketplace because you are gifted at relating to secular people you meet outside the saltshaker.

Chapter Four
Anointed in the Marketplace

When you know you are called and commissioned to the marketplace, and when you are equipped to articulate and share the Gospel in the marketplace, you need to be anointed for your ministry in the marketplace. The Apostle Paul places a benediction on his theological masterpiece, his letter to the believers in Rome, with these words: *"For of Him and through Him and to Him are all things, to Him be glory forever. Amen"* (Romans 11:36).

THREE ABSOLUTES OF THE WORK OF GOD

Paul uses the two words "*all things*" frequently, but never lightly. As he concludes his greatest and most comprehensive statement of the Gospel of salvation, he eloquently tells us that God is the ***Source*** of all the things he has written. God is the ***Power*** behind all the things he has shared with us, and the glory of God is the ***Purpose*** for everything he has described in this letter. When we think in terms of having a ministry for God and Christ in the marketplace, we absolutely must learn these three basic facts about a work of God.

In many ways these three truths are an enormous consolation for us. The assurance of this truth enables our particular call to ministry. They have become three absolutes that guide me as I decide how to spend the little bit of energy and life I have to spend. I have lived with chronic fatigue since 1978, and my doctors can't believe I am still here. I can't afford to be involved in any ministry unless I am assured that God is the *Source* of that ministry. Since I have no power of my own, I must know that He is the *power* behind that ministry, and I must be convinced that His glory alone is the *purpose* of that ministry.

I reject the terms people use when they refer to a bed-fast quadriplegic like me. The derivation of the word handicapped has to do with a person with their cap in their hand begging. Invalid means "not valid," or a person who is not a valid human being. And disability means without ability.

I like to refer to people like me as limited. We all have to accept the limits of our limitations and the responsibility for our ability. Even Olympic athletes have limits. They call them records. They can only run or swim so far, so fast. And they can only jump so high or throw things so far. The only difference between people like me and others is that we live with a different set of limits.

FOUR SPIRITUAL SECRETS

My limits have led me to discover four spiritual secrets. The first one is "I'm not but He is." The second one is "I can't but He can." The third one is "I don't want to but He wants to." And when He uses me, I must remember a fourth spiritual secret, "I didn't but He did." These four secrets are not just cognitive propositions that make all the difference for me. They must have an ignition factor, described by Jesus in one of His most profound metaphors.

THE VINE AND THE BRANCHES

In the last retreat He had with His apostles before He was

arrested and crucified, Jesus explained that they were intrigued with His words and His works. He told them the key to the dynamic ministry they had observed for three years was that He and His Father were one. Every word He spoke and every work He did were an overflow of the reality that He was at one with His Father. He told them He was leaving them but He was going to send them the Holy Spirit. Through the Holy Spirit they would have a closer relationship with Him than they had experienced while He was present with them. And if they would be as at one with the Spirit as He was with His Father, they would speak the words of Jesus and do the works of Jesus after He was gone.

They then took a break and went out into a garden. He pulled down a vine with many branches loaded with fruit. He then said something like, *This is what I have been telling you at this retreat. I am like this vine and you are these branches. The way these branches are aligned with this vine makes it possible for the life-giving power of the vine to pass through them and produce this fruit. I am the Vine and I'm looking for branches who will align with Me and make it possible for Me to do My work and speak My words after My death and resurrection* (John 15:1-16).

The inspired metaphor of the vine and the branches describes the ignition that makes these four spiritual secrets a reality as we serve Jesus Christ in the marketplace. We're not simply serving Him there with His blessing upon us. We are in alignment with Him and He is actually dwelling within us and working through us while we serve Him in the marketplace.

THE LIFE OF MOSES

The greatest illustration of these spiritual secrets in the Old Testament is the life and ministry of Moses. Moses lived for 120 years in three periods of 40 years. In the first 40 years, God taught him he was nobody. Through some unusual providential circumstances he lived the first 40 years of his life in the palace of the Pharaoh of Egypt.

At the end of that period he learned he was not an Egyptian prince, but one of the Hebrews, like the slaves he worked and saw badly treated. On one occasion he saw an Egyptian taskmaster mistreating a Hebrew slave, so he killed the Egyptian and became public enemy number one in Egypt. He had to flee into the desert where he tended sheep for 40 years. During that second period of his life he lived with the reality that he was nobody.

After that second 40 year period, God appeared to him when an acacia bush burst into flame (Exodus 3:1-10). That happens in the intense heat of the desert but the bush is usually consumed in five seconds. This bush kept burning without being consumed. God spoke to him out of that bush.

"Now Moses was tending the flock of Jethro his father-in-law, the priest of Midian. And he led the flock to the back of the desert, and came to Horeb, the mountain of God. And the Angel of the Lord appeared to him in a flame of fire from the midst of a bush. So he looked, and behold, the bush was burning with fire, but the bush was not consumed. Then Moses said, 'I will now turn aside and see this great sight, why the bush does not burn.'

"So when the Lord saw that he turned aside to look, God called to him from the midst of the bush and said, 'Moses, Moses!' And

he said, 'Here I am.' Then He said, 'Do not draw near this place. Take your sandals off your feet, for the place where you stand is holy ground.' Moreover He said, 'I am the God of your father – the God of Abraham, the God of Isaac, and the God of Jacob.' And Moses hid his face, for he was afraid to look upon God.

"And the Lord said: 'I have surely seen the oppression of My people who are in Egypt, and have heard their cry because of their taskmasters, for I know their sorrows. So I have come down to deliver them out of the hand of the Egyptians, and to bring them up from that land to a good and large land, to a land flowing with milk and honey, to the place of the Canaanites and the Hittites and the Amorites and the Perizzites and the Hivites and the Jebusites. Now therefore, behold, the cry of the children of Israel has come to Me, and I have also seen the oppression with which the Egyptians oppress them. Come now, therefore, and I will send you to Pharaoh that you may bring My people, the children of Israel, out of Egypt'" (Exodus 3: 1-10).

To summarize, God told Moses at the burning bush that he had seen the problem and that was good. It was commendable that Moses cared about the suffering of the children of Israel. Moses wanted to get involved and become part of the solution and God thought that was great.

But God informed Moses that the important thing was that He, God, saw the problem of their slavery and terrible treatment. He cared about their awful slavery. He wanted to be part of their solution and He had come to be that Solution. Just as Moses was thinking about returning to his sheep, God said the most amazing thing. God said, *"Come now, therefore, and I will send you to*

Pharaoh that you may bring My people, the children of Israel, out of Egypt" (Exodus 3:10).

In effect, God was telling Moses "You are not their deliverer. I am their Deliverer. You can't deliver them but I can." After Moses raised five objections, God said to him, "You don't even want to deliver them but I do, and I am with you Moses" (Exodus 3:11-4:17). When they were delivered right through the Red Sea, which parted for them, nobody had to tell Moses that he did not deliver the people of God, but that God had delivered them.

If you can identify with Moses, was there ever a more unlikely candidate for a deliverer for the children of Israel? He was public enemy number one. He was a murderer (Three of the greatest men of God in the Bible were murderers: Moses, David and the Apostle Paul.). Moses was also an ungrateful adopted son. And He was an Israeli and a shepherd. We're told in the book of Genesis that Egyptians hated shepherds even more than they hated the children of Israel. Imagine how Moses felt when God told him to go into the presence of Pharaoh with a shepherd's staff. When you feel that you are not qualified to present the Gospel to a secular person in the marketplace, think of Moses and his qualifications.

In his 120 years of life the three lessons God taught Moses in three periods of 40 years each were first, that *he was nobody*. At the end of the second period at the burning bush God taught Moses he was somebody. And in the last 40 years of his life God taught Moses what God can do with somebody who has learned that he is nobody. The personal application is that God wants to teach you and me these same lessons. Has God taught you that you are nobody, that you are somebody and what He can do through you when you are somebody who knows they are nobody?

If He has I want to share with you what I heard an old pastor say many years ago when I was learning these 4 spiritual secrets: "When Jesus rode that donkey into Jerusalem on the first Palm Sunday and all the people shouted such wonderful things about Him, now wouldn't it have been silly for that little old jackass to think that was all for him?"

ABSOLUTE SECRETS

It's more difficult for achievers and over-achievers to learn the *four spiritual secrets*. But even achievers must learn that though they can do many things, there are still many things they absolutely cannot do. When it comes to the work of God they continuously hit a wall of the impossible. They cannot give the new birth experience to another person. Nor can they put faith into somebody else's life. The new life experience cannot be given to another person. They cannot raise the dead or heal the sick. Only God can do those miraculous happenings in the lives of the people we intersect in the marketplace.

A pastor was told by his Elders that he should visit one of his Elders, whom we shall call "Farmer Joe," because he had fixed up an old run-down farm and was proud of his beautiful farm. So the pastor called on the farmer. At the appropriate time, the pastor said to the farmer, "Joe, you and the Lord have really done a great job out here haven't you?" Farmer Joe responded "Yes pastor we have. And pastor, you should have seen this place when the Lord was running it all by Himself!"

I'm personally very grateful that the Lord does not do it all by Himself. It gives my life so much meaning, purpose and value to co-labor with the Lord in doing what only He can do. It is critically important for you to realize that only the Lord can do what He has commissioned, called and equipped you to do in the marketplace. Your goal is to see the grace of God changing lives in the marketplace. Only He can do that, but He is a Vine looking for branches without which He will not do what He wants to do in the marketplace.

THE LIFE OF PETER

A great example in the New Testament of these four spiritual secrets is the life of the Apostle Peter. Jesus uses the metaphor of fishing to spell out these four secrets for Peter. He calls Peter to follow Him and He promises Peter that when he does, he will become a fisher of men and not just fish.

"And Jesus, walking by the Sea of Galilee, saw two brothers, Simon called Peter, and Andrew his brother, casting a net into the sea; for they were fishermen. Then He said to them, 'Follow Me, and I will make you fishers of men'" (Matthew 4:18-19).

Luke shares his version of this call of Peter in chapter 5 of his Gospel and it may be a follow-up of the call we read about in the passage from Matthew above.

"So it was, as the multitude pressed about Him to hear the word of God, that He stood by the Lake of Gennesaret, and saw two boats standing by the lake; but the fishermen had gone from them and were washing their nets. Then He got into one of the boats, which was Simon's, and asked him to put out a little from the land. And He sat down and taught the multitudes from the boat.

"When He had stopped speaking, He said to Simon, 'Launch out into the deep and let down your nets for a catch.' But Simon answered and said to Him, "Master, we have toiled all night and caught nothing; nevertheless at Your word I will let down the net." And when they had done this, they caught a great number of fish, and their net was breaking. So they signaled to their partners in the other boat to come and help them. And they came and filled both the boats, so that they began to sink. When Simon Peter saw it, he fell down at Jesus' knees, saying, 'Depart from me, for I am a sinful man, O Lord!'

"For he and all who were with him were astonished at the catch of fish which they had taken; and so also were James and John, the sons of Zebedee, who were partners with Simon. And Jesus said to Simon, 'Do not be afraid. From now on you will catch men.' So when they had brought their boats to land, they forsook all and followed Him" (Luke 5: 1-11).

In this context Jesus gave Peter a two word version of the Great Commission when He told Peter he was to catch men rather than fish. We know Jesus was using the word "men" generically because when Peter became the great catcher of men on the Day of Pentecost the 3000 who were converted and the many thousands later who were converted when Peter preached were men and women.

Peter had been fishing all night and had caught nothing. While he was washing his nets, a crowd of people backed Jesus right up to the water's edge because they were eager to hear Him teach the Word of God. Peter continued the work of cleaning up after a fruitless night of fishing, while Jesus taught the crowd.

While Jesus was teaching, He had His eye on this big fisherman who was probably not in a very good mood. Jesus knew, of course, that in about three years this fisherman was going to preach to thousands of religious pilgrims from all over the world, and 3,000 would be converted because of the powerful sermon they heard him preach. Seminaries should give a lot to know what Jesus had to teach this fisherman, so that miracle might happen in just three years.

When the Bible class is over, Jesus suggested to Peter that they cast off into the deep water and go fishing again. When they actually came to the place where the water was deep, Jesus told Peter to let down his nets. But Peter gave Him some static. We read: "*But Simon answered and said to Him, 'Master, we have toiled all night and caught nothing; nevertheless at Your word I will let down the net*'" (Luke 5:5).

I like to imagine a thirty-second pause right after Peter said they had caught nothing, when his eyes met the eyes of Jesus. Peter then said he would let down the net as Jesus had requested. The miracle was that net was so filled with fish that it began to break and Peter had to frantically call his partners in the Zebedee Seafood Corporation, James and John, for backup. The fish nearly sank both boats!

When Peter objected to the directive of his Lord, he addressed the Lord as Master. This meant teacher. It's possible that Peter was saying to Jesus "You are the teacher. I am the fisherman." But of course Jesus was saying to Peter, "If you are going to catch men you must learn that you are not the fisherman. I am the Fisherman!"

WHO OWNS THIS BUSINESS?

Peter might have been saying to the Lord, "This is my business. Stay out of my business." But Jesus was saying to Peter, "I would like the chance to prove to you I can work for you in your business life." We're so prone to think that the risen living Christ can work in us and through us while we lead people to Christ, but we might not really think we have a right to ask Him to work in and through us while we are at work in our profit-making business. This story teaches us He can indeed work in and through us and make us a success in our business. Of course, the important issue is that when He does, He owns the business and all the profits are His.

As He teaches Peter the four spiritual secrets, they spell out this way: "You're not the fisherman I am. You can't catch men. Why you can't even catch fish. You don't want to catch men. I can and I want to catch men. I am the Fisherman and I am in your boat with you, Peter."

When the supernatural catch of fish was sinking both boats, we read: *"When Simon Peter saw it, he fell down at Jesus' knees, saying, 'Depart from me, for I am a sinful man, O Lord!'"* (Luke 5:8). Why did Peter react to the miracle in that way? I believe it was because Jesus was calling him to catch men and Peter was saying to the Lord something like, *You don't want somebody like me doing that. I am a sinful man. I swear a lot and I have a terrible disposition. You couldn't possibly want somebody like me catching men!*

WHO WAS THE FISHERMAN?

On the Day of Pentecost Peter boldly proclaimed that the resurrected Jesus Christ was causing all the miracles and wonders people could see on that glorious day:

"This Jesus God has raised up, of which we are all witnesses. Therefore being exalted to the right hand of God, and having received from the Father the promise of the Holy Spirit, He poured out this which you now see and hear" (Acts 2:32-33). When Peter preached that great sermon and 3,000 were converted, Peter knew who the Fisherman was that day. On all the days that followed, Peter understood it was the resurrected Christ present when he preached, and thousands more were converted every time.

There is another passage of Scripture that parallels this experience Peter had with Jesus. It is found in the third chapter of the book of Revelation. Jesus is writing a letter to a group of apathetic believers in Asia Minor. We read He writes to them:

"As many as I love, I rebuke and chasten. Therefore be zealous and repent. Behold, I stand at the door and knock. If anyone hears My voice and opens the door, I will come in to him and dine with him, and he with Me" (Revelation 3: 19-20).

There are many applications we can make to this passage of Scripture. A Presbyterian pastor named Dr. Robert Munger wrote a beautiful little booklet on this passage which he entitled, *My Heart, Christ's Home.* His thesis was that Christ was inviting Himself into our lives as if each area of our life were represented by the rooms in this house. That is the application I would like to make to this Scripture. Jesus is asking apathetic believers to let Him come into the very real, practical areas of their lives, like their business work life, that He might prove the reality of His presence to them there.

As He did with Peter, He would like to be invited into your business life so He might prove to you that He can not only be real to you there, but can also make you a success there. And He wants to prove to you He can make you a success there as a marketplace disciple. He wants to prove to you He can be the Fisherman through Whom you "*catch men*," (Luke 5:10) or businesspeople, for Christ in the marketplace.

TWO WAYS THE HOLY SPIRIT WORKS

In his book *Joy Unspeakable*, Dr. Martin Lloyd Jones gives us a wonderful perspective on the Holy Spirit. He teaches us there are different dimensions of the work of the Holy Spirit. There is the miracle work of the Holy Spirit within us, which is the new birth. The evidence or proof of that miracle in our lives as we have seen is what Paul calls the fruit of the Spirit (Galatians 5:22-23).

However, that is not the only dimension of the work of the Holy Spirit. Another distinct dimension of the work of the Holy Spirit is the anointing of the Holy Spirit *upon* us. That is described in the Scripture as the baptism of the Spirit. "*Upon whom you see the Spirit descending, and remaining on Him, this is He who baptizes with the Holy Spirit*" (John 1:33). On the Day of Pentecost, Peter described the Baptism of the Holy Spirit by quoting the Prophet Joel: "*And it shall come to pass in the last days, says God, that I will pour out of My Spirit on all flesh...*" (Acts 2:17).

Observe in the book of Acts how frequently the prepositions *on* and *upon* are used to describe this dimension of the ministry of the Holy Spirit. This is what Paul describes in chapter 12 of his first letter to the Corinthians, where we read: "*There are diversities of gifts, but the same Spirit. There are differences of ministries, but the same Lord. And there are diversities of activities, but it is the same God who works all in all*" (1 Corinthians 12:4-6).

When he tells us there are diversities or different kinds of gifts, ministries and activities, the word *activities* refers to operations or activities of the Holy Spirit. That means when a believer exercises a spiritual gift or ministry like preaching or teaching, the Holy Spirit comes upon them in different ways.

In summary, the miracle work of the Holy Spirit *within* us is the new birth or regeneration. The evidence or proof of that work is the fruit of the Spirit. The second dimension of the work of the Holy Spirit is the miraculous baptism of the Spirit *upon* us. The proof, or evidence of that miracle, can be seen in the gifts of the Spirit, which enable us to have ministries of the Spirit.

The members of the Church in Corinth were not ignorant of the reality of the Holy Spirit, but they were ignorant about the function of the Holy Spirit. Paul therefore taught (in chapter 12) very eloquently what I have just summarized. This is the greatest chapter in the Bible on the subject of how the Holy Spirit functions in a church.

I once had the opportunity to speak at a Thanksgiving service on a late Sunday afternoon in the historic Bruton Church in Colonial Williamsburg, Virginia. The College of William and Mary choir was tremendous and the sanctuary was packed. When I finished my message, my wife (who is my most honest but encouraging critic) said to me, "What happened?" My teenage children said, "You blew it, dad!" The anointing in the famous Church was so weak and I was so discouraged as I drove back to Virginia Beach, I felt as if I never wanted to preach again.

However, I was scheduled to give the same message the next evening to several hundred Law Enforcement Officers in Norfolk,

Virginia. The anointing as I spoke to the police officers was so strong I felt as if I were preaching like Elijah. I told the Lord I thought His timing was off. In the same chapter from which I have just quoted the quality and quantity of these activities of the Holy Spirit upon us are given "*as He wills*" (1 Cor 12:11) or *as it pleases Him, not us.*

I thoroughly agree with the distinguished scholar Martin Lloyd Jones who preached for 40 years at Westminster Chapel in London, England. There are at least two dimensions of the work of the Holy Spirit: His miracle work *within us* and His miracle blessing *upon us* as we serve Him in the Church, in the marketplace or anywhere else.

Anytime we serve Him, no matter where that may be, it is critical that we pray for the miracle work of the Holy Spirit within us and the energizing-anointing of the Holy Spirit upon us. This not only applies when we are exercising one of the ministries made possible by the gifts of the Holy Spirit. It is also true when we serve the Lord in any and every possible way and place. We should pray for this when we enter into an important business transaction. Every day we should pray for enabling spiritual power upon every transaction and activity on our agenda for the day.

Chapters 12, 13 and 14 in Paul's letter to the Corinthians are the most profound and eloquent New Testament Scriptures about these two dimensions of the work of the Holy Spirit. We cannot have the work of the Holy Spirit upon us, as evidenced by the gifts and ministries of the Holy Spirit, without the work of the Holy Spirit within us, as represented by the primary fruit of the Spirit, which is love. He makes that point in what most people consider the love chapter of the Bible, chapter 13. Then in chapter 14, he describes the order that should prevail among us as people who have the ministry of the Holy Spirit upon us and within us.

His work within us is also where we get the wisdom to know how to set our priorities and agenda in place. This work also gives us the wisdom we need to expedite each item on our agenda for the day. If we are honest and humble, no matter how gifted we may be, there are many times when we simply do not know what to do. James instructs us when that happens to ask God for wisdom. He promises God will give us all the wisdom we need, and then some (James 1:5).

SOME EXAMPLES OF MARKETPLACE DISCIPLES

In my teaching of Bible breakfasts for businessmen, I often emphasized the truth that God is our Mentor and He does His most effective mentoring when we are in a difficult place or when we are suffering. Two men often approached me after a message like that and said to me, "What about us? We don't have any problems. Does God not love us?"

One of them was the founder of that breakfast, a man named Caleb West, who owned the Savings and Loan and had extensive investments through his own private company. The other man was Jerry Hogge, Caleb's personal assistant who had been mentored by Caleb right out of college. When they responded the way they did, I said to them, "May I pray for you?"

As a result of a lot of dynamics I will not share with you, almost overnight they found themselves being prosecuted by bank examiners in Washington, DC. Their pictures were on the front page of the newspaper sometimes more than once a week. When that happened to them I sent them a card in which I wrote, "Welcome to the fellowship of hurting hearts."

There followed several months of daily court sessions, with legal fees of more than a million dollars. Caleb was completely exonerated and the one who brought the suit had to pay the legal fees. It was the first time anyone had ever won a case in court against those bank examiners. While Caleb and Jerry were going through that awful trial in their lives, I had a fruitful time ministering to them. Jerry became interested in teaching a Sunday school class in his large Baptist church, which he did for some time. He would often come to my home to get tapes of messages he had heard me give, to help him with his large class. He was even praying about the ministry. He appeared to be in great physical condition. But one night while he was playing tennis, he had a stroke on the tennis court and went to be with the Lord. Only the Lord knows how much the stress of that trying time contributed to his stroke.

Caleb often came to my home, where we went over, again and again, a teaching I had given on twelve conditions for personal peace (I will share those twelve conditions for peace in chapter 8 of this book). That teaching ends by working those twelve conditions into a prayer. Since he was the chairman and the MC for the breakfast, he always opened the breakfast with prayer. For many weeks Caleb opened the breakfast with that peace prayer.

When I congratulated Jerry and Caleb because they had not missed a breakfast throughout that entire crisis, they both assured me that the blessing of God's Word and the fellowship they experienced there was their spiritual and emotional lifeline.

I learned from my relationship with Jerry and Caleb how enormous the stresses can be in the marketplace today. To be a fruitful marketplace disciple, you simply must be an anointed marketplace disciple. That anointing is necessary not only to be fruitful and successful, but also to survive the pressures and stress of the marketplace.

I have a son-by-marriage named Woody Perry, who has just finished seven years of litigation. He had a wealthy older man as a partner for years, but when that partner died, Woody had to work with his children. When Woody wanted to withdraw from the partnership, it went into litigation. He has spent just under a million dollars on legal fees and learned first-hand how slowly the court system can move. The court finally ruled in his favor, but it took seven years for that to happen.

I'm so proud of him because he has not let the incredible pressure of this experience blow him out of the water spiritually. Rather, it has driven him deeper and deeper into the Lord and His Word. He has lived with Psalm 37, which exhorts us to rest in the Lord, trust in the Lord and wait on the Lord. He has also practically memorized my booklet, *A Prescription for Peace*, in which I wrote about those twelve conditions for personal peace I describe in chapter 8 of this book.

I gave an invitation at every one of those Thursday morning breakfasts. One morning an automobile dealer named Charlie Fletcher responded to my invitation and trusted Jesus Christ to be his Lord and Savior. As he tells it in his God story, his decision didn't stick. One evening, he watched Monday night football with his adult son, whom he and his wife Margaret had adopted while he was still in diapers. About three o'clock in the morning, Charlie was blown out of bed when his son shot him with a shotgun. His wife was also shot. She saw their son leaving the room with his shotgun and thought he was pursuing the one who had shot both of them. When she called out to him he shot her a second time.

They both miraculously survived their tragedy. Passing through that awful trial was what drove Charlie deeper into the Lord and His Word. He and Margaret were two of the best students I ever had in my Mini Bible College, which I taught on a weeknight in my church. I had actually become their pastor by this time and I was involved in deep counseling with them. This was especially needed when their son was later released from a hospital for the criminally insane.

The mental health professionals never established an explanation or motive for their son's actions. After he was released, I met with him regularly for some time and I was never able to hear from him anything like a motive or reason for what he had done. Naturally, his father, and especially his mother, were apprehensive about him living with them again. He did live with them for several years before he established his own life, living separately from them.

I share this story for two reasons. As I got to know really well, men who attended my breakfasts and who worked in the marketplace, I was amazed at the personal problems they brought with them that had nothing to do with their work in the marketplace.

Secondly, as I taught these men, I was made aware that the most deeply spiritual people I knew, and those who were also my best Bible students, were people who had survived great calamities. In Isaiah 45:7, God tells us He creates calamity. Over many decades, God has reinforced my conviction that He is our Mentor. He does His most effective mentoring when we are going through those calamities, such as suffering and enduring the pressures and stresses of economic downturns.

One day a Jewish man named Herman approached me and asked if I would counsel his son. I shared the Gospel with him and told him I would be counseling his son from that perspective. He told me I would have to meet with his brothers, Sam and Harry, because the oldest had taken the place of the father when his father died. We had lunch and after about an hour and a half, Sam, the oldest brother, said I could counsel Herman's son.

As I did that over an extensive period of time, several times I needed to meet with Herman. We became friends and began jogging together. I invited him to my Thursday morning Bible breakfast and his response was that his Rabbi had a Bible study luncheon. If I would attend that luncheon with him, he would come to my breakfast. We did that for over a year. A group of men from the breakfast started a small group Bible study at night, which Herman also attended.

One day Herman called me from his furniture store. He was having a big holiday sale, but took the time to call and say "I have decided to make 'Yeshua my Messiah. How do I do that?" I went by the store and told him I was having a baptismal service that Sunday morning and I would be happy to baptize him. He said to me, "Man you really know how to close a sale!"

But then he turned as white as his shirt and said, “Do you realize what this would mean to me? For starters, Sam and Harry will put me out of the business. If my orthodox parents were living, they would have a funeral service for me and no longer have a son named Herman.” I responded that I did not make the rules; I just kept them. Jesus was the One who commissioned that every professing disciple should go public with their faith by being baptized.

Sam and Harry did put him out of the business. He was successful in starting his own business and also started a Messianic Synagogue in Norfolk, Virginia, known as Beth Messiah. His coming to faith was precipitated by that small group of men with whom he attended the Bible study.

One night while we were studying Romans chapter 9, I made the statement that God loves Jews so much that an anti-Semitic Christian was a theological monstrosity. This is primarily true because Jesus was a Jew. Herman responded, “Do you mean to say that Christians are supposed to love Jews?” The men in that group then thoroughly affirmed their love for him. As that group meeting came to a close with prayer, they all had their arms interlocked in love for him. Prior to that evening, he thought Hitler was a Christian and that all Christians were anti-Semitic.

I’m telling you his story to show how difficult it is and how greatly it can impact our marketplace if we become a professing marketplace disciple from another faith. People think it was so extraordinary for a Jewish man like Herman to become a disciple of Jesus Christ. In the book of Acts, the inspired Church history book of the Bible, Peter could not believe it when he was given the commission to take the Gospel of Christ to non-Jewish people. God had to give him a vision and repeat it three times to convince Peter it was true. In the first ten chapters of Acts, all the believers we read about in the New Testament Church were Jewish.

My relationship with Herman is an example of friendship evangelism in the context of the marketplace. For collateral reading I recommend my book *4 Spiritual Secrets*, which teaches about the anointing we all need to function as marketplace disciples.

Chapter Five

The Values of Christ in the Marketplace

It may be because Luke is a medical doctor that he is the only Gospel writer who gives us The Parable of the Good Samaritan. In that parable Jesus tells the story of a man who is mugged and left to die by the side of the road:

"And behold, a certain lawyer stood up and tested Him, saying, 'Teacher, what shall I do to inherit eternal life?' He said to him, 'What is written in the law? What is your reading of it?' So he answered and said, 'You shall love the LORD your God with all your heart, with all your soul, with all your strength, and with all your mind,' and 'your neighbor as yourself.' And He said to him, 'You have answered rightly; do this and you will live.' But he, wanting to justify himself, said to Jesus, 'And who is my neighbor?'

"Then Jesus answered and said: 'A certain man went down from Jerusalem to Jericho, and fell among thieves, who stripped him of his clothing, wounded him, and departed, leaving him half dead. Now by chance a certain priest came down that road. And when he saw him, he passed by on the other side. Likewise a Levite, when he arrived at the place, came and looked, and passed by on the other side.

"But a certain Samaritan, as he journeyed, came where he was. And when he saw him, he had compassion. So he went to him and bandaged his wounds, pouring on oil and wine; and he set him on his own animal, brought him to an inn, and took care of him. On the next day, when he departed, he took out two denarii, gave them to the

innkeeper, and said to him, 'Take care of him; and whatever more you spend, when I come again, I will repay you.'

"'So which of these three do you think was neighbor to him who fell among the thieves?' And he said, 'He who showed mercy on him. 'Then Jesus said to him, 'Go and do likewise'" (Luke 10:25-37).

THREE PHILOSOPHIES OF LIFE AND NEIGHBOR

The context of this parable helps us to interpret the parable. We are told the motive of this lawyer was to test Jesus. When Jesus answered the lawyer's initial question so clearly and wisely again, we are told his motive was to justify himself when he asked that question, "Who is my neighbor?" The Pharisees believed your fellow Jew was your neighbor and everyone else was your enemy. It was a controversial question because all Jews did not define their neighbor that way. Jesus completely ignored that issue and answered the lawyer's question with this profound parable which He followed with His own question about who is a neighbor.

We all have a *philosophy of life* whether we think it through and put it in writing or not. In the same way we all have a *philosophy of neighbor*, or how we believe we should relate to those we classify as our neighbor. To be a fruitful marketplace disciple, we simply must work out a Christ-like philosophy of neighbor as we intersect with and relate to the people in the marketplaces where we do business.

The road in this story leads from Jerusalem to Jericho. Priests and Levites often traveled that road to retreat in Jericho from their duties in the Temple of Solomon. A Levite was a professional employee of the Temple. Some of them were like our ministers of music or education. One at a time, this priest and Levite came by and observed the awful condition of this dying and helpless man. They each said, *You've really got a problem there, bleeding to death in that ditch, but I am not going to get involved.* We read that they passed by on the other side.

However, a Samaritan also travelled that road. When he saw the dying man, he stopped and treated his wounds, put him on his animal, and took him to an inn. After giving the innkeeper money, he said, *If you need more, when I come back again I will pay it.*

Remember the question Jesus was answering when He taught this story: "*Who is my neighbor?*" This profound answer of Jesus presents three philosophies of life or of neighbor. After telling this story, Jesus answered the lawyer's question with: *Which of these three was a true neighbor to the man who fell among thieves?*

Jesus first answers the lawyer's question with the example of the bandits who robbed and mortally wounded this man. Their philosophy was, "What's mine is mine, and what's yours will be mine just as soon as I can take it." There are many people in the marketplace with that philosophy of life and neighbor. That is why we have government, police, and a military. Most governments today will not negotiate with those who have that *philosophy of neighbor.* During the Cold War in the early sixties, John Kennedy said that you cannot negotiate with people who believe "What's mine is mine and what's yours is negotiable."

The priest and the Levite – the religious people in the story – profile a second answer to this question of Jesus: Their philosophy of neighbor was, *What's mine is mine and what's yours is yours. I have my blessings and you have your blessings. I have my problems and you have your problems. Mine is mine; yours is yours. I don't get involved in these things.* Too many religious people have that philosophy of life and neighbor today.

In this story, there is a third answer to the question of Jesus about our philosophy of life and neighbor. The absolute Master of the use of parable threw this story alongside a truth He wanted to teach us. That truth is expressed in the way the Samaritan answers the question of Jesus. The Samaritan's philosophy of life and neighbor was: "What's yours is yours and what's mine is yours any time you need it."

THE PHILOSOPHY OF AN AUTHENTIC DISCIPLE

The Samaritan's philosophy of neighbor will not make you rich, but this is the philosophy of Jesus about life and neighbor. Putting this statement of personal philosophy next to a realistic and biblical definition of a disciple spells out the hard reality that a marketplace disciple of Jesus is not in the marketplace to get rich, but to be an effective witness and disciple-maker for Jesus. A friend of mine said, "That might be tight, but that is right!" This message may be a hard reality to apply, but it is the philosophy of a marketplace disciple of Jesus.

The dictionary defines a value as "that quality of any certain thing by which it is determined by us to be more or less important, useful, profitable and therefore, desirable. " Jesus had an inspired set of values. When we are told in the Scripture to confess Jesus Christ, that means we are to follow behind Him as we read Scriptures. When He identifies and declares a value, we need to declare the same thing about that value He does: "*Every spirit that confesses that Jesus Christ has come in the flesh is of God, and every spirit that does not confess that Jesus Christ has come in the flesh is not of God"* (1 John 4:2-3).

In 1 John 1:9, we are instructed to confess our sins. In the previous passage I quoted that we are told every spirit that confesses that Jesus has come in the flesh is of God. It is explained that we confess Christ with our spirit when we love.

The word *confess* is a compound Greek word that combines the words for speaking and sameness. I warn you that confessing the values of Jesus Christ is revolutionary, as you can see in the dynamic parable we have just considered. If you identify yourself in the marketplace as a disciple of Jesus Christ, it is imperative that you both speak and own His values as you serve Him there.

THE MANIFESTO OF THE MESSIAH

The author of the third Gospel presents the life and ministry of Jesus through the grid of His Nazareth Manifesto:

"Then He came to Nazareth where He had been brought up. And as His custom was, He went to the synagogue on the Sabbath day, and stood up to read. And He was handed the book of the prophet Isaiah. And when He had opened the book, He found the place where it was written, 'The Spirit of the Lord is upon Me, because He has anointed Me to preach the Gospel to the poor: He has sent Me to heal the broken-hearted, to proclaim liberty to the captives, and recovery of sight to the blind, to set at liberty those who are oppressed; to proclaim the acceptable year of the Lord."

"Then He closed the book, and gave it back to the attendant and sat down. And the eyes of all in the synagogue were fixed on Him and He began to say to them, 'Today this Scripture is fulfilled, in your

hearing'" (Luke 4:16-21).

Many world leaders have begun their mission by writing a Manifesto a declaration of their answers to the problems people have in this world. When we hear Jesus begin His three years of public ministry by declaring what scholars call "The Nazareth Manifesto," we should realize we are hearing the greatest Manifesto the world has ever heard. This is not only true because its content is inspired Scripture and the fulfillment of prophecy. The Nazareth Manifesto is the greatest Manifesto this world has ever heard, because it was implemented perfectly by the One Who declared it.

We should also realize Jesus was declaring the Manifesto of the Church today by the way Luke tells us His ministry began. The Nazareth Manifesto not only shows us what Jesus Christ was doing when He lived out His life here in the flesh, but it also shows us what He desires to do through those of us today who call ourselves "the Body of Christ." How should the body of Christ function in the marketplaces of this world today?

The metaphor that we are the body of Christ today means the risen living Christ is literally living in and through His disciples in this world right now. If He was committed to meeting the needs of the blind, the bound and the broken people of this world when He had a body of His own, then He wants to do through us, who are His body, the same things He did when He was here.

The Communist Party had very few members for many years after their Manifesto had been written by Marx and Engels. Then one member named Lenin wrote a pamphlet entitled, "What Is to Be Done?" The thrust of this tract was, *What should be done by those who believe our Manifesto?* That little pamphlet mobilized many millions of people into the Communist Party movement.

I have often thought it would be a good thing for a disciple of Jesus to read the Gospels and the Bible and then decide what is to be done if one really, truly believes the Gospel and the teachings of Jesus Christ. It was pointed out to me by an outstanding spiritual statesman that no one believer could write that statement for us all. Each of us must personally write that statement for ourselves as we ask the question the Apostle Paul asked Jesus: "*Lord, what would you have* ***me*** *to do?*" (Acts 9:6).

The life and teachings of Jesus Christ are the Manifesto of the disciple of Jesus Christ. Authentic followers of Jesus Christ believe the risen, living Christ has the only solutions to the needs and problems of the people of this world. This declaration of purpose by Jesus at the outset of His ministry is His capsule Manifesto that not only tells us what He purposed to do, but tells us what is to be done by every disciple of His in this world today.

Jesus' Nazareth Manifesto declared He was anointed by the Holy Spirit to bring Good News to the poor. He described the poor as the people in this world who are blind, bound, bruised and brokenhearted. He was dedicated to giving sight to the blind and He did this primarily through His teaching ministry.

We're told in several places in the Gospels that when He saw the multitudes, Jesus wept over them. The Greek word suggests that His whole body convulsed with sobs. That was caused by the reality of His seeing people as sheep having no shepherd, not knowing their right hand from their left. Jesus placed great value on His teaching ministry. We read so very many times in the Gospels that He opened His mouth and taught them. That was when He gave sight to the blind.

Jesus could never walk on by those who were not free. An anonymous poet has written: "A famished bear, whose foot was clenched within a murderous trap, wrenched about in fright and pain around the tree that held the chain emitting many a hideous howl. His state was noticed by an owl who, perched above him, fat and free philosophized from out of the tree, 'To what avail this fuss and noise? The thing you need good bear is poise!'"

The author of this poem tells us there are two kinds of people in this world: Those who are free and those who are not free. He further tells us that those who are free often look down in detached and apathetic condescension on those who are not free. The Gospel of Luke tells us emphatically that Jesus was no fat owl in His relationship to those who were not free. We should realize He wants to express Himself in the same way through us, as we live out our life in the marketplace.

Jesus gave freedom to the bound, or to what He described as "the captives." He set captives free as the cumulative effect of His teaching ministry (John 8:30-36). He also brought freedom to the bound, through what He called being *born again*, which for them was like getting out of jail.

He related to the bruised and brokenhearted people through His miraculous healing ministry. The dynamic application of this Nazareth Manifesto of Jesus is that the Christ Who lived on earth now lives in us. He still wants to relate to the blind, bound, bruised and brokenhearted people of this world today as He intersects with them while living in us.

As you move among people each day in the marketplace, learn

to view all the people who intersect your life as the blind, bound, bruised and brokenhearted people for whom Jesus came. Luke presents Jesus as reaching out and inviting people to participate with Him in the implementation of His great Manifesto.

THE PARABLE OF THE LOST THINGS

Luke describes Jesus reaching out to people through parables as He enlists them to participate in the implementation of His Manifesto. Luke prioritizes an entire chapter showing the tremendous value Jesus places on the lost things of this world. In chapter 15, Jesus describes secular people as lost sheep, lost valuable coins, and two lost sons. The religious establishment of His day did not understand why He spent so very much time relating to these lost people. But Luke understood Jesus' Manifesto, and why He cared so much for the lost people of this world.

At the end of Luke chapter 14, Jesus preached a hard hitting and dynamic sermon. Chapter 15 begins by telling us that in response to that great sermon, an enthusiastic crowd of publicans and sinners, who liked what they heard, gathered around Him. In contrast, the religious leaders took about thirty steps back and withdrew from Jesus, showing their strong disapproval of what they heard and saw happening in that inner circle.

Jesus faced two concentric circles of people when He gave the teaching found in chapter 15. He actually addressed this teaching to the outer circle of religious leaders. His objective was to explain to them what was going on in that inner circle, and why it was so important to God and should be to them. He was actually reaching out to them, earnestly and sincerely inviting them to participate with Him in His Nazareth Manifesto.

Saul of Tarsus could have been in that outer circle. We can almost be certain that men like Nicodemus and Joseph of Arimathea, who came to claim the body of Jesus after His crucifixion, would have been in that outer circle. Jesus loved Pharisees like these men and all three of them became disciples of His. Saul of Tarsus, of course, became the greatest missionary for Jesus the Church ever had. It is exciting to imagine that he might have been there.

Jesus begins this teaching by telling us a little allegory about lost sheep:

"What man of you, having a hundred sheep, if he loses one of them, does not leave the ninety-nine in the wilderness, and go after the one which is lost until he finds it? And when he has found it, he lays it on his shoulders, rejoicing. And when he comes home, he calls together his friends and neighbors, saying to them, 'Rejoice with me, for I have found my sheep which was lost!' I say to you that likewise there will be more joy in heaven over one sinner who repents than over ninety-nine just persons who need no repentance" (Luke 15:4-7).

Since it was a pastoral culture, they would all resonate with this short allegory. His point is that all heaven is rejoicing when one of the sinners in this inner circle here repents. Jesus is asking, *What is your problem? Why are you not rejoicing with Me when these sinners repent?*

Jesus then follows with another profound metaphor:

"Or what woman, having ten silver coins, if she loses one coin, does not light a lamp, sweep the house, and search carefully until she finds it? And when she has found it, she calls her friends and

neighbors together, saying, 'Rejoice with me, for I have found the piece which I lost!' Likewise, I say to you, there is joy in the presence of the angels of God over one sinner who repents" (Luke 15:8-10).

One explanation of this *coin*-metaphor of Jesus is that in the Hebrew culture, a woman had a headdress that presented ten coins across her forehead. The significance of this jewelry was much like our custom of a wedding ring. If she was unfaithful to her husband, she informed him of her infidelity by detaching one of these ten coins. If she inadvertently lost one of these ten coins, can you understand how frantically she would search until she found that coin she had lost? Think of how, when she finds it, she gathers her lady friends together and exclaims, "*Rejoice with me! I found the coin I lost!*"

By application, Jesus says to the outer circle that all they see in the inner circle are publicans, sinners, thieves, prostitutes and pimps. But Jesus makes the application that some of these in the inner circle are like that woman with a lost coin. His first metaphor made the claim that some of those in the inner circle were like lost sheep being found by their Shepherd. In this second metaphor of the coin headdress, He could be illustrating sanctification. Some people are lost in the sense that they can't keep the ten coins together. They cannot seem to find the secret of victory over sin, so they come to their Shepherd for sanctification.

Since it is a woman who has lost her coin and the Church is sometimes referred to in the feminine, this could be picturing those who have been lost by the religious establishment. I have often found myself ministering to people who had a bad church experience that caused them to throw away the Church. But, they have not thrown away God or the Bible.

THE REDEMPTION OF A LOST COIN

When I was a teenager, on a day that was cold, windy and filled with sleet, I waited for a trolley, having a coin that would pay for my trolley ride to my home several miles away. Suddenly, I accidentally dropped my coin, which rolled into a drain covered by heavy iron grating. While I could see the coin about 18 inches from the surface, I could not reach it. The thought of walking several miles to my home in that awful weather gave me a rush of anxiety.

An old gentleman who was also waiting for the trolley had an umbrella and could see my predicament. He folded up his umbrella, took his chewing gum and stuck it on the tip. Passing the umbrella through the iron grating and attaching the chewing gum to the coin, he withdrew the umbrella and dropped the coin in my hand. That coin seemed to be ten times more valuable to me than it was before I lost it. To get something back that you have lost is the pure definition of redemption. Redemption is the essence of all these metaphors Jesus gives of lost things that are found or recovered again.

A word synonymous with redemption is the word *rehabilitation*. The Latin root of this word means "to invest again with dignity." As a pastor for nearly six decades, I found myself deeply involved in the rehabilitation of people. One of the most beautiful experiences of a pastor is to watch the grace of God change lives and give people a second chance at life while they invest again with dignity.

We cannot even begin to imagine the emotions Jesus

experienced when He was surrounded by that inner circle of sinners receiving the grace of God to invest again with dignity. That outer circle of people, who were supposed to be the spiritual leaders of God's people, were angry and would not come into that inner circle and participate with Jesus in the redemption and rehabilitation of those in the inner circle.

The point Jesus makes several times is that all heaven rejoices when redemption happens. His challenge to the outer circle, as He profiles what is happening in the inner circle, is this: all heaven is rejoicing because of the redemption that is happening in this inner circle. What is your problem? Why are you not rejoicing?

He then continues the pattern with one of His most well-known parables. We call it "The Parable of the Prodigal Son." Many of the people you meet in the marketplace today are like this prodigal son.

"Then He said: 'A certain man had two sons. And the younger of them said to his father, 'Father, give me the portion of goods that falls to me.' So he divided to them his livelihood.

"And not many days after, the younger son gathered all together, journeyed to a far country, and there wasted his possessions with prodigal living. But when he had spent all, there arose a severe famine in that land and he began to be in want. Then he went and joined himself to a citizen of that country, and he sent him into his fields to feed swine. And he would gladly have filled his stomach with the pods that the swine ate, and no one gave him anything.

"But when he came to himself, he said, 'How many of my father's hired servants have bread enough and to spare, and I perish with hunger! I will arise and go to my father, and will say to him, 'Father, I have sinned against heaven and before you, and I am no longer

worthy to be called your son. Make me like one of your hired servants.

"And he arose and came to his father. But when he was still a great way off, his father saw him and had compassion, and ran and fell on his neck and kissed him. And the son said to him, 'Father, I have sinned against heaven and in your sight, and am no longer worthy to be called your son.' But the father said to his servants, 'Bring out the best robe and put it on him, and put a ring on his hand and sandals on his feet. And bring the fatted calf here and kill it, and let us eat and be merry; for this my son was dead and is alive again; he was lost and is found.' And they began to be merry" (Luke 15:11-24).

This parable clearly shows us the love God has for the lost people of this world. Seminary professors tell you when you are learning to preach that every sermon should have three points, three points under each of those three points and a conclusion.

A good way to outline this sermon would be to have these three main points: *His Madness, His Sadness* and *His Gladness.* Under the first point of *His Madness* three points could be: *He Rambled, He Scrambled and He Gambled.* Under the second point of *His Sadness* in the far country, three points could be: *He went to the dogs, He lost his togs and He slept with the hogs.* Under that third point, *His Gladness* when he returned to his father, you could have three points: *He ate the veal, He wore the seal and He did the reel.* A good conclusion could be *Turn or Burn*!

This eloquent sermon outline summarizes the truth Jesus was teaching to that outer circle about what was happening in that inner circle and why. The point this sermon makes is that Jesus loves all those secular people you will meet in the marketplaces of this world. The critical truth found in this touching story is the unconditional love of the Father for His Son. The love of God is pictured here as an old man running. There is nothing in all the world as undignified as an old man running. And there is no picture of the love of God in the Bible more touching than this picture of the unconditional love of God for His prodigal son. While his son is still a long way off, the old man father runs to enthusiastically smother him with loving embraces and kisses.

At the heart of this story is the awful banquet of consequences faced by this Jewish boy in a hog pen. It was as he found himself feeding hogs and wishing he could have the food he was slopping them that he was brought to his senses. God used the harsh consequences of his own choices to bring him to himself and to a realization of how far he had fallen away from the love of his Father. In the opening verses of the book of Proverbs, according to the *Living Bible-Paraphrased*, this wonderful book of wisdom tells us young men need to experience the full terrors of the way they have chosen when they choose not to walk in the ways of wisdom.

The word *self* is defined in the dictionaries as "the uniqueness, the individuality of any given person that makes them distinct from every other living person." I find it intriguing that when the prodigal came to himself and decided to return to his home and his father's love, it was this decision that brought him to himself. This, in turn, would make him the person his father wanted him to be, distinct from every other living person.

We are told the wages of sin is death. That means the consequences of sin are the awful pits we dig for ourselves when we are running away from God. "Soon or late every man must sit down to a banquet of consequences." So wrote the poet Longfellow, and so taught our Lord Jesus Christ when He explained to that outer circle what was happening in that inner circle. We sometimes fail as a parent when our prodigal children are about to learn something from the awful consequences of the way they have chosen, when we intervene and rescue them from those consequences.

THE ELDER BROTHER

But that was not the whole story Jesus was teaching:

"Now his older son was in the field. And as he came and drew near to the house, he heard music and dancing. So he called one of the servants and asked what these things meant. And he said to him, 'Your brother has come, and because he has received him safe and sound, your father has killed the fatted calf.'

"But he was angry and would not go in. Therefore his father came out and pleaded with him. So he answered and said to his father, 'Lo, these many years I have been serving you; I never transgressed your commandment at any time; and yet you never gave me a young goat, that I might make merry with my friends. But as soon as this son of yours came, who has devoured your livelihood with harlots, you killed the fatted calf for him.'

"And he said to him, 'Son, you are always with me, and all that I have is yours. It was right that we should make merry and be glad, for your brother was dead and is alive again, and was lost and is found'" (Luke 15:25-32).

The most intriguing metaphor in this entire chapter, which is collectively called "The Parable of the Lost Things," is the elder brother of the prodigal son. This older brother is angry and will not go in and enjoy his brother's welcome home celebration party. His refusal to join the party is a profound profile of that outer circle that was angry and would not come into the inner circle and rejoice like the angels in heaven when these lost sheep, coins and prodigal son repent. Those in the inner circle are being found by the unconditional love of God for the *lost things* of this world, yet the elder brothers, those in the outer circle, will not participate in the celebration.

We might even say the outer circle and the elder brother are the most lost of all the lost things described by Jesus here. They are completely out of touch with the heart of their Father and His passion for the *lost things* of this world. This chapter shows us in such a beautiful way the love of God for the lost secular people we encounter in the marketplaces of our part of the world. My prayer is that we will not only see His love by example, but realize the risen living Christ indwells us as we move out into the marketplace. The important thing is not our love for the secular people we encounter there. We are called to the marketplace that the love of Christ in us might reach out and touch the lost people we encounter.

TWO RICH MEN

Luke next follows this great chapter on the lost things of this world with a story about two rich men. The first rich man demonstrates how to participate with Jesus in the implementation of His Manifesto. The second of these two stories about rich men in many ways describes a rich man who does not care at all about the lost and hurting people of this world and demonstrates for us what it looks like when we do not participate with Jesus in His Manifesto. This is pictured by a beggar who lies in pathetic condition at the rich man's gates, and for whom the rich man does not care at all.

Chapter 16 begins with a parable that is controversial, because it is difficult to interpret. Many people think Jesus is commending a crooked, dishonest embezzler who steals from his employer. A close look at the teaching of Jesus in this first story will show us this is not the case. This somewhat negative story actually teaches a positive truth about what it looks like when someone actually partners with Jesus in the implementation of the Nazareth Manifesto:

"There was a certain rich man who had a manager handling his affairs. One day a report came that the manager was wasting his employer's money. So the employer called him in and said, 'What's this I hear about you? Get your report in order, because you are going to be fired.'

"The manager thought to himself, 'Now what? My boss has fired me. I don't have the strength to dig ditches, and I'm too proud to beg. Ah, I know how to ensure that I'll have plenty of friends who will give me a home when I am fired.'

"So he invited each person who owed money to his employer to come and discuss the situation. He asked the first one, 'How much do you owe him?' The man replied, 'I owe him 800 gallons of olive oil.' So the manager told him, 'Take the bill and quickly change it to 400 gallons.'

"'And how much do you owe my employer?' he asked the next man. 'I owe him 1,000 bushels of wheat,' was the reply. 'Here,' the manager said, 'take the bill and change it to 800 bushels.'

"The rich man had to admire the dishonest rascal for being so shrewd. And it is true that the children of this world are more shrewd in dealing with the world around them than are the children of the light.

"Here's the lesson: Use your worldly resources to benefit others and make friends. Then, when your earthly possessions are gone, they will welcome you to an eternal home. If you are faithful in little things, you will be faithful in large ones. But if you are dishonest in little things, you won't be honest with greater responsibilities. And if you are untrustworthy about worldly wealth, who will trust you with the true riches of heaven? And if you are not faithful with other people's things, why should you be trusted with things of your own? No one can serve two masters. For you will hate one and love the other; you will be devoted to one and despise the other. You cannot serve both God and money" (Luke 16:1-13 NLT).

SO, WHAT'S A PARABLE?

Jesus was the master of using parables to communicate truth to those He was teaching. The word *parable* is a compound Greek word that divides into a combination of the word *para* which means "alongside of," and the Greek word for throwing, which is the word *ballo* (That's why we call that thing a quarterback throws a *ball*). A parable is a story a teacher throws alongside a truth he wants to teach because the story can make the complex simple and easy to understand. When you find Jesus throwing a story alongside what He teaches, always ask yourself, "What is the truth this story is trying to make very clear to me?"

The truth Jesus teaches in this somewhat negative parable,

in one word, is *stewardship*. The rascal in this story has control over wealth that is not his own. This crooked but clever manager learns from his employer that the control is being taken away from him. Before that happens, this unscrupulous but smart manager uses that control and wealth to make friends who will show him hospitality and support him after he has been fired. The J.B. Phillips translation reads that his employer commended him because he was careful for his future.

Every time you find a character study in the Bible, you are to meet yourself in that character. Jesus makes that clear when He gives His interpretation of this story. We are stewards or managers of our wealth, and we are to use this wealth we temporarily manage, realizing it all belongs to our Lord. We are to use this wealth to make friends in the eternal dimension of life, knowing full well that one day we will hear the summons, "*You may no longer be steward. Now give an account of your stewardship!*" (Luke 16:1).

In the Bible, we are told to give God the first tenth of all we have. The emphasis is upon the reality that the tithe is the *first* tenth of everything we earn. This is one way we have of measuring our commitment to God. A theme that summarizes the teaching of many passages of Scripture is *God First*. God knows if He is first in our hearts, but we need the tithe to measure that reality for ourselves. When it comes to giving, tithing is like the training wheels our children use when they are learning to ride a bicycle. Beyond the tithe, we are instructed to give offerings and sacrifices. An offering is anything we give to God above our tithes. David defined a sacrifice for us when he wrote he would not offer to God as a sacrifice that which cost him nothing (2 Samuel 24:24).

However, when we come to this magnificent parable we learn that *all* our wealth accumulation belongs to God. My partner in ministry, Dois Rosser, tells publicly that for years he had a legal pad with a line down the middle of the top page. On the left side of that line he had what he labeled "God's business" and on the other side of that line he had written "my business." One day God made him know that he should erase that line. That is when he decided that his life was all about God's business and everything he had was God's. That is the primary truth Jesus presents when He teaches this parable. But there are many other applications to this powerful story. Being a steward is all about faithful management of what Jesus calls your "*worldly resources.*" Just as this unfaithful steward owned none of this wealth he controlled, we own none of the wealth we control. If we are not faithful in the way we manage our wealth, which all belongs to God, God will not trust us with the true riches. We are to use all of our worldly resources to make friends in the next dimension of this life. As the unfaithful rascal in this story used his master's wealth while he had control of it to cultivate people who would welcome him to their homes when he was fired, we are to use the wealth we are managing to make friends who will welcome us into their eternal dwelling places.

By application, this parable also teaches we should be faithful and very successful managers. Many think that a devout disciple is not to be caught up in the affairs of business but this parable makes the statement that a faithful disciple in the marketplace should be successful. Of course when he or she is successful, who is the owner of all the wealth accumulation? There is even a thinly veiled implication that the devout disciple in the marketplace should be more clever and shrewd than the secular people in the marketplace.

SUMMARY APPLICATIONS

What is the truth Jesus wants to teach when He tells this story? The interpretation and application of the parable is truly profound. Jesus is basically teaching: *You are just like that steward. Everything you have really belongs to God. You are simply managing what you have been given. As that steward knew he was going to be fired, you should know that one day you are going to die and you are then going to lose control of all the money and assets God has given you to manage. Then you will hear those sobering words: 'You may no longer be steward. Now, give an account of your stewardship'* (Luke 16:2).

The steward lived in two dimensions. In the first dimension he had control of his master's money and assets, but he knew he was soon going to move into another dimension when he would lose that control. While he was in the first dimension, he used his control over that wealth in such a way that he made friends who were willing to receive him when he was fired into the next dimension.

Just as the unjust steward used wealth that was not his to make friends in the next dimension, we should use what has been entrusted to us to make friends in the next dimension, meaning the eternal state. When we are "fired" or die, we will have friends who will be waiting to welcome us into their eternal habitations, or living places.

This parable teaches "*He who wins souls is wise*" (Proverbs 11:30). Use what you have been given in this dimension in such a way that when you die there will be people in the eternal state who will say to you, "You gave money to a missionary, making it possible for that missionary to make a missionary journey. On that missionary journey, I found Christ. I would not be here in this eternal state if you had not been a faithful steward."

In other words, this parable is saying, all you have is not really your own, and you cannot take it with you. But, you can buy shares in heaven. One way you buy shares in heaven is to manage your money and assets in such a way that the kingdom of God is extended and Jesus Christ builds His Church by your faithful stewardship. People can come to a saving knowledge of Christ because you faithfully managed that which God has entrusted to you. That means you should be highly motivated to be successful in the marketplace, but when you are, it all belongs to the One for Whom you are managing it.

After Jesus tells this story, He makes this somber application: *"He who is faithful in what is least is faithful also in much; and he who is unjust in what is least is unjust also in much. Therefore if you have not been faithful in the unrighteous mammon, who will commit to your trust the true riches?"* (Luke 16:10-11).

This application means God will not bless us spiritually if we are not faithful in the way we manage money in the marketplace. This is not really a focus on how much we give but, rather, on how well we manage what has been given to us as stewards. Faithful, responsible management or stewardship is the thrust of this teaching.

This teaching is to be applied by every disciple of Jesus Christ, regardless of how wealthy they may or may not be. I shall never forget a young man named Lonnie Gunter. He was a sailor who attended the church I was leading when we were building our first church building. Lonnie was married with two children; he had reenlisted and was living on the entry-level income of a sailor, struggling to make ends meet. One Saturday night there was a knock at my door and when I answered it Lonnie was there holding a beautiful shotgun. He had tears in his eyes and could not even speak. He simply placed his beautiful shotgun it my hands and left.

That Monday I took his beautiful weapon with a hand carved stock to a local gunsmith. I told him the story and asked him if he could sell it for me. He looked at me as if he could not believe what I had told him. Then he asked, "What are you preaching in that little church of yours that would make a man give up his beautiful bird gun for the Lord? That gunsmith did get our church a good price for the gun.

Shortly after that I was invited to speak to a retreat for some Presbyterian Elders. They did not assign me a topic so when we began the retreat I asked them what they wanted to hear. After a long pause a familiar voice said "Just tell us how you got the man's bird gun!" It was the gunsmith!

The Holy Spirit worked in a powerful and effective way at that retreat. Their church was in crisis. They were given the opportunity to move out of a dying neighborhood into a new flourishing residential development, but members who had not attended in years did not want to see their real estate values drop, so they came to a membership meeting and voted to block the opportunity the church had to relocate. As a result of the retreat, the remaining members decided to relocate anyway leaving all their assets in the old neighborhood. The Church flourished for decades in that new location.

God moved so effectively in that Elders retreat that I was convinced of the reality that God uses the widow's mite proportionately because it comes by way of a total commitment from the giver. I cannot prove this, but I believe God can use a sacrificial gift like Lonnie Gunter's bird gun more fruitfully than He does a large check of a wealthy person that does not represent sacrifice.

I repeat that stewardship applies to every believer regardless of how poor they may be. If you will think about it we all have a *bird gun* we can give to God. David defined a sacrifice when he told us that he would not offer to God as a sacrifice that which cost him nothing (2 Samuel 24:24).

Are you participating, by way of stewardship, with Jesus in the implementation of His Manifesto? Are you partnering with Christ in the application and implementation of His great ministry in and to this world? You can do that as a missionary, evangelist, pastor, or as a faithful steward and witness for Jesus Christ in the marketplace. According to this parable, you can also do that by faithfully investing what God has committed to your trust to finance those who are partnering with Christ as missionaries, evangelists, pastors, and faithful witnesses for Christ.

There are many ways to partner with Christ, but I must ask if you are in reality partnering with Christ, as the risen, living Christ carries out His mission objectives in our world today? Many of the teachings of Jesus tell us that we are going to live for all eternity with the awesome reality of how we answer that question today.

Remember there is a sense in which no material thing we are going to leave when the Lord calls us home is worth living for while we are here.

THE RICH MAN AND LAZARUS

In His second story about a rich man, Jesus told a story about *a certain rich man who fared sumptuously every day; he was clothed in purple and fine linen, lived in a mansion and could not have had it better in this life. Lying at his gate, there was a man named Lazarus. Lazarus could not have had it worse in this life* (Luke 16:19-20 paraphrase).

Thinking of this story as if it were a three-act play, we would see Act One opening with the rich man sleeping between silk sheets every night and feasting at his banquet table every day. And every morning, when he goes out through his gate, a beggar lies there with dogs licking his sores. In Act One, this rich man could not have it better in this life; the poor man Lazarus could not have it worse.

Act Two is about the death of both men. Death is their great common denominator. The rich man dies between silk sheets in his mansion and is buried with great pomp and ceremony. Lazarus dies lying at the gate. Because we do not read that he is buried, we can assume the sanitation crew comes, picks up his carcass and throws it on a cart. His body is probably dumped outside Jerusalem on the awful refuse site known as *Gehenna*. The main point in Act Two is that death takes the life of both men.

When the curtain goes up on Act Three, we discover the truth Jesus wants to teach with this story. Now both men are in the eternal state. The beggar, Lazarus, who could not have it better, is in Abraham's bosom, meaning he is in intimate fellowship with Abraham. The rich man, who could not have it worse, is in hell.

We read the rich man is in torment. There is a great separation, a great abyss fixed between these two men that is final and permanent. Nothing can be done about it. When the rich man realizes this finality, he cries: "*Oh, Father Abraham, let Lazarus dip his finger in water and come and touch my tongue. I am tormented in this great flame.*"

But he is told: *No, there is a great abyss fixed between you and Lazarus, and those that would come from where Lazarus is to you, cannot. And those that would go from where you are to Lazarus cannot. It is fixed* (Luke 16:24-26 paraphrase).

Now, when he accepts this, he has great concern for his five brothers. He says, "*Oh, Father Abraham, let Lazarus be raised from the dead and let him go tell my five brothers so that they will not come to this place of torment.*" He is told, "*They have Moses and the prophets. Let them hear them.*" *The rich man responds: "Oh, but if somebody were raised from the dead, they would believe.*"

Jesus places great value on the inspired writings of Moses and the Prophets by sending this word back through Father Abraham to the rich man: *If they will not believe Moses and the prophets, they would not believe somebody who was raised from the dead* (Luke 16:27-31 paraphrase). This is literally fulfilled when Jesus is raised from the dead and He is not believed when He proclaims the Gospel, which can keep people from the fate of the rich man.

This awesome story is the most graphic picture of the eternal state in the Bible. It is from this story we get the concepts of hellfire, eternal damnation, eternal retribution, and eternal torment. However, Jesus taught about hell in other places. That great garbage dump, to which I referred earlier, *Gehenna*, represents the favorite word of Jesus for His concept of Hell. The word is the name of a huge valley right outside Jerusalem, where every kind of garbage was discarded, including the bodies of animals and poor people like Lazarus.

When some dark chapters of Hebrew history were being written, Jewish parents offered their children as human sacrifices to pagan Gods in that valley. Jesus taught that if we call our brother a fool, we are in danger of Hell. When He gave that teaching, Jesus used the word *Gehenna*. The word conveys the concept of waste. According to Jesus, being saved from Hell means being saved from a wasted life.

The story about the rich man and Lazarus is also His most definitive description of the eternal state of those who are not saved. One of the worst things about this vivid profile of the eternal state is that the rich man has a memory. He has an endless eternity to remember his lifetime, the sixty or seventy years he lived out his life here on earth. What did he do with his lifetime? He exists eternally tormented with that question, incited by the words "*remember your lifetime.*" Imagine having an eternity to think about how you spent your personal life and your business life in the marketplace.

This story follows the *Parable of the Unjust Steward*. God gives each of us a lifetime of which we are managers – not only of our money, which may actually be the least important dimension of our stewardship. Our life, our time, our energy, our gifts, our talents, our health – these are the essence of our lifetime. The eternal question facing this rich man is, "What did you do with your lifetime?"

In The Parable of the Unjust Steward, Jesus asks you and me, "Will you partner with Me in the implementation and the application of My Manifesto by faithfully managing your life and everything that is entrusted to you?" This second story about a rich man is the awesome illustration of the man who answered that question of Jesus with a resounding, "No!"

The application of this second rich man story also focuses the social conscience of Jesus and of the compassionate, beloved physician Luke. When we read this story, the details about the eternal state are so graphic and tragic we might miss the social applications.

A man named Albert Schweitzer said it was this teaching of Jesus that changed his life forever. Schweitzer gave up all the status symbols and creature comforts he enjoyed as one of the greatest organists, philosophers, medical doctors, and theologians in Europe, when he went to Africa to be a medical missionary. Once there, he practiced medicine in a remote part of Africa where those who were sick would not have had access to medical care at all if he had not provided it. As Schweitzer went to Africa, he said, "I finally decided who Lazarus is. Lazarus is Africa."

A man named Norman Cousins traveled to Africa to spend time interviewing Schweitzer. A definition of humility I shall never forget was Cousins' description of how one evening Schweitzer met for devotions with his staff on the porch of his modest home and headquarters. To see one of the greatest organists in Europe sitting down at an old mildewed piano, with keys stuck together and playing a simple hymn, defined humility for Norman Cousins.

When Schweitzer went to Africa he said, "Your life is your argument." I think that is a profound way of describing the essence of a person's life. With his life, he made the statement I have quoted earlier: "What we really believe, we do. All the rest is just religious talk." His ministry as a medical missionary all started when he realized who Lazarus is. I wonder if you and I know who Lazarus is. What kind of a statement are you and I making by the way we live our lives in the marketplace?

The challenge of this great teaching of Jesus is to consider the graphic and tragic portrait Jesus paints of the eternal state of the lost. This perspective of eternal retribution and condemnation should motivate us to present the Gospel to all those who have never heard that Gospel. Like the Apostle Paul, we should be motivated by this summary paraphrase of his three mission absolutes: One died for all, all are lost, and all must hear the Good News (2 Corinthians 5:13-6:2).

The primary application is this: will you and I become partners with Jesus in the implementation and the application of His mission objectives in this world as they are profiled in the Manifesto of the Messiah? Will we partner and participate with Him in giving sight to the blind, freedom to the bound and healing to the brokenhearted and bruised people of this world?

Learn to see the people of this world as the lost sheep, coins, sons, and the great "Lazarus" lying at the gates of the Church. Realize that the Christ Who lives in you and me would like to reach out to them through us, and make us part of the solution for their needs in this life and in eternity.

It has been said that the Church today is like a World Cup Soccer match. When you attend or watch the World Cup on television, you join millions of spectators who desperately need exercise getting more rest, while they watch men who desperately need rest, getting more exercise!

As you consider the world mission of Jesus today, make the deliberate commitment to the risen, living Christ that you are not going to be a spectator but a partner, a participant and an impact player in making disciples for Him in every nation beginning with those who live under your roof, your neighbors and those you encounter in the marketplace.

Chapter Six
Integrity in the Marketplace

As I have already referenced in chapter two, when the outstanding teaching Rabbi in Jerusalem came to see Jesus at night his first words were, "*Rabbi, we know that You are a teacher come from God; for no one can do these signs that You do unless God is with him*" (John 3:2). Later in the Gospel of John, Nicodemus challenged the religious leaders not to form their opinion of Jesus until they considered what He does. Jesus obviously earned His hearing with the outstanding Rabbi by what the Rabbi had seen Him do. We must also earn our hearing that way with people in the marketplace.

Are you aware of the emphasis in the Word of God upon the personal righteousness of a disciple of Jesus Christ? The word *righteousness* is synonymous with the concept of integrity. While the Scriptures make it abundantly clear that we are not forgiven or saved from our sins by any personal righteousness of our own, there is a strong emphasis in Scripture that we are to live a righteous life as a result of our salvation.

The prophet Isaiah told us that as the people of God, we are to be "*trees of righteousness, the planting of the Lord that He might be glorified*" (Isaiah 61:3 KJV). That has always been the intent of God for His people. The fall of the human race into sin has made that purpose of God for us impossible but the purpose of salvation is that we might be restored to be those trees of righteousness.

In His greatest discourse, the Sermon on the Mount (Matthew

5-7), Jesus placed a strong emphasis on the righteous living of His disciples. The essence of this great discourse was *eight blessed attitudes* that would make His disciples part of His answer and His solution to what's wrong with this world.

The biographical Scriptures that tell the story of the people of God who distinguish themselves also tell us they had a pattern in the way they knew and served God. They had experiences that brought them to God. We might call them *the coming experiences.* Then they had experiences when God told them to go for him. We could label those *the going experiences.*

These eight blessed attitudes divide into two different sets of four attitudes. The first set describes the coming attitudes of a disciple. There are some things we can learn in private. For example, as a pianist, we could learn to be a concert performer in private … that is, in our studio, for instance. But there are other things, like character, that can only be developed when we relate to the people in this world. These coming attitudes can be learned and developed in our prayer closets. But the going attitudes can only be learned and applied when we come out of our solitude and mix with people.

The first attitude relates to what we think of ourselves; that we are blessed when we have learned to be poor in spirit. In a word, it means to be humble. Like Moses, we must learn that we are nobody and then that we are somebody, because we have learned what God can do with somebody who has learned he is nobody.

The second attitude is we are blessed when we mourn … possibly that we mourn while we learn we are poor in spirit. God is our Mentor and He does His most effective mentoring while we mourn. We cannot expect to be part of the solution to the problems people are living with if we never suffer ourselves.

The third attitude is meekness. This is not weakness. It's like a horse that has learned to take the bit and accept the control of the bridle and the rider. Meekness is strength under control, or tameness. We hear Jesus say He is meek and we are told Moses was the meekest man who ever lived. As we get to know these two men, we understand they're not weak men.

The fourth blessed attitude is: "*Blessed are those who* ***hunger and thirst for righteousness*** *for they shall be filled*" (Matthew 5:6). Once a person has been tamed or made meek, they then hunger and thirst to know what God wants them to do. Righteousness is simply *rightness* or doing what is right. To hunger and thirst after righteousness is to hunger and thirst to know what is right – especially to know what is right for them as a disciple.

The Apostle Paul became meek when he met the risen Lord Jesus Christ on the road to Damascus. He then hungered to know what his Lord wanted him to do. This illustrated the third and fourth blessed attitudes. The promise with this fourth attitude, according to the original language, is they will be so filled with righteousness they will choke on it.

Later in this chapter Jesus teaches: "*For I tell you, unless* ***your righteousness*** *exceeds that of the scribes and Pharisees, you will never enter the kingdom of heaven*" (Matthew 5:20). And at the beginning of the sixth chapter He teaches: "*Be careful not to do your* ***acts of righteousness*** *before men, to be seen of men.*" In the second half of the sixth chapter He teaches values. He reaches the zenith and the conclusion of His values clarification when He prescribes the number-one priority value of a disciple of His: "*But seek first the kingdom of God* ***and His righteousness***" (Matthew 6:33).

When we have experienced the first four coming attitudes, we can experience the fifth blessed attitude when we are filled with mercy or unconditional love. In Psalm 23:6, David writes that the mercy of God will follow him all the days of his life. The Hebrew word for *follow* can also mean *pursue.* Many scholars believe David therefore claims that the unconditional love of God will pursue him all the days of his life.

A man named Thompson wrote a profound poem called *The Hound of Heaven*, in which he compares God to a relentless hound dog, yapping at our heels as we live out our life here on earth.

That seems to be the spirit of what David means when he tells us the mercy of God will pursue him all the days of his life. When a disciple is filled with righteousness, he or she is filled with love, because love is right and right is love.

It is so wonderful to realize the word mercy is found 366 times in the Bible. God knew we would need it every day of the year, with an extra day for leap years. Two hundred and eighty of those references to the mercy of God are found in the Old Testament. My favorite is the last verse of David's Shepherd Psalm.

Next Jesus describes the sixth blessed attitude, being *pure* in heart. The word for pure here is a Greek word, from which we get our word *catheterized.* When a disciple is filled with unconditional love or mercy, the Holy Spirit catheterizes out of his heart and life anything that is not the unconditional love of God. All selfish motives, un-forgiveness or anything that is in conflict with the unconditional love of God is purged out of the heart of a merciful disciple.

This leads to blessed attitude number seven, which is to be a peacemaker – the peacemakers ("*called sons of God*" Matthew 5:9) who are persecuted ***for righteousness sake***. The core meaning of this attitude is that a disciple is now a reconciler. Paul tells us in 2 Corinthians 5 that every disciple who has been reconciled to God through Christ has committed to him a message and a ministry of reconciliation. That is fulfilled in the seventh blessed attitude.

Lastly, we read that the disciple with all of these attitudes is persecuted. You would think the world would gather around such a person and sing, "For he's a jolly good fellow." However, since these attitudes profile what a person *should be*, secular people have two choices when they meet this disciple. They can confess this is what they should be, or they can attack such a person for being something they do not want to be. For centuries, secular people have been exercising that second option.

Dr. Martin Lloyd Jones writes that the beatitudes are like climbing a mountain: The first two – poor in spirit and mourning – take us half-way up the mountain. Meekness takes us three-fourths of the way, while hungering, thirsting and being filled with righteousness takes us to the top of the mountain. In other words, we climb the mountain while we learn the coming attitudes.

When disciples learn the four *coming attitudes* that lead them to the top of the mountain, what kind of people will they be before beginning their descent down the other side of the mountain and learning the going attitudes Christ wants to teach them? Because they have been filled with righteousness, are they like the Pharisees?

Do they look down in detached, apathetic and smug condemnation on people and quote chapters and verses that condemn their behavior? The going attitudes will answer these questions.

The promise that accompanies the attitude about hungering and thirsting for righteousness is that the disciple will be filled with the righteousness for which he hungers and thirsts. This also means he will be filled completely with the Holy Spirit of God, Who is Righteousness and he will be filled with a hunger and thirst to know the right things He wants the disciple to do.

Observe that the beatitude here is not *Blessed are those who hunger and thirst after happiness for they shall be made very happy.* It is not a *hunger and thirst* to be happy. It is a hunger and thirst to be holy. It is not, *Blessed are those who hunger and thirst for fulfillment.* It is not, *Blessed are those who hunger and thirst to be rich, for they shall be very prosperous.* That is not what is promised here. The beatitude is, "*Blessed are those who hunger and thirst after righteousness.*"

A concept often believed by some professing disciples is that when we become a disciple of Jesus Christ He will make us prosperous in the marketplace. As you understand this core teaching of Jesus in His eight blessed attitudes, please make the observation that Jesus does not make the promise to fill His disciples with riches, but with righteousness.

He promises they shall be filled full of rightness, a passion to do what is right and to put right what is wrong in this world. Many of the great champions who have addressed injustice – like Wilberforce and those who accomplished the abolition of slavery – were devout disciples of Jesus Christ. With a hunger and thirst for that which was right, they also had a passion for attacking what was not right.

Nobel Peace Prize winners, such as Nelson Mandela and Martin Luther King Jr. demonstrated their hunger and thirst for righteousness by peacefully crying out against the injustice of racism. If you trace the word *righteousness* through the Bible, you will see Jesus was consistent with Scripture when He emphasized the concept that the disciple who is filled with righteousness confronts unrighteousness.

As Jesus emphasizes the personal integrity and righteousness of His disciples, He states that one reason why those people at the bottom of the mountain are miserable and unhappy is because they are doing what nearly everybody else does. They are doing that which is expedient rather than what is right.

It is the plan of God – and therefore the strategy of Jesus in this discourse – to recruit disciples who will be conduits of rightness as they return to that multitude of people at the foot of the mountain … those who represent the secular people of the marketplace. His strategy is that His disciples should be planted in the marketplace like trees of righteousness to the glory of God.

The promise of Jesus to the merciful that "*They shall obtain mercy,*" does not only mean they will receive mercy from God and from those to whom they show mercy. It also means they will become channels or conduits of God's unconditional love to people who need to be loved unconditionally.

If we are going to go down from the mountain where Jesus taught His Sermon on the Mount and be part of Christ's solution to those who hurt, we must be filled with the unconditional love of God. Those disciples who seek to be the solutions and answers of Jesus are not self-righteous Pharisees, but conduits of the unconditional love of God and of Christ. This is what disciples are like who climb to the top of the mountain while learning the four coming attitudes which culminate in being filled full of righteousness. According to Jesus, to be filled with righteousness is to be filled with the unconditional love of God. Love is right and right is love. To be filled with one is to be filled with the other as we work in the marketplace.

MARKETPLACE RIGHTEOUSNESS IN THE BOOK OF ROMANS

A wonderful scholar and pastor/teacher of the Word of God, Dr. David Stuart Briscoe, summarizes part of the argument presented by the Apostle Paul in the first four chapters of Romans in this way: "Paul's letter to the Romans tells us what God is. God is righteous. That means God is right on. He further tells us that God wants us to be righteous. In fact, God commands that we be righteous. He actually condemns anyone who is not righteous. Paul also tells us what God knows. God knows that we could never in a million years be righteous enough to save ourselves. He then tells us what God did. God became a man and that God/Man died on a cross to present the only sacrifice that could make it possible for our sins to be forgiven.

Finally Paul tells us what God wants us to do. God wants us to believe Him when He tells us Who and what He is, what He wants us to be, what He condemns, what He knows, what He has done and what He wants us to do. God not only wants us to believe He died on the cross that we might have peace with Him through our Lord Jesus Christ. He also wants us to access the grace that makes it possible for us to be righteous and live a life of integrity in the marketplace that glorifies Him."

The key word in the entire letter of Paul to the Romans is the word *justified*. When we believe, we are not only forgiven or pardoned. We are declared righteous. Some hyphenate the word this way: *just-as-if-I-had* never sinned. When David confessed his sin of adultery and murder, in the original language he asked God to *un-sin* his sin. That is exactly what God does every time we believe, according to the Apostle Paul in his letter to the Romans.

David used the word *justified* in Psalm 51 where he confessed his sin. In chapter 18 of the Gospel of Luke, Jesus declares the good news that any person who confesses "*God be merciful to me a sinner*" is justified in the sight of God (Luke 18:9-14). The Apostle Paul, in his theological masterpiece to the Romans, explains comprehensively how God does that and what we have to do to receive that justification and live it out every day in the marketplace.

The second four chapters of this letter tell us how a person who has been declared right, lives right. The theological masterpiece of the Apostle Paul is all about what God does to make it possible for us to get right, be right and do right as we serve God in the marketplaces of this world.

Jesus taught we are to love our enemies. Before He taught that highest ethic of any religion in the world, He asked a profound question: "*What do you do more than others?*" (Matthew 5:47). As a dedicated disciple of Jesus Christ in the marketplace, when you do business is there anything you do, or about you, that is more than or different from the way secular people do business? Is there anything different about your ethics when you do business that would impress them and make them want to hear your *religious talk*?

On the negative side, is there anything about the way you do business that would turn off the people you deal with and make them decide they definitely do not want to hear your religious talk? "What you do speaks so loudly I cannot hear the things you say" (or your religious talk). That is the way one person expressed the negative effects of doing business with a professing disciple of Jesus Christ, when that disciple businessperson played hardball with him in the marketplace.

A DISCIPLE OFFERS THE SACRIFICES OF RIGHTEOUSNESS

"Then Jesus entered and passed through Jericho. Now behold, there was a man named Zacchaeus who was a chief tax collector, and he was rich. And he sought to see who Jesus was, but could not because of the crowd, for he was of short stature. So he ran ahead and climbed up into a sycamore tree to see Him, for He was going to pass that way.

"And when Jesus came to the place, He looked up and saw him, and said to him, 'Zacchaeus, make haste and come down, for today I must stay at your house.' So he made haste and came down, and received Him joyfully. But when they saw it, they all complained, saying, 'He has gone to be a guest with a man who is a sinner.'

"Then Zacchaeus stood and said to the Lord, 'Look, Lord, I give half of my goods to the poor; and if I have taken anything from

anyone by false accusation, I restore fourfold.'

"And Jesus said to him, 'Today salvation has come to this house, because he also is a son of Abraham; for the Son of Man has come to seek and to save that which was lost'" (Luke 19:1-10).

This is one of my favorite stories of Jesus because it ends with what could be known as His vision statement and mission objective: "*The Son of Man has come to seek and to save that which was lost.*" The first line of this story tells us Jesus is only passing through Jericho. He is only spending one day in this city and He spends that whole day with the godfather of the publicans, a man named *Zacchaeus.*

Many times in the Gospels, the authors make reference to publicans and sinners. This is not making the statement that publicans were not sinners. This designation means that publicans were sinners in a class all by themselves. They were Jews who collected taxes for Rome from their fellow Jews. They were hated as traitors because they were the employees of their Roman conquerors. They often added a percentage for themselves to the taxes people owed. The people were helpless and could not do anything but pay the publican.

The sinner in this story was not only a publican. He was the chief of the publicans and was rich because he was the successful godfather of the publicans in Jericho. Zacchaeus had a whole syndicate of publicans who worked for him and regularly poured money into his coffers. I often like to think of these great Gospel stories as if they were a three-act play. Although we used this approach in the story of the rich man and Lazarus, I would like to use it again here. Act One in this play dramatizes Jesus meeting

Zacchaeus in Jericho.

A scholar named H. Griffith Thomas made an intriguing connection with this chief publican and a publican we met in the previous chapter of the Gospel of Luke (we are now in chapter 19). In chapter 18, Jesus taught a parable about a publican and a Pharisee. The Pharisee stood in a prominent place and prayed "*with himself.*" That was the satirical way Jesus described the prayer this Pharisee prayed. His prayer was actually a little speech about what a great person he was, as he used the personal pronoun "I" five times in two sentences (He had *I-trouble*!). And he asked for nothing. To pray literally means to ask. So he actually did not really pray at all. According to Jesus his prayer started with himself, it was all about himself, and it went no further than himself.

The publican however was off by himself in an inconspicuous part of the Temple. With sincere contrition, which means being exceedingly sorry for sins, and genuine repentance, he pleaded with God for mercy and confessed he was a sinner, asking for mercy. Dr. Thomas believed Zacchaeus was that publican and Jesus was there when he prayed that prayer. This means that Jesus had a mission in Jericho. That mission was to seek out this publican He met the day before and do what we think of as follow-up, or disciple making. When He spoke with the publican in the tree He already knew him and called him by name. It may be they had some form of contact in the Temple, which made Zacchaeus so anxious to meet Jesus when He came to Jericho.

As we consider this story which demonstrates the mission statement of Jesus, consider the way meeting Jesus had a dynamic impact on the way Zacchaeus did business. As you serve the Lord by doing business in your marketplaces, ask yourself if meeting Jesus has dynamically impacted the way you transact your affairs. Have the people you do business with noticed any change in the way you do business because you have met Jesus?

Act Two in this play takes place in the home of Zacchaeus. We are not told anything about what happened in Act Two, but we know it was not merely a short tea as some of us learned in a little song we were taught, as children, in Sunday school. This interview between Jesus and the chief of the publicans lasted all day. What did they talk about? We simply do not know. But one thing we do know is that when the door opened and their visit ended, the first words came from the biggest sinner in Jericho, who said, *Lord, half of my wealth I will give to the poor and I will use the other half to make restitution to anyone I have cheated in Jericho. I will give them four hundred percent on the dollar of whatever I have taken from them!*

You see, as Jesus met with this publican everybody hated, He must have said something like, "Did you really mean it, Zacchaeus? If you did, you must repent and this is what repentance looks like for you." We can be certain Jesus must have spoken to him about Zacchaeus' wealth, because the first thing the publican says to Jesus when the door opens is what he plans to do about his wealth. Repentance means something different for everybody, but this is what it meant for Zacchaeus. This does not mean Jesus wants everybody to get rid of their wealth. It was true for this publican because he accumulated his wealth by stealing it from his fellow Jews. And they were helpless to do anything about it when he added a percentage for himself to their Roman taxes.

Imagine the impact this had on the population of the city of Jericho. Try to think of receiving a summons from the chief of the publicans. With your heart pounding in your chest, you deeply fear what he will take from you now. You can hardly believe it and stand there shaking in your sandals as they count out to you four hundred percent of what he has stolen from you over the years. Don't you think it shook things up in the business community and the marketplaces of Jericho when this happened? The whole city was probably buzzing with lively conversations about nothing else but this story.

One strategy Jesus used when He was simply passing through a city or a village was to reach someone everybody knew. The person may be a sinner like the woman at the well in Samaria. After Jesus passed through Samaria, this woman reached the men of Samaria for Jesus. These were probably men she knew professionally. Long after Jesus passed through, the influence of the Living Water He gave to that woman impacted Samaria. They may not like the person we might think of as the hard case or the impossible convert, as they did the chief of the publicans in Jericho, but they all knew him. Long after Jesus passed through Jericho, the impact of the way Zacchaeus did business there made a dynamic impact on that city.

If I were an artist, I would love to do a painting of Jesus walking down that street in Jericho, with His arm around this little crook Zacchaeus. I would be sure to capture all the people, especially their religious leaders, griping about the fact that Jesus is going to spend His one and only day in Jericho with the biggest crook in town.

Josephus was a Jewish historian who wrote much Hebrew history, including the period of history in which Jesus lived. This historian described Jesus as a big man Who was usually surrounded by big men like Peter, but Who could always be seen head and shoulders above them. Under my painting of the big-man Jesus with His arm around the little chief publican, Zacchaeus, I would write those words of Luke that describe the vision statement of Jesus: "*The Son of Man has come to seek and to save that which was lost.*"

I realize you are not the godfather of the publicans, but think of the ways your integrity would impact the communities where you do business because you have decided to follow Jesus. Is it possible you may need to make some restitution, like the chief of the publicans did in Jericho?

When you truly understand what it means to be a disciple of Jesus, it should impact your ethics, your values and your vision of why God has placed you in the marketplace. If it does not make any difference in your vision statement or mission objectives in your marketplace, you need to ask yourself if you have actually become an authentic disciple of Jesus Christ?

ANOTHER RICH MAN JESUS ASKED TO REPENT

"Now as He was going out on the road, one came running, knelt before Him, and asked Him, 'Good Teacher, what shall I do that I may inherit eternal life?' So Jesus said to him, 'Why do you call Me good? No one is good but One, that is, God. You know the commandments: 'Do not commit adultery, do not murder, do not steal, do not bear false witness, do not defraud, honor your father and

your mother.'

"And he answered and said to Him, 'Teacher, all these things I have kept from my youth.' Then Jesus, looking at him, ***loved him****, and said to him, 'One thing you lack: Go your way, sell whatever you have and give to the poor, and you will have treasure in heaven; and come, take up the cross, and follow Me.'*

"But he was sad at this word, and went away sorrowful, for he had great possessions" (Mark 10:17-22).

Here is the story of another rich man Jesus told to repent by giving away all his wealth. In many ways this rich man is like the publican in Jericho. They were both Jews. They were both rich and they were both anxious to meet Jesus. Zacchaeus ran and climbed a tree and we're told this rich man came running and fell at the feet of Jesus. Jesus told both of these men to get rid of all their wealth.

Comparing these two men becomes intriguing when you consider their profound differences. Zacchaeus was a traitor and a crook, with a whole syndicate of publicans making him rich. This second man whom we call "the rich young ruler" is a fine, religious and moral man who has kept the commandments since he was a boy. He would have been loved by every Jewish mother and if he were single, a man they would want to introduce to their daughters. Zacchaeus was hated by all and the last person in the world any Jewish family would want to meet socially.

The most striking comparison of these two men is that one of them repented and did what Jesus asked him to do, and the other did not. This means the little godfather of all the publicans in Jericho is in heaven, and unless he reconsidered, the fine, upstanding religious and moral man is in hell.

PERSONAL APPLICATIONS

Does this mean the religious and moral man is in hell because he did not do the *six things* Jesus told him to do? When he asked Jesus what he had to do to inherit eternal life, Jesus did not tell him he did not have to do anything but believe. Jesus told him to *go, sell, give, come, take up your cross* and *follow Me* as one of My disciples. Was Jesus telling him he would earn eternal life if he did these six things?

There is an old hymn entitled *Only Believe.* According to the Apostle James, there is no such thing as to only believe. Faith is always validated by actions. Faith alone can save, but the faith that saves is never alone according to the second chapter of the letter of James. When Zacchaeus told Jesus what he was going to do with his wealth, Jesus announced that salvation had come to his house that day. In the presence of many people, Jesus announced that this publican was a child of Abraham. That must have been part of His mission objective in this follow-up of the publican He met the day before. Jesus wanted to confirm this publican as a whole new person who had been converted and committed to be one of His followers.

Does this mean that the publican was saved because he gave away his wealth? No. It means he was saved because giving away his wealth was an evidence of the faith that saved him. His faith was validated when he gave away his wealth and by making restitution to those he had cheated in Jericho.

Jesus does not tell everybody to give away their riches. Jesus told Zacchaeus to give away his wealth because he had stolen it from those helpless people in Jericho. He told the religious and moral man to give away his riches because his riches were his god. Anything that takes first place in our life, a place that is reserved for God alone, is an idol. That is the biblical definition of an idol. We are to have no other gods but our one true and living God. Riches had taken first place in the life of this religious and moral man.

Only God knows our hearts. Jesus knew the heart of this religious and moral rich man. He knew that he had this kind of problem with his riches. It is not wrong to be rich. It is wrong for a devout disciple of Jesus to be rich if, like the publican, they stole their riches from others. As a marketplace disciple, it is imperative you have a godly perspective on your riches. Just as Jesus knew the heart of Zaccheus and exactly what he had been stealing, and that the rich man worshipped his money, Jesus knows your heart's condition with regard to your wealth. His instruction about riches is meant to help you live a life of great worth and personal integrity.

When the words *eternal life* are used as they are in the story of this religious and moral rich man, they are not merely referencing the eternal state where we will experience our ultimate salvation. They are not only referring to a *quantity* of life, but are also referring to a *quality* of life we experience here in our life span. Observe the way these words are used all the way through the Gospel of John.

There is a sense in which Paul writes that we will not have the best quality of life if we are consumed with a strong desire to be rich in terms of money. It is when we understand that biblical concept of stewardship and the management of our wealth for our risen, living Lord and Savior, that we will have the values of Christ and enjoy the true riches.

AN INTERESTING OBSERVATION

There is an interesting detail in the interview between Jesus and this religious and moral rich man. According to the Gospel of Mark, just before Jesus told this rich man to do six things, we read, "*looking at him He loved him.*" Since Mark was the only Gospel author who records that detail, Ray Stedman, a scholar who mentored me, believed Mark was that rich man. This would mean that he reconsidered his decision to walk away.

Scholars believe he was mentored by Peter and became the author of the second Gospel. And they believe Mark was the first written Gospel about the life and ministry of Jesus Christ, on which Matthew and Luke built their Gospels. Perhaps all this happened because Jesus challenged him to give away his wealth and Mark decided to think again, have a change of mind, heart, will and direction, and in these ways repent because he met Jesus.

THE CHURCH OF THE THREE EPIPHANIES

"*For the grace of God that brings salvation has <u>appeared</u> to all men, teaching us that, denying ungodliness and worldly lusts, we should live soberly, righteously, and godly in the present age, looking for the blessed hope and glorious <u>appearing</u> of our great God and Savior Jesus Christ, who gave Himself for us, that He might redeem us from every lawless deed and purify for Himself His own special people, zealous for good works*" (Titus 2: 11-14).

The Apostle Paul placed Titus on the island of Crete and commissioned him to plant and shepherd the church there in that difficult place. As he wrote to Titus, he emphasized that when you plant a church in a difficult culture, it is imperative that the people of God in that church adorn the doctrine you teach with good works. Paul is emphatic in all his writings that we are not saved by good works. Rather, here and in many other places in his writings, he emphasizes the fact that we are saved *for* good works (Ephesians 2:8-10).

With great inspired eloquence, he uses the word *appearing* in three ways. This appearing is a translation of the Greek word *epiphany*, which means appearing the way God appeared to Abraham. He describes the first Christmas when he tells us the grace of God that brings salvation *appeared* to all men (Titus 2:11).

Then he tells us that as believers, we look forward to the great appearing of God when Jesus Christ returns in His Second Coming (Titus 2:13).

His third reference to an epiphany is when he writes that the grace of God that appeared, and will appear again, very much wants to *appear* to this world today through the godly and righteous integrity of those who make up the Church today.

He describes this third appearing as God purifying for Himself a special people (Titus 2:14). This is translated by some as a peculiar people. This is meant to convey the thought that the marketplace disciple of Jesus is like a rare painting. He or she is a one of a kind unique person through whom the risen Christ makes His appearance to the world today.

By application, no matter how sinful and ungodly your marketplace may be, God wants you to be part of the Church of the Three Epiphanies as you interact with secular people today.

Integrity in your business dealings is a vital dimension of your witness, as God appears to this secular world through you and all His people He has called to the marketplace. As you run up your flag and identify yourself as an authentic disciple of Jesus Christ in the marketplace, it is imperative that you bring integrity to all your business transactions. You must show you are one of those people God has redeemed because He wants to purify for Himself a special people who are zealous for good works in the marketplace.

Chapter Seven

Blueprints for Burnout in the Marketplace

God has told us so much in His Word by way of character studies. He knows people are interested in people and we learn from the experiences of others. There are several extraordinary men of God in the Bible who experience what today we call *burnout.* Under the extreme stresses of the marketplace, many marketplace disciples get tired and some get *tired of.* There is a difference between tired and *tired of.*

We get tired when we spend more energy than we have stored up through sleep, a proper diet, exercise and recreation. *Tired of* is when we do the same thing over and over and over again for a long time. We can also get *tired of* because we're not overworked but we are under motivated. And we can get *tired of* because for a long time we do not accept the limits of our limitations.

WHAT MOSES CONTRIBUTED TO THE WORK OF GOD

In my opinion, the greatest man of God in the Bible is Moses. The greatness of a man of God is measured by the contribution he made to the work of God. Moses gave people who were not free the thing they wanted more than anything else in the world. He gave the people of God freedom when they were slaves. Then he gave them the thing newly emancipated people need more than anything else. He gave them law and government. Spiritually, he gave them the Word of God and he gave them worship.

However, he led them around in circles in the desert for nearly 40 years and during that time he became a classic example of burnout. Listen to his words as recorded in Numbers 11, as they demonstrate what it means to be burned out:

"So Moses said to the LORD, 'Why have You afflicted Your servant? And why have I not found favor in Your sight, that You have laid the burden of all these people on me? Did I conceive all these people? Did I beget them, that You should say to me, 'Carry them in your bosom, as a guardian carries a nursing child,' to the land which You swore to their fathers? Where am I to get meat to give to all these people? For they weep all over me, saying, 'Give us meat that we may eat.' I am not able to bear all these people alone, because the burden is too heavy for me. If You treat me like this, please ***kill me here and now****—if I have found favor in Your sight—and do not let me see my wretchedness!"* (Numbers 11:11-15).

Imagine the stress Moses endured all those years in the wilderness wanderings. There were more than 600,000 fighting men, plus their women and children. This means Moses was leading somewhere between two and three million people around in circles in that desert. He was the only legal judge they had to settle all their squabbles. And he had no rules with which to guide them or make his decisions regarding their problems. His frustration reached the level of exasperation. He is so *tired of* and burned out, he actually asks God to kill him.

Do you sometimes feel as if you are leading people around in circles as you work in the marketplace? The experience of Moses shows us the absolute reality that we must have some structure and rules as we lead or are part of a staff that follows a leader in the marketplace.

AN INTRIGUING WORD FROM THE APOSTLE PAUL

One of the most profound things the Apostle Paul wrote was his Romans 8:26-28 message to the believers in Rome:

"In the same way, the Spirit helps us in our weakness. We do not know what we ought to pray for, but the Spirit himself intercedes for us with groans that words cannot express. And he who searches our hearts knows the mind of the Spirit, because the Spirit intercedes for the saints in accordance with God's will. And we know that in all things God works for the good of those who love him, who have been called according to his purpose" (Romans 8:26-28 NIV).

There are times when God's people are so weak they don't know how to pray because they don't know what they should ask God in their prayers. In effect, Paul teaches that when we are burned out like Moses was and we don't even know what to ask God, we should pray anyway. The Spirit of God knows the mind and will of God. When we are so weak we don't know how to pray, the Spirit will make intercession for us according to the will of God. He does this even when we cannot express ourselves in words. We can only groan. Then even if we ask for the wrong things, our loving heavenly Father God will give us the right things.

When Moses asked God to kill him, he was so weak, *tired of* and burned out he did not know what to pray. He prayed anyway and even though he asked for the wrong things, God knew his heart and so He gave him the right things. God made Moses know that His work requires a team effort. Serving God is a team sport.

The marketplace can burn you out big time if you have not learned that running a business is a team sport. Other players on your team have gifts and skill sets that you do not have and you have what they do not have. Therefore, it is a good blueprint against burnout to accept the reality of the beauty in diversity. Diversity should be celebrated rather than resolved.

SOME PERSPECTIVES ON VISION

There are *let it happen* people, *make it happen* people, *don't know what's happening* people and *don't know anything is supposed to be happening* people. *Let it happen* people absolutely must be teamed up with *make it happen* people because *let it happen* people need *make it happen* people. The *let it happen* people are often the visionary type of leader but they often need others to make their vision a reality.

Another perspective is to say that for a work of God to happen there must be a vision. There must be a plan because without vision the people perish and without a plan the vision perishes. The vision must be shared and that means there must be a vision caster. For the vision to continue there must be keepers of that vision. All these roles are not fulfilled in one person. It takes a team effort for all this to come together and stay together.

THE MBA APPROACH

When you study for a master's degree in business administration, you are taught to do five things: analyze, organize, deputize, supervise and agonize. That was the blueprint God gave to Moses when this great man of God was so burned out he had no idea what to do, or even how to pray. In Moses' prayer, as recorded in Numbers chapter 11, one thing he said that was so true was that he could not lead all those people by himself. The truth is we cannot do the work of God without God, and we cannot do His work without a team of others who share the work with us.

Moses was given 70 men to help him. Scholars tell us this was the beginning of the Sanhedrin, the ruling body of 70 leaders for the Jewish people, which continued up to the time of Jesus Christ, as noted in the Gospels. The blueprint Moses was given by God for his burnout was in place for many thousands of years, and not only benefitted Moses, but also blessed many Jewish leaders and the people of God for whom they were responsible.

THE BURNOUT OF ELIJAH

Another man who burned out royally was the great prophet Elijah. He reached the zenith of his career as a prophet when he challenged the people of God to stop being spiritual schizophrenics. This is one of the greatest challenges we pastors address in our congregations today. Elijah challenged them to decide if the Lord was God or if the false god Baal was God. When that happened on Mount Carmel, as recorded in chapter 18 of 1 Kings, the people experienced a great revival and committed themselves to serving the true and living God. They also slaughtered 850 false prophets of the wicked Queen Jezebel. Then the very next day we read these unbelievable words about Elijah:

"But he himself went a day's journey into the wilderness, and came and sat down under a broom tree. And he prayed that he might die, and said, 'It is enough! Now, LORD, take my life ..."

"Then as he lay and slept under a broom tree, suddenly an angel touched him, and said to him, 'Arise and eat.' Then he looked, and there by his head was a cake baked on coals, and a jar of water. So he ate and drank, and lay down again. And the angel of the LORD came back the second time, and touched him, and said, 'Arise and eat, because the journey is too great for you.' So he arose, and ate and drank; and he went in the strength of that food forty days and forty nights as far as Horeb, the mountain of God.

"And there he went into a cave, and spent the night in that place; and behold, the word of the LORD came to him, and He said to him, 'What are you doing here, Elijah?'" So he said, 'I have been very zealous for the LORD God of hosts; for the children of Israel have forsaken Your covenant, torn down Your altars, and killed Your prophets with the sword. I alone am left; and they seek to take my life.

"Then He said, 'Go out, and stand on the mountain before the LORD.' And behold, the LORD passed by, and a great and strong wind tore into the mountains and broke the rocks in pieces before the LORD, but the LORD was not in the wind; and after the wind an earthquake, but the LORD was not in the earthquake; and after the earthquake a fire, but the LORD was not in the fire; and after the fire a still small voice."

In that still small voice God made Elijah know: "*Yet I have reserved seven thousand in Israel, all whose knees have not bowed to Baal …*" (1 Kings 19:12-18).

Elijah was one of the greatest prophets who ever lived and preached. Many are not aware of him or his greatness because he is not one of what we call "the writing prophets." The amazing and drastic changes we see in him between these two chapters of the first book of Kings are due to a lot of things. One factor in his burnout is that he was at the peak of his triumph as a man of God. After a servant of the Lord has a great victory, the evil one likes to discredit the source of what people have just seen. Sometimes the Lord also likes to discredit the source of a great victory because it brings more glory to God when people see the flaws, or cracks, in the earthen vessel that was at the center of the miracle.

Still another factor is that Elijah had neglected what I like to call his *Temple Maintenance*. When I was out jogging, I often told my children if anyone called to tell them their father was doing *temple maintenance*. I was a pastor so that sounded like something official around the church. The Apostle Paul tells us that our body is the temple of God. Therefore, anything we do to maintain our body could be described as temple maintenance. We are only issued one body this side of heaven and we must take care of that body. If we neglect our temple maintenance, it can have serious consequences for our health and our ministry. That was one of the explanations of the burnout of this great prophet Elijah.

If you carefully read chapter 18 of this Old Testament history book, observe in that dramatic victory Elijah won on Mount Carmel all the physical stress and effort he put out that day. We read Elijah dug a deep ditch around that altar and filled it with water. Have you ever dug a deep ditch? Have you ever handled enough water to fill a ditch as deep as that ditch probably was? This prophet then spent the entire day challenging and taunting the false prophets. We are told Elijah personally took charge of the execution of 850 false prophets. At the end of that long day he ran in front of a chariot for 17 miles. Our hero must have been completely exhausted physically, mentally, emotionally and spiritually.

When you are the owner of a business you never delegate responsibility. You delegate authority to many, but the responsibility is always yours. If you do not accept the reality Moses learned in his burnout and you have no team approach to your work, you may burn out big time. With all the responsibility, you may not realize how hard and how many hours you are working. You may not put out all the dramatic and traumatic effort of Elijah on Mount Carmel, but it is possible to put out an enormous physical effort before you learn to accept the limits of your limitations and balance that with a realistic responsibility for your ability.

You may find yourself in a position where your family and close associates are trying to tell you that you need to lighten up. When physical symptoms show up that are sufficient enough to drive you to a doctor's appointment, that's the time to consider the example of Elijah. When you are a diagnostic challenge to your doctor, always consider the possibility that your suspected illness may begin with a physical explanation. That was the blueprint God gave Elijah for his burnout. God made Elijah know that he had neglected his temple maintenance and his problems began in the physical dimension of his life.

The physical dimension of our life directly affects our mental, emotional and even spiritual perspective. The word neurotic has been defined as "thoughts and feelings for which there is no basis in fact." Elijah was obviously allowing his physical stresses to affect him mentally, emotionally and spiritually. We know that all his blubbering about being the only true servant of the Lord that was left was neurotic when God made him know He had 7,000 faithful servants like him, who had not bowed their knees to Baal.

THE PROPHET JONAH

Another prophet God has placed on the pages of Scripture, to teach us vital truth about how to cope with burnout, is Jonah. One of the greatest challenges we have as serious and authentic disciples of Jesus in the marketplace is that we are told to love all those we meet and do business with in the marketplace. We live in a secular world and most of the people we meet in the marketplace are secular people. We should not be shocked when we realize that most of our political leaders and the leaders in the corporate structure are secular people with secular values.

The values of Jesus we are to communicate in all our dealings are summarized in the one concept of love. When you make a careful study of precisely what the love of God is in a great passage like chapter 13 of 1 Corinthians, it can be overwhelming as you search for the dynamic to love in that way. At the heart of that chapter Paul lists 15 virtues. If we have Christ in our heart we will find ourselves loving in those fifteen ways. The prophet Jonah teaches us that God's love, like that Paul describes, is unlike any love we've known. We cannot love as God loves, but He can express that love through us.

Jonah lived when the greatest enemy Israel ever had, the Assyrian World Empire, was threatening Israel. Assyria was to Israel as Nazi Germany was to Jews in the 1940s. The cruelty of the Assyrians has been chronicled in ancient history and it was far, far worse than that of the Nazis. When Jonah was commissioned to go to Nineveh, the capital city of the Assyrian Empire, he flatly refused to go. He explained in his tiny prophecy that he refused because he knew God was a loving God, and if he preached to the people of Nineveh, the love of God would surely save them (Jonah 4:2). Since he hated his enemy intensely, his response to God's commission to go to Nineveh was a "No!" You can write across the first chapter of the prophecy of Jonah the three words "I will not!"

GOD'S WILL AND OUR WILL

There is a sense in which God will never make us do anything we do not want to do. But God will lean on us like an elephant until the only sensible thing for us to do is to obey God. God created a great sea monster just for the purpose of swallowing Jonah. It is never called a whale. He was thrown into a raging sea from the ship he chose to take him as far away from Nineveh as it was possible to travel, according to the maps of his day.

In the belly of that great fish, Jonah prayed and he remembered every psalm he could think of. This means he sang every hymn he could remember. In the belly of that great fish three times, perhaps one time for each of the three days he was in that awful situation, Jonah said the words God wanted to hear. Those words were "*I will!*" At the end of the three days and nights, God spoke to the fish and it regurgitated Jonah on a beach near Nineveh.

Regenerated and regurgitated, Jonah went to Nineveh, looking like a bleached out freak of a prophet and probably smelling something awful. When he preached in that city, the greatest evangelistic crusade in the history of God and man took place in the capital of Israel's worst enemy. We know this only happened because God showed up. The greatest evidence of this is that Jonah became so angry he sat on a hill overlooking the city. He joined Moses and Elijah when he asked God to kill him, preferring to be dead than to see the salvation of that city. This proves beyond the shadow of a doubt that the greatest evangelistic crusade this world has ever known had very little to do with the evangelist.

The most important insight we have into this bizarre story is that Jonah wrote this book that makes him look like an awful jerk. A nutshell summary of what he is writing in his short prophecy of only four chapters would go something like this (I call this the F*our Spiritual Secrets of Love*):

I was not the love of God when I was in Nineveh, but God was and He was with me. I could not love the way God loves when I was in Nineveh, but God could. I did not want to love as God loves when I was in Nineveh, but Oh how God did want to love that way in that city. I did not love as God loves when I was in Nineveh, but God did love that city through me when I was there.

DEVOTIONAL AND PRACTICAL MARKETPLACE APPLICATIONS

I realize the cities in which you do business are not Nineveh. We are told that all the things that happened to the Old Testament people of God happened to them for examples and warnings for us today (1 Corinthians 10:11). Therefore, we must try to extract from the story of Jonah, principles of truth that are relevant to your life and mine. The big truth Jonah has shared with us is we cannot love as God loves and has commanded us to love. Only God loves that way and He wants to love that way with us, in us and through us.

The signature of every authentic disciple of Jesus Christ in the marketplace today is the love of God and the risen, living Christ. We must recognize and apply these *spiritual secrets of love* Jonah learned in Nineveh, and shared with us, if we are to have any hope of leaving that signature on all the business transactions we make in the marketplaces where our Lord strategically places us.

FEAST AND FAMINE IN THE MARKETPLACE

A businessman I know well did some research and told me that since 1790, in 222 years of American history, we have experienced thirty-six recessions and eleven depressions. That averages out to a downturn every 4.7 years. The economic downturn we are currently experiencing in America, and around the world, is putting great pressure on marketplace disciples everywhere. Why is it that we have always had good times and bad times economically?

If you bring that question to the Old Testament you will find that God often gets the attention of His people and brings them back to Himself by turning off His growing processes. Famine and drought often bring the people of God to their knees and back to God and His will for their lives.

THE MESSAGE OF THE PROPHET HAGGAI

One of the roles of a prophet was to show up when a problem was blocking the work of God. This is exemplified in the preaching and ministry of the prophet Haggai. The people of Judah had been given permission by their conquerors to return to their land and rebuild their Temple, their city and their broken lives. The people who were placed in their land by their conquerors when the Jews were taken in chains to Babylon remembered that the Jews were a mighty military force and their religion had much to do with their military successes. They, therefore, opposed their efforts to rebuild their Temple and their religion.

For 15 years the people of Judah stopped working on the Temple they had returned from captivity to rebuild. During those years they became obsessed with the building of their own comfortable houses. Enter the prophet Haggai!

Half of the short book of Haggai records, and then describes, the results of Haggai's first sermon. In this sermon, Haggai challenged the people of Judah: *Consider your ways*! Haggai's challenge to these exiles was something like, "Consider your time and God's time. You have time for your houses, but you have no time for the house of God" (Haggai 1).

Speaking for God, Haggai then preached: "*Consider My ways! You look for much, but behold, it comes to little; when you bring it home, I blow it away. Why?' declares the Lord of hosts, 'Because of My house which lies desolate, while each of you runs to his own house!*'" (Haggai 1:9).

Another translation tells us they were living in houses with ceilings while God's house had no roof. When I was a young pastor, my congregation was building a church building on a pay-as-you go basis. When we reached the point on a Saturday workday of laying the ceiling structure in place but having no roof to cover it, the next day I preached this question/message of Haggai: "*Is it right for you to live in your houses with ceilings and My house has no roof?*" We got our roof that day!

One translation quotes Haggai as saying they were putting their money in a sock with holes in it. When the prophet challenged them to consider the ways of God, the Word from God was that He was the One Who was putting the holes in their socks.

Haggai challenges these exiles to consider what they are doing, and what God is doing. As a consequence of their flawed priorities, God has called for a drought on all their work and on the people of Judah themselves (Haggai 1:10-11). He did not send them rain but, instead sent them famine. All their hard work produced nothing, and it was all a direct result of their refusal to put God first.

Haggai must have been a powerful preacher, because the people were stirred to obedience. They refocused their priorities and resumed work on the Temple. The first sermon of Haggai actually came in two parts. The second part was in response to their obedience. The essence of part two of the first sermon was: "*I am with you says the Lord!*" (Haggai 1:13). Once they realigned their priorities, God was with them. God blessed them and their work when they put God first.

PERSONAL APPLICATIONS

Apply the preaching of this great prophet to your life today. What are your priorities? Is God blessing your business? And how are you doing in your spiritual life? The worst part of the judgment of God on the flawed priorities of these exiles was that God had called for "*a drought upon men, and the works of their hands*" (Haggai 1:10-11). Have you ever felt you were experiencing a spiritual drought? Is God blessing the hard labor of your hands? Are you in one of those spiritual dry places? Then the devotional and practical application of the message of Haggai for you is: *Consider your ways*, and *Consider God's ways*!

Remember, based upon the Parable of the Unjust Steward taught by Jesus (Luke 16), the critical issue is always your faithfulness as a manager of that for which God has made you responsible. If you are a faithful steward of what Jesus called "*the mammon of unrighteousness*" (which is a way He described money), God will bless you. He will not only bless you economically, but will also bless you with what Jesus called "*the true riches*" (Luke 16). The best way to cope with a spiritual drought or dry place is to have a personal revival of your faithful management of all He has appointed you to manage. Remember that the bottom line of that great parable is that all you are and have belongs to God. And the key issue is faithful management.

A PROFOUND ALLEGORY

We find a formula for the new birth and a personal revival in chapter 2 of the Gospel of John. Read this passage and see if you can find those formulas in this passage.

"*On the third day there was a wedding in Cana of Galilee, and the mother of Jesus was there. Now both Jesus and His disciples were invited to the wedding. And when they ran out of wine, the mother of Jesus said to Him, 'They have no wine.' Jesus said to her, 'Woman, what does your concern have to do with Me? My hour has not yet come.'*

"*His mother said to the servants, 'Whatever He says to you, do it.' Now there were set there six waterpots of stone, according to the manner of purification of the Jews, containing twenty or thirty gallons apiece. Jesus said to them, 'Fill the waterpots with water.' And they filled them up to the brim. And He said to them, 'Draw some out now, and take it to the master of the feast.' And they took it.*

"When the master of the feast had tasted the water that was made wine, and did not know where it came from (but the servants who had drawn the water knew), the master of the feast called the bridegroom. And he said to him, 'Every man at the beginning sets out the good wine, and when the guests have well drunk, then the inferior. You have kept the good wine until now!'

"This beginning of signs Jesus did in Cana of Galilee, and manifested His glory; and His disciples believed in Him" (John 2:1-11).

Let me share some perspective on the Gospel of John. The Apostle John has also written the three short letters at the end of the New Testament, ones named for him, as well as the Bible's last book, titled *The Revelation*. In all his writings, he likes to tell us his purpose for writing, as he states at the end of chapter 20:

"And truly Jesus did many other signs in the presence of His disciples, which are not written in this book; but these are written that you may believe that Jesus is the Christ, the Son of God, and that believing you may have life in His name" (John 20:30-31).

When John uses the word *signs*, he is using a term that means "miraculous evidences." By this he means that Jesus performed miracles that should convince us He was the Christ and the Son of God. He tells us in the last verse of this Gospel that if all the signs Jesus did were recorded, the whole world would not be able to hold the books that would have to be written. At the end of chapter 20, he writes that from among all these signs, he has carefully chosen the ones he has shared with us because he is convinced that if we will carefully consider those he has chosen, we will believe and as a result of believing that Jesus is the Christ, the Son of God, we will have eternal life.

The story of the Cana wedding is the first of the many signs John shares with us. John tells us that as a result of that miraculous sign, His disciples first believed in Jesus. The fourth Gospel can be read on two levels. On the first level, we have simple one syllable words. I taught my children to read from this book in the New Testament.

But there is a second level and the most gifted minds in this world cannot truly fathom the depths of this Gospel on this level. We might call this an allegorical level, which does not mean it is fiction or not true. It just means John is teaching us allegorically. An allegory is a story in which the people, places and things have a deeper meaning.

In 20 years of speaking to and meeting with businessmen in the marketplace, I have found the Gospel of John to be very effective and fruitful as an evangelistic tool. I always began a breakfast with a verse-by-verse study of this book. Many, many businessmen in the marketplace came to faith through the simplicity and the profound truth that is presented in this Gospel. I highly recommend Bible studies from this wonderful presentation of the life and teachings of Jesus Christ when you are sharing the Word of God with secular people in the marketplace.

A FORMULA FOR THE NEW BIRTH

With that in perspective, consider with me the allegory I see in this beautiful story. First of all, it is an allegory of the new birth. The first step in this formula of the new birth is when Mary says to Jesus, "*They have no wine*" (John 2:3). In the Bible, wine is a symbol of joy and happiness. This can therefore be saying that they have no joy or happiness. This would mean the first step toward being born again is to confess you are not born again.

THE SECOND STEP IN THIS FORMULA

The second step toward being born again is pictured by the command of Jesus to fill the water jars with water. The Word of God is often described as water. This would be in connection with the cleansing power of the Word of God. Consider what Peter wrote as he describes the importance of the Word of God and the role it plays in the new birth:

"*Since you have purified your souls in obeying the truth through the Spirit in sincere love of the brethren, love one another fervently with a pure heart, having been born again, not of corruptible seed but incorruptible, through the word of God which lives and abides forever,... Now this is the word which by the gospel was preached to you. Therefore, laying aside all malice, all deceit, hypocrisy, envy, and all evil speaking, as newborn babes, desire the pure milk of the word, that you may grow thereby, if indeed you have tasted that the Lord is gracious*" (1 Peter 1:22-23, 25; 2:1-3).

Peter describes the new birth in retrospect for the people to whom he is writing. He writes that they heard the Word of God when the Gospel was preached to them. They purified their souls by obeying the truth, which resulted in a sincere love of the brethren. They are exhorted by Peter to love one another fervently.

While this process was happening to them, they were being born again. The Agent of their new birth was the Holy Spirit, Who used the Word of God. This process was conceived in them by an incorruptible seed (he uses the word sperm), which is the Word of God. Having been born again, they are to "*desire the pure milk of the word*" that they may grow thereby.

When he exhorts them to "*desire the pure milk of the word*," he uses Greek words which mean they are to go after the Word of God the way a newborn baby goes after the nipple, because the baby knows their sustenance depends upon what they are receiving from their mother's breast. The Word of God is the "prenatal" dynamic of the new birth experience from its conception through the "gestation" period, to the crisis of the new birth and into the growth process. That is why it is critical that we get people into the Scriptures and the Scriptures into people.

And that is what is expressed beautifully and allegorically in this metaphor of filling the vessels with water. Recall the connection of the Word of God being like cleansing water. Since the Word of God is such a significant dimension in the process of being born again, when we want to be born again, we should come to the Bible and fill our minds and hearts and souls with the Word of God.

THE THIRD STEP IN THIS FORMULA

The next step in this process of being born again is pictured in the advice of Mary to the servants, who were actually giving out the wine to the guests at this wedding. She told them, "*Whatever He says to you, do it*" (John 2:5). The application here is obvious.

While you are filling your vessel with the water of the Word of God, whatever God tells you to do, do it! In the passage where we have quoted the Apostle Peter, observe it was when the people to whom he was writing obeyed the Word that their souls were purified and they were empowered to love while being born again. The key that makes the Scriptures a powerful enabling force in the life of a believer is our obedience to what the Scriptures tell us to do.

THE FOURTH STEP IN THIS FORMULA

The fourth part of this formula is pictured for us in Jesus' instruction to those servants to draw out of the large vessels some of the water, which would now be wine. This would mean, by application, that when we have confessed we have no wine, filled our vessel with the Word and obeyed what God tells us to do, we are to share this life-changing experience of new birth with others. To carry the application a little further, since the water we are to share represents the Word of God, we are to share the Word of God with them. The two greatest experiences in this life are the experience of being born again and the experience of leading others to the new birth.

You will never be a fruitful marketplace disciple until you are born again. This formula for the new birth could guide you into that experience. It could also present to you the guidelines you must follow if you want to experience the second greatest experience in life. As you reach out to people you meet in the marketplace, realize they must confess they have no wine. They may be already doing that as they share their problems with you. Then try to get them into the Word in some way. Perhaps in the context of friendship, you could invite them to join you and perhaps others for a Bible study in your home. As you share the Word with them, emphasize the importance of their applying the Word to their real life situations. When they are truly born again, you may not even need to encourage them to share the Gospel with others.

A FORMULA FOR PERSONAL REVIVAL

You can also find, in this story of the first miracle of Jesus (John 2:1-11), the formula for personal revival . If you have experienced the new birth and a personal relationship with God that made you very fruitful, and you believe you have entered into a dry place in your walk with God, you should prioritize some time and a place to get alone with God and apply this formula. Confess that you are in a dry place and you do need a personal revival. Fill your vessel with the Word of God and while you are doing that, whatever He tells you to do, do it! Then be sure you are not selfish or egocentric with your revival. Draw out the results of your revival in a way that will make you a fruitful servant of the Lord again in the marketplace.

Chapter Eight
Peace in the Marketplace

Economic downturn can turn up the heat of an already hostile marketplace. A poet described the rat race and dog fight of the ethics in the marketplace today with this verse: "All nature is red in tooth and claw." Some describe the chaos of buyouts and downsizing taking place today as "we're taking no prisoners and we're shooting our wounded."

Two thousand years ago, Jesus taught that the context in which we live and do business is only a dogfight if we are dogs, and only a rat race if we are rats. He taught that His disciples are to be peacemakers. According to Jesus, there is a peace that can be experienced by His followers, which they can then pass on to others. That peace is not because of a lack of storms. The peace Jesus taught can be found and experienced in the middle of the storms that come into all of our lives. Consider this Gospel of Mark story that illustrates what I am proposing:

"On the same day, when evening had come, He said to them, 'Let us cross over to the other side.' Now when they had left the multitude, they took Him along in the boat as He was. And other little boats were also with Him. And a great windstorm arose, and the waves beat into the boat, so that it was already filling. But He was in the stern, asleep on a pillow. And they awoke Him and said to Him, 'Teacher, Do You not care that we are perishing?'

"Then He arose and rebuked the wind, and said to the sea, 'Peace, be still!' And the wind ceased and there was a great calm. But He said

to them, 'Why are you so fearful? How is it that you have no faith?'" (Mark 4:35-40).

I experienced crossing the Sea of Galilee in a small boat when a great storm formed in about twenty minutes. It was amazing to realize how quickly a storm like the one described in these verses can take place. Jesus suggested they get in their boat and take this little sea voyage. In the middle of the worst part of that great storm, they came to Jesus, who was asleep on a pillow.

They frantically asked Him if He didn't care that they were all (including Jesus) about to perish and drown at the bottom of the Sea of Galilee. Jesus supernaturally turned that great storm into a great calm and then He asked His disciples a great question: "*How is it that you have no faith?*" And He prefaced that question with, "*Why are you so fearful?*"

If you think about it, they were professing to believe Jesus and all Jesus was teaching them about the Kingdom of God – about who Jesus was, why He was here, and that He had chosen each of them to be His disciple. His question implied, *Do you really believe all of these things are going to end up at the bottom of the Sea of Galilee? "How is it that you have no faith?"* One translation reads: *"When are you going to get some faith?"*

Jesus was the greatest Teacher Who ever lived. His teaching methods were superb and His subject that day was faith. Jesus did not print up a syllabus labeled *Faith 303*. That day the classroom of Jesus was a boat and a great storm that could be reduced to a great calm with His great question. The result was a lesson about faith these men would never forget. Scholars believe Peter remembered it and shared it with John Mark, who wrote this Gospel account of the event.

Jesus concluded His greatest discourse by describing for us the difference between an *authentic disciple*, who both understands and applies His teaching, and a *non-authentic disciple*, who merely understands but never applies His teaching. He compared these two disciples to two houses. These houses stand side by side looking exactly alike until storms come down and pound upon both of them. The house that represents the disciple who does not apply His teaching collapses under the storms, and the fall of it is great.

The house that represents the *authentic disciple* withstands the storms because there is a foundation under it. The disciple can relate the teaching of Jesus to all the storms or problems he encounters in life and in work. It's important to realize that storms beat down on both houses in this metaphor.

There are people who think that following Jesus guarantees us immunity from storms or problems. Following Jesus does not assure us of immunity from storms. In fact, being a disciple of Jesus assures the hard reality that we will encounter storms. Let me tell you why. Jesus wants us to be a witness for Him. One way He works that out is to show the world of secular people that while we are enduring storms, there is a foundation under our life. Storms are a vehicle He uses to that end.

PERSONAL APPLICATIONS

By application, Jesus has promised to take us to the other side of this life. When we encounter a great storm, in the marketplace or anywhere else in our life, are we afraid and struggle to apply our faith to that great storm? The peace Jesus invited His disciples to experience, and then pass on to others, is a conditional kind of peace. After being a believer and a pastor for many decades, I finally acknowledged I did not have this peace and became determined to do whatever I had to do to get it and be a peacemaker.

After a whole day of extensive tests by a godly cardiologist named Ken Cooper in Dallas, Texas, I met with him in his office. He had all the results of the tests I had taken all day. He asked me the question, "On an anxiety scale of one to ten, how would you rate yourself?" I responded, "Probably one or one and a half. I mean, I'm a sweet little brown-eyed pastor." He responded that I was actually about eight and a half, nine or even ten sometimes.

He then said that if I wanted to tell myself I had the peace that every believer is supposed to have, I could go ahead and do so. But if I did I would be living in denial because his examination showed that I was not at peace. He joked that de Nile is not just a river in Egypt. He held up all his test results and said, "These things don't lie. You are uptight, Dick, and you'd better find out how to get down loose or you're not going to be with us very long."

I then began a study of peace in the Bible, and I would like to share with you some of the results of my study. The impact on my health of the peace that resulted from my study, when I worked it in with Dr. Cooper's prescribed regimen, was phenomenal. I lost forty-two pounds, seven and a half inches off my waist and corrected all kinds of symptoms that said I was headed for a heart attack or a stroke.

I discovered there are several kinds of peace mentioned in the

Bible. There is world peace, and there is peace with God, which we experience when we believe the Gospel. Then there is a state of peace known as the peace *of* God. This state of peace, in which we are told God can keep His people, is the peace on which I wish to focus. I was encouraged to discover this state of peace is conditional and it can be learned. Isaiah the prophet wrote: "*You will keep him in perfect peace whose mind is fixed on You because he trusts in You*" (Isaiah 26:3).

In this one verse of Isaiah there are two conditions to be met if we are to be kept in this state of peace. We must keep our mind fixed on God and we must trust in God. It encouraged me to discover that the peace of God is conditional, because I then realized I could have His peace by meeting His conditions. I was further encouraged when I discovered from reading the Apostle Paul that the peace of God can be learned.

In chapter 4 of the letter of Paul to the Philippians, I found twelve *peace of God conditions*, either directly stated or implied. These conditions are clearly focused, especially as the J.B. Phillips translation expresses Paul's heart and intent in this chapter. I have quoted these verses for you in that translation that you might read through them and reflect on them. I have also numbered the verses because that translation does not number verses. As you read, see if you can spot these twelve conditions for peace:

4"*Delight yourselves in the Lord; yes, find your joy in him at all times.* 5*Have a reputation for gentleness, and never forget the nearness of your Lord.* 6*Don't worry over anything whatever; tell God every detail of your needs in earnest and thankful prayer, 7and the peace of God, which transcends human understanding, will keep* *constant guard over your hearts and minds as they rest in Christ Jesus.*

[8]Here is a last piece of advice. If you believe in goodness and if you value the approval of God, fix your minds on whatever is true and honorable and just and pure and lovely and praiseworthy. [9]Model your conduct on what you have learned from me, on what I have told you and shown you, and you will find that the God of peace will be with you.

[10]It has been a great joy to me that after all this time you have shown such interest in my welfare. I don't mean that you had forgotten me, but up till now you had no opportunity of expressing your concern. [11]Nor do I mean that I have been in actual need, for I have learned to be content, whatever the circumstances may be. [12]I know now how to live when things are difficult and I know how to live when things are prosperous. In general and in particular I have learned the secret of facing either plenty or poverty. [13]I am ready for anything through the strength of the One Who lives within me. (Philippians 4:4-13, J.B. Phillips).

PAUL'S FIRST CONDITION

"Don't worry over anything whatever!" (Verse 6)

If you want to have this peace Paul prescribes, you must meet this first condition: "*Don't worry about anything whatever.*" Jesus taught the same thing in the sixth chapter of the Gospel of Matthew: "*Therefore I say to you, do not worry. Which of you by worrying can add one cubit to his stature?*" (Matthew 6:25, 27).

So, Jesus and Paul taught *Don't worry*!

You may be thinking to yourself, "I'm no apostle. I work in the marketplace and I have plenty to worry about!" Neither of them told us *not to worry because they had nothing to worry about*. If you are familiar with their lives, you know they both had plenty to worry about. Jesus taught us not to worry about the things we cannot control. They both tell us this because worry is not only non-productive – it is counterproductive. Worry simply doesn't accomplish anything, and worry uses the emotional and spiritual energy we need to cope with our problems. The bottom line is that by being anxious, we don't solve our problems. Therefore, Paul and Jesus agree that we should not worry about anything.

PAUL'S SECOND CONDITION

"Pray about everything!" (Verse 6)

In his peace prescription, Paul also writes, "*Tell God every detail of your needs in earnest and thankful prayer.*" It's easy to say "don't worry," but what are we going to do about our problems if we don't worry about them? Paul does not leave us in a vacuum here. His exhortation, that we are not to worry, is just the first of his twelve conditions for the peace of God. He goes on to prescribe: "*Pray about everything!*"

The Word of God exhorts us to pray when we are in a crisis situation. The New American Standard Bible has a beautiful alternate reading for the first verse of Psalm 46. The verse reads: "*God is our refuge and strength, a very present help in trouble.*" But, if you check the alternate readings suggested in the margin, the first verse reads that our God is "*abundantly available for help in tight places*." As a result of our prayers, God can deliver us from our tight places.

Paul had experienced that many times. He was delivered from many, many tight places. For example, he asked the Philippians to pray that he might be delivered from prison. They prayed, and he was delivered from the imprisonment he was experiencing when he wrote this inspired letter to them.

But Paul knew God does not always deliver us from our difficult circumstances. From personal experience he learned God does not always take our problems away. He had a physical condition, which he described as "*a thorn in the flesh*." Three times he asked God to take it away. This man saw many people healed as he became a channel of the healing power of the Holy Spirit to them. Yet when he asked God to solve his own health problem, three times God said, *No. No. No*. God said to Paul, *I'll tell you what I am going to do, Paul. I'm going to give you the grace to cope with the problem* (2 Corinthians 12:8-9).

When God did give Paul the grace to cope with the problem, Paul not only accepted his physical problem, he gloried in it! He discovered the power of Christ was upon him in such a mighty way that he said, in effect, *I would rather have this power of Christ upon me than to be delivered from the problem.* So Paul not only accepted the will of God regarding his thorn, but he gloried in the whole experience of learning that the will of God will never take us where the grace of God cannot keep us. Paul's weakness became a showcase in which God exhibited His grace and strength.

Paul learned from his own personal experience that, while worry is not productive (and may even be counterproductive), prayer is always very productive. Prayer may deliver us from our problems, or it may give us the grace to cope with our problems – but in any case, pray. Always pray about everything. I like the JB Phillips translation of these words of Paul: "*Tell God every detail of your needs in earnest and thankful prayer.*" Especially when you hit the wall of the impossible in your life and in your marketplace work, always pray about everything.

PAUL'S THIRD CONDITION

"Think about all the good things" (Philippians 4:8, Isaiah 26:3)

Paul and Jesus agree we should think our way to peace. Jesus said (my paraphrase), *You can have a body filled with darkness or a body filled with light. It depends on how you see things* (Matthew 6:23). Jesus was talking about how we think and how we look at things – our mindset, or our outlook. According to Him, one of the most important questions we ever ask or answer is the question, "How do you see things?"

Paul gives us precisely the same counsel here in his prescription for peace. In essence, Paul and Jesus tell us our thoughts are like sheep and we are the shepherds of those sheep thoughts. We can decide how we are going to think and how we are not going to think.

I have been told, "Five percent of the people think, ten percent think they think, 85 percent would rather die than think, and the ten percent who think they're thinking are merely re-arranging their prejudices and not really thinking at all!" In his prescription for peace, Paul challenges us to join the five percent and really think. He primarily tells us to decide how we are going to think. Specifically, he instructs us to think about the things that are true, honorable, right, pure, lovely, and those things that are good news.

Some scholars believe this part of Paul's peace prescription is a paraphrase of that sermon preached by Isaiah: "*You will keep him in perfect peace whose mind is stayed upon You because he trusts in You*" (Isaiah 26:3). According to Isaiah, if we will keep our eyes fixed on the Lord and if we will trust in the Lord, God will keep us in this state of personal peace. Since Isaiah also calls this "the peace of God," scholars believe Paul was quoting and expanding the teaching of Isaiah.

Paul and Isaiah agree we must keep our minds continuously fixed on God and we must continuously trust in God to experience this state of perpetual, personal peace. You see, if the trust is always, the peace is perfect and perpetual. If the trust is spasmodic, then the peace is imperfect and inconsistent. If the trust is up and down, the peace is up and down. If the trust is on and off, then the peace is on and off. If there is no trust, there is no peace, because the peace of God is absolutely conditional.

What does it mean to have our minds *stayed or fixed on God*? Well, for starters, it could mean that we should think about His attributes. The concepts Paul prescribes for our disciplined thought life are all attributes of God.

A good illustration of what it means to keep our eyes on the Lord is the negative example of Peter. Jesus challenged Peter to walk on water in the middle of the night during a terrible storm. As long as Peter kept his eyes on the Lord, he walked on water! But Peter took his eyes off the Lord, and when he did, he began to sink

(Matthew 14:28-30).

Paul wrote to these Philippians when he was in prison. He actually spent much of his dynamic life in prison, and the imprisonment from which he wrote this letter is described in the last chapter of the book of Acts. Although this is considered his mild imprisonment, and he was treated relatively well, he was chained between two soldiers 24 hours a day. Would that arrangement challenge your state of personal peace?

Because it applies in this context, I'm repeating that one benefit of that arrangement was his witnessing to those soldiers, leading many of them to Christ, and impacting the whole palace guard of the Caesar. (Paul probably thought of this as *a chain reaction.*) Although Paul was the captive, he more than likely considered these guards to be his captives. If you were chained to the Apostle Paul for four hours every day, do you think you would know the Gospel?

Since these Roman soldiers were probably profane men, Paul had to practice this condition for peace continually: "*Think about the things that are true, honorable, right, pure, lovely and good*" (Philippians 4:8). He tells us that if we will think this way, then the peace of God, which transcends human understanding, will stand guard (just like these soldiers guarded Paul) over our hearts and minds.

Paul's last imprisonment was in a horrible dungeon in the Mamertine prison in Rome, where he spent his last days on earth before he was decapitated. In that dungeon, this condition for peace probably became his personal prescription for sanity. Do a little research on the prison in which Paul spent his last days. Then read Paul's last words to Timothy in the Living Bible Paraphrase (Second Timothy), dictated to Timothy from that awful setting. You will then understand why I say that this prescription for peace became Paul's prescription for sanity.

In the context of terrifying stress such as combat, a terrible accident, surgery, prison, or the final stages of a malignancy, this prescription can preserve our sanity – and give us peace. In the chaotic pressures and stresses of the marketplace caused by economic downturns, buyouts and downsizing, it is critically important that you make Paul's third condition for the peace of God your own. How you think is critical for maintaining your peace.

PAUL'S FOURTH CONDITION

"Do all the right things" (Verse 9)

Paul also agreed with Jesus when he wrote, "*Do all the right things.*" The Old King James Version is clearer: "*Those things which you have learned and received* [believed] *and heard and seen in me, do, and* [then] *the God of peace will be with you*" (Philippians 4:9). JB Phillips translates this verse: "*Model your conduct on what you have learned from me and what I have told you and shown you, and you will find that the God of peace will be with you.*"

Is there anything we can do to attain and maintain the peace of God – especially when we are facing one of life's storms? Oh you bet your life there is! "*Do the right things.*" That's what Paul prescribes if we want to experience the peace of God.

When Jesus taught about anxiety, He said, *Don't worry. Simply seek first the kingdom of God and His righteousness and all these things you are worrying about will be provided by your heavenly Father* (Matthew 6:33). In other words, *don't sweat the small stuff; sweat the big stuff. The big stuff is your commitment to God as your King, and what He wants you to do. The small stuff is what you need to do the will of your God, and God will provide those things. The number one priority is to seek first the kingdom of God and what He shows you to be right* (Matthew 6:33).

According to Jesus and Paul, if we just put God first, let Him show us the right thing to do, and then get on with doing what God calls us to do, He will provide all those things we are worrying about. Jesus agreed with Paul that the best way to address our anxiety is to do the right things. We might call this constructive and productive worry.

This counsel of our Lord is the best therapy I have discovered as a bedfast quadriplegic. Most of the quadriplegics, stroke victims and retired people I know, and sometimes counsel, do not have meaningful work. Their disability or retirement means they cannot or do not work, and as a result they feel useless and worthless.

God has blessed me with meaningful work. I have voice-activated computer software which makes it possible for me to author written materials that supplement the four year Mini Bible College I have already mentioned. I am so fulfilled and excited about providing these studies and written materials, like this book, that I cannot wait for the alarm clock to sound in the morning.

As a pastor emeritus of a church I served for twenty-three years before I became housebound and bed fast, I also have the opportunity to meet with the pastors, elders, staff members, and interns who are being apprenticed in our church. I find that doing this meaningful work does more for my peace than just about anything I know. When I am involved in productive ministry, I have no time to have a *pity party* and think about the onset of disability or the disease that keeps coming on with its relentless symptoms.

Doing what is right, or the work of God, is very therapeutic. Although I realize my circumstances are the exception and not the rule, how I wish every person who lives with the limitations that challenge me every day, or with anxiety rooted in boredom and being useless, could find some kind of meaningful work. That is at least one reason why Paul and Jesus, as part of their peace prescriptions, both say to us, "*Do the right things*!"

While making the claim that His teaching was the teaching of God, Jesus gave us a wonderful insight into the value of doing: "*Anyone who chooses to* ***do*** *the will of God will find out whether my teaching comes from God or whether I speak on my own*" (John 7:17 NIV). The intellectual person often takes the stance, *When I* ***know*** *I will* ***do***. *But Jesus says, "Oh no, when you* ***do*** *you will* ***know****!* There are so many things that are resolved by doing, and one of them is to do what is right when you wrestle with doing what is expedient. If you are a spiritually-oriented marketplace disciple, it is imperative you realize the importance of this condition that maintains the state of peace known as the peace of God.

Sometimes the *peace thief* that robs us of our peace is the hard reality that we are not doing what is right. In Psalm 4, the psalmist cannot sleep because he struggles with a hard choice. He can do the right thing, but if he does, he believes he won't make it through the crisis he faces. Or, he can do the expedient thing, which is what almost everybody does. But since the psalmist has decided to do the expedient thing and he is a man of spiritual integrity, he cannot sleep. He is not comfortable with the mindset of expediency or mediocrity, and he is suffering from Holy Spirit conviction.

My years as a pastor have convinced me that God does more work in the lives of people in the hospital waiting rooms of our communities than He does in the sanctuaries in our communities. God also does more work in the lives of people in the middle of the night when they can't sleep than He does throughout the busy hours of their working days.

You have probably heard about the man who dreamed he swallowed a ten-pound marshmallow and when he woke up he couldn't find his foam-rubber pillow! Another man said he slept like a log. In fact, when he woke up, he was in the fireplace!

It seems as if the author of Psalm 4 is having that kind of night. In the middle of the night, after hours of intense moral conflict, he resolves to "*Offer the sacrifices of righteousness and put his trust in the Lord*" (Psalm 4:5). In other words, he makes up his mind he is going through with whatever sacrifices he must to do what is right, and then trust God to see him through what he perceives to be his hopeless dilemma of consequences. His motivation for doing right is that he is surrounded by people looking for something good – like a man willing to do what is right even if it costs him everything!

When he begins his psalm, he is so uptight as a consequence of his moral and spiritual schizophrenia, he cannot sleep. But, after he resolves that awful dichotomy, he experiences peace and sleep! We can assume his emotional and spiritual climate was transformed because the peace of God and the God of peace are with him. I believe this summary of Psalm 4 shows us why Paul's prescription for peace involves doing the right things.

A marketplace disciple shared with me that his staff informed him they were marketing a Christmas decoration that was flammable and should be recalled. Since the recall would result in an enormous loss, he told them he wanted to sleep on it and pray about it. When he got home he changed to his jogging suit, put on his earphones to listen to Mini Bible College on his Walkman, and went for his evening run as he did every night. As he ran, his next Mini Bible College lesson *happened* to be on Psalm 4.

He could hardly wait to get to his place of business the next morning to tell his people they were going to recall. The newspaper in his city got hold of the story and his motivation for the decision. It was a tremendous witness to the city, and so many people were touched by the story that the company did not lose money on the recall.

PAUL'S FIFTH CONDITION

"Believe in goodness" (Verse 8)

These three words focus on another "peace thief," especially in the lives of believers who invest four or five decades of service for the Lord. As a young social worker, I once visited with an elderly couple who had spent 50 years as missionaries in China. They were in poor health and living in welfare housing for indigent people. As these dear white-haired saints, who were what I consider

Spiritual Nobility, reflected on the banquet of consequences they had personally gained from their lifetime of sacrificial service, they were discouraged. They were beginning to doubt the value of all the good they had done for Jesus in their 50 years in China.

I will never forget the way their example inspired me. I shared this part of Paul's prescription for peace with them. Paul was emphatic in his teaching that we are not saved by good works. Here he references the good works for which we were saved (Ephesians 2:8-10). Paul teaches here that our good works are not always rewarded in this life, but all the good works of the believer will be rewarded in the eternal state. We should always believe in the value of the good we have done for Christ in our span of life.

I heard the story of another old missionary who returned from half a century of service in Africa. He had buried his wife in Africa and was returning alone. There was a brass band to welcome Teddy Roosevelt, who was on the same ship returning from a safari. But not one solitary soul was there to welcome the missionary home. Very discouraged, that night from a small rented room, he called an old friend who had returned the year before to a similar lack of welcome. After some conversation and a commitment to meet the next day, the friend said to his fellow missionary, "We're not home yet, George!"

Paul certainly could have identified with this dear couple and with these two servants of God who realized their *welcome home and well done* would be waiting for them in heaven. From the time of his conversion, when Paul met Jesus on the road to Damascus, he had committed himself to doing what his Lord and Savior wanted him to do. He had completely dedicated himself to the work of Jesus. And what did it get him but prison after prison, each one worse than the last. Most of them were foul smelling dungeons. And yet, he writes that he experienced joy and peace in those prisons.

Again, let me emphasize Paul does not present goodness here in the context of salvation by good works. The emphasis that we are not saved by good works was one of the first theological priorities of this great apostle. In his prescription for peace, when Paul writes, "*If you believe in goodness*," he focuses on the lifetime of goodness faithful servants have invested for the Lord.

These spiritual heroes might forget that even though they may not be rewarded by people for their faithful service in this life, their reward waits for them in the eternal state. They must believe that every good thing they did was for their Lord. He saw it all and they will hear Him say, "Well done good and faithful servant!" That's what Paul meant when he made these words part of his prescription for peace: "*Believe in goodness*!"

PAUL'S SIXTH CONDITION

Be thankful! (Verse 6)

Paul prescribed "*earnest and* ***thankful*** *prayer*." Do you know what thankful prayer is? My definition of thankful prayer is *grateful worship*. I have found effective peace therapy in a litany of thanksgiving that has evolved in my devotional life over the last several decades, and I have been praying through Paul's peace prescription while gradually becoming a bedfast quadriplegic.

When we are thankful, we have automatically moved our minds

from the negative to the positive issues of our lives. When suffering from a disability that causes us to lose our mobility one body part at a time, we have two choices: we can continuously think about what we have lost, or are losing, and be depressed about it, or we can think about what we still have, and be grateful!

If you have suffered great loss in your investments or your business in the marketplace, you have these same choices I am describing. A man who had experienced great wealth accumulation in his lifetime, as a lawyer and a wise investor, asked to see me. When we had our appointment and I asked him why he wanted to see me, he told me he had suffered great losses and he simply wanted to ask me one question. "How can you lose as much as you have lost and still be happy and even joyful as you serve the Lord?" What I have just shared was my answer. He told me that answer was worth the time and the distance he had traveled to ask me his question.

As I have experienced this gradual loss over the last few decades, I have personally found that second option to be an effective part of Paul's prescription for peace. When I think about it, I have so many blessings for which to be thankful. I discover regularly that when I begin to focus on them, I move my mind from the negative to the positive – and the peace returns! I highly recommend this therapy of thanksgiving. Picture a scale in your mind and place all your problems on the left side of the scale. Then place all your good things on the other side. When you do this, most of us, most of the time, will find that our good things far outweigh our problems.

Next to the value of meaningful work, I find that I get more peace mileage out of the *attitude of gratitude* than any of these eleven other conditions for peace.

PAUL'S SEVENTH CONDITION
"Be patient!" (Verses 11 and 12)

As part of his prescription for peace, Paul mentions patience. Throughout the history of the church, patience has been considered a great virtue by spiritual heavyweights like Augustine, Thomas à Kempis and Francis of Assisi. Why is patience such an important virtue? For starters, patience is one of the nine fruit of the Spirit we find revealed in Paul's letter to the Galatians (Galatians 5:22-23).

In our relationship with God, we might call patience *faith waiting*. In the Bible we are exhorted to "*Wait on the Lord*" (Psalm 27:14; 37:7). There are few spiritual disciplines that will focus our faith like those times when we must wait. When we pray for something and receive no answer, God may be guiding us to a patience that will grow our faith while we wait on the Lord. There are times when what God does in us while we wait is more important than that for which we wait.

In our relationships with people, patience could be called *love waiting.* I had no idea how selfish I was until I got married. I had no idea how impatient I was until I became a father and found myself waiting for teenage children to grow up. I have found the Lord wants to grow two dimensions of patience in my life: He grows what I call *vertical patience* by teaching me to have a faith that waits on Him, and He grows *horizontal patience* by teaching me that in relationships, love waits.

You may be asking, "How does patience relate to a prescription for peace?" It may help if we think of the opposite of patience – impatience. I once heard a father give this advice to his son who was leaving home for the first time: "Remember, son, if it doesn't go your way, force it!"

We all eventually find ourselves facing circumstances beyond our control. When that happens to us, how much peace will we gain because our philosophy of life is to *force it*? Imagine Paul chained in that awful prison in Rome. Would he find and maintain the peace of God because his formula for peace was to rattle his chains and "force it?" Biblical patience is the opposite of what that father told his son. That is especially true of the patience which is the supernatural fruit of the Holy Spirit, and which gives us the grace to accept the things we cannot control.

There are so many times in the marketplace when we must have patience. If we do not learn the spiritual discipline of waiting on the Lord, we can lose out on wonderful things God has for us. This is especially true when we hit the wall of the things we cannot control or make happen. If we believe the *4 Spiritual Secrets* that empower my life and make the things happen that are impossible without the Lord showing up, we simply must learn to be patient. Since only He can do the impossible, we must cultivate the patience which is the fruit of the Spirit.

PAUL'S EIGHTH CONDITION

Be Gentle! (Verse 5)

When Paul speaks of having a reputation for gentleness, he does not mean weakness or milquetoast gentleness. The Greek word for gentleness here is actually the word meekness. Meekness is not weakness. Biblical meekness is closer in meaning to tameness. When a powerful stallion is broken, finally takes the bit, and yields to the control of the bridle and the rider, it is not weak. That powerful animal could be described as "strength under control." That is what the biblical word "meek" means and that is the essence of this concept of gentleness.

When Saul of Tarsus met the risen Jesus Christ on the road to Damascus, Jesus asked him, "*Why are you persecuting Me? It is so hard for you.*" The Old King James Version reads: "*It is hard for you to kick against the pricks.*" That is King James English that means, *It is hard for you to pull against the bit. It is tearing up your mouth.* When Paul asked this great question, "*Lord, what will You have me to do?*" he took the bit in his mouth, so to speak (Acts 9:1-6). That is when Paul became meek, and that is what he means when he exhorts us to be gentle. This kind of biblical meekness is evidenced in the fruit of the Spirit, expressed as gentleness. "*But the fruit of the Spirit is love, joy, peace, longsuffering, kindness, goodness, faithfulness, **gentleness**, self-control*" (Galatians 5:22-23).

When I mounted a horse, I would always ask, "Is this animal gentle?" I did not mean, "Is this a weak, milquetoast animal?" Instead I meant, "Does this horse submit to the control of this bit and bridle?"

Another word for biblical gentleness is acceptance. Paul teaches us by precept, and by his example, that we must accept the discipline of the will of God until we are so meek we experience this gentleness. In other words, Paul prescribes that we accept

God's will for our lives. Paul's prescription here is, *Don't pull against or fight the will of God for your life.* Words that summarize this condition for peace could be: *Unconditional Surrender*!

There are times when the peace of God will flood our hearts because we rest in the assurance that if He had wanted to, God could have prevented our circumstances. We will experience the peace of God because we surrender to and accept issues and circumstances that must, at the very least, be the permissive will of God. The well-known serenity prayer then becomes a prayer of acceptance: "God, grant me the serenity to accept the things I cannot change, the courage to change the things I can, and the wisdom to know the difference."

PAUL'S NINTH CONDITION

"Never forget the nearness of the presence of the Lord" (Verse 5)

As the chaos of marketplace conflicts swirl all around you, to maintain your spiritual equilibrium you must have a relationship with the Lord, like the relationship Paul describes as he spells out his ninth condition for maintaining the peace of God in your life.

When Paul was experiencing his last horrible Roman imprisonment, visiting him was very dangerous. The Romans might chain you next to Paul if you came to see him. And nobody came. He writes: "*They all forsook me. May God not lay it to their charge." But he also writes: "Notwithstanding the Lord stood by me and strengthened me*" (2 Timothy 4:16-17 KJV). That is what Paul means when he prescribes: "*Never forget the nearness of the presence of the Lord.*"

This is why I am continuously emphasizing the ground rule that a personal relationship with the Lord is an absolute if you are serious about understanding and applying Paul's prescription for the peace of God. The Presbyterian catechism, which millions of believers learned as children, states that the chief end of man is not only to glorify God, but also to enjoy Him forever. You cannot enjoy the Lord if you do not have a relationship with Him.

If you do not have a relationship with Christ, follow the Lord's directions. He was speaking about a relationship with God when He taught:

"Ask and keep on asking and it shall be given you; seek and keep on seeking and you shall find; knock and keep on knocking and the door shall be opened to you. For every one who asks and keeps on asking receives; and he who seeks and keeps on seeking finds; and to him who knocks and keeps on knocking, the door shall be opened" (Luke 11:9-10 Amplified Bible).

PAUL'S TENTH CONDITION

"Delight yourselves in the Lord; yes, find your joy in him at all times." (Verse 4)

Misery is optional even though pain and suffering are inevitable. Those words were written by a man who lives with excruciating pain every day. How can misery be optional for someone in pain? How is it Paul can mention joy seventeen times in a short letter he wrote from prison? For those who experience and express the fruit of the Holy Spirit, as well as have a relationship with the risen, living Christ, there is a joy that is not controlled by their circumstances.

The peace Paul experienced and prescribes for you and me can be called *the peace that doesn't make good sense.* It is a peace that "*transcends human understanding*" (Philippians 4:7). The joy of which Paul writes can be called the happiness that doesn't make good sense. This is true because the peace and joy are the fruit or the evidence of the Spirit Who lives in us and they are not controlled by our circumstances. What is the foundation of that joy? According to Paul, that foundation is the Lord. We are to delight ourselves in the Lord and find our joy in Him at all times.

What is the foundation of your serenity and joy? If the foundation of your serenity is your spouse, your children, or some special human being with whom you have a relationship, then the foundation of your serenity is very fragile. There is no relationship on earth you cannot lose.

If the foundation of your serenity and joy is your health or your athleticism, I can bear witness to the sad reality that you have an extremely fragile foundation for your peace and happiness. Many thousands of people, who had a physical orientation around which their lives revolved before an illness or an injury destroyed that foundation, will join me in warning you that health, athleticism and youth are fragile foundations for joy and happiness.

Jesus commended Mary when her sister Martha was upset because she chose to sit at His feet and hear His Word rather than help with the dinner preparations. With as much love for Martha as He had for Mary, Jesus said to Martha, "*Mary has chosen the good part that will never be taken away from her*" (Luke 10:38-42).

When Paul writes these words about joy, he agrees with

what Jesus told Martha about Mary, and he directs us here to a foundation for serenity and joy that is not fragile: "*Delight yourselves in the Lord; yes, find your joy in him at all times.*"

Like Mary, you should prioritize a regular structured time in the Word of God before you enter into the rush and whirlwind of another day in the marketplace. Time in the Word is like sitting at the feet of Jesus. The communion with Him you can experience will never be taken away from you. It will set your sail for whatever adverse winds may blow against you that day.

PAUL'S ELEVENTH CONDITION

"If you value the approval of God" (Verse 8)

Have you made the observation that Jesus asked a lot of questions? Jesus asked 83 questions recorded in the Gospel of Matthew. He asked a profound question of the religious leaders in the Gospel of John when He asked, "*How can you believe since you look to one another for approval and are not concerned with the approval that comes from God?*" (John 5:44 Jerusalem Bible).

Abraham was told by God, "*Walk before Me*" (Genesis 17:1). Do any of us actually do that? Do we really walk before God, all day long, every day? How many of us walk through a 24 hour day holding in focus how God feels about who we are, what we are, and all the things we do – or don't do?

There are times in this life when we simply cannot have the approval of God and the approval of man at the same time. There are times when we are not able to explain to people what is going on in our lives. When those times come, if our peace depends on the approval of people, we will discover that the foundation of our peace is very fragile.

More than 150 times, these three words are found in the New Testament: "*In His sight.*" That concept should be important to us in this life. One day when we all face the certainty of judgment, the way we have lived our lives in His sight will be the only thing that matters.

PAUL'S TWELFTH CONDITION

"Rest your heart and mind in Christ!" (vv. 7, 13)

I conclude my summary of Paul's prescription for the peace of God with this condition for attaining and maintaining the peace of God: "*The peace of God, which transcends human understanding, will keep constant guard over your hearts and minds* ***as they rest in Christ Jesus.***"

What does it mean to rest in Christ Jesus? What does it mean to be *in Christ*? To be in Christ is the favorite description chosen by the authors of the New Testament when they want to describe our relationship to our Lord and Savior. They tell us that we are "*in Christ.*" Paul uses that description 97 times in his writings.

The expression means we are in union with Christ, as a branch is in union with a vine. To be so aligned with Him means we are in fellowship with Him. To be "*in Christ*" means we can draw from Him, the Vine, all the life-giving spiritual power we need for everything we do for Him, with Him and through Him, if we will rest in Him. And that means to rest in His power to do the things He calls us to do, all day long, every day.

I have tried to convey what it means to be *in Christ* by wrapping the concept in a package I call, "Four Spiritual Secrets." I referenced them in chapter 4 and do so again for emphasis, I could not function as a human being, I could not function as a pastor, and, as a bedfast quadriplegic, I could not possibly be teaching the Bible all over the world without these insights. My four spiritual secrets are:

> *I'm not, but He is, and I am in Him, and He is in me.*
> *I can't, but He can, and I am in Him, and He is in me.*
> *I don't want to, but He wants to, and I am in Him, and He is in me.*

When the good things happen because He did something through me, I always try to remember this fourth spiritual secret:

> *I didn't, but He did, because I was in Him, and He was in me.*

That is my way of expressing what it means to rest in Christ Jesus. So much of the anxiety, and perhaps the greatest *peace thief* devout disciples of Jesus experience, is the result of thinking we must do the work of Christ in our own strength. If we are in the will of God, then all day long we will face things we cannot do because they are His works and we cannot do His work. We can only be vehicles through which He does His work. But, if we lose sight of the fact that it is His work, and only He can do His work, and if we think it all depends on us, we will hit a wall of the impossible and lose our peace … big time!

In the sixties, I knew an old elder in a church in Florida who was a godly man. He would sometimes wait until everybody had left because he loved me. Then he would say, "You were laboring today, Richard. You were laboring." He did not have to tell me that because I was exhausted. There is nothing more exhausting than trying to do the work of God in your own strength.

But then, once in a while on a Sunday morning, he would wait until everybody had left and he would come to me, and he would smile and hug me and say, "He was laboring today, Richard! He was laboring!" He did not have to tell me that, either, because when He is laboring, it is as if you start out tired, or even exhausted, and then the wind of the Spirit is in your sails and you are energized! Because of His Word, the vehicle of His Word is energized when He is doing His thing in and through you. Then the people who hear your word are energized.

This is the last part of Paul's prescription for peace: acknowledge that you can't but He can, as you rest your heart and mind in Christ and in what only He can do. Enormous stress relief will be experienced when we realize the challenges we face are a matter of what He can do and not what we can do. Overwhelming physical and emotional problems that crush the life out of us, difficult relationships and all the challenges of everyday living will be manageable when we realize that facing them is not a matter of who and what we are, or what we can or cannot do. They are simply an opportunity to prove and demonstrate who and what He is and what He can do.

I have now profiled twelve conditions of a prescription for peace that I find in the fourth chapter of the letter of Paul to the

Philippians. If you want to meet these conditions and apply them in your experience of the marketplace, I would like to share a prayer with you that can be the vehicle of your application. I invite all of you to pray this prayer with me if you seek the personal and perpetual state of peace the Bible calls "*the peace of God.*"

Father, you tell us in Your Word that You can keep us in a state of perfect personal peace if we will meet your conditions for that state of peace. Because I seek this peace in my life, give me the wisdom to worry about nothing, and the faith to pray about everything.

May I have the mental discipline to think about all the good things and the moral integrity to do all the right things.

Even though it seems as if everything is on the downturn in the marketplace, may I always have that incurable optimism that believes in goodness, and give me such an insight into what You have been doing and what You are now doing in my life and in my world that I will give thanks always and in all things.

May I never try to push You or run before You, but always wait on You, experiencing and expressing the gentleness and patience that are the fruit of Your Spirit living in me.

As I sort out my priorities, may I always value Your approval of who and what I am and what I do, and not walk before men to be seen of men or to please men.

Never let me forget how near You are to me as I draw near to You, worshipping and enjoying You each day and forever.

And finally, Father, realizing that it is not who I am, but Who You are that is important; acknowledging that it is not what I can do, but what You can do that really matters; agreeing that it is not what I want, but what You want; and remembering that in the final analysis it will not be what I did, but what You did that will have lasting eternal results, give me that absolute trust in You and that total dependence on You that will truly rest my heart and my mind in Christ.

Enable me to meet these conditions for personal peace in the name of Jesus Christ, for my peace and for Your glory. Amen.

Chapter Nine
Prayer in the Marketplace

In the mid-fifties, I made a discovery about prayer. I came to the conclusion we are praying even when we don't close our eyes, fold our hands and bow our heads. In the words of an old hymn, I discovered that "Prayer is our soul's sincere desire, uttered or unexpressed."

Martin Luther told us the sigh of a believer is a prayer. He meant when we come to the end of our hoarded resources and throw ourselves across a bed and sigh or cry, that is a prayer.

God sent the Prophet Isaiah to tell a sick King Hezekiah that he was going to die. Hezekiah turned his face to the wall and cried. When God saw the tears of King Hezekiah, God sent Isaiah back to him with another message: "*I have seen your tears. I have heard your prayer.*" And God added fifteen years to his life (Isaiah 38).

When we express the sincere desire of our soul, which is often too deep for words, leaves us in tears, or produces a sigh of despair, that is a prayer God hears and answers. In that spirit, when you have problems and burdens in the marketplace that make you want to sigh or cry, offer those sincere desires of your soul to God. He will respond to your authentic prayers as He did to good King Hezekiah.

LEARNING TO PRAY

As a young pastor, I found the hardest meeting to get a man to attend was a small prayer meeting. I soon learned that one reason men were reluctant to join others for prayer was because they did not know how to pray.

There is so much to learn about prayer. I always told the men who would not attend a prayer meeting how the apostles came to Jesus and asked Him to teach them how to pray. Our Lord uses storms to teach us how to pray. I heard about a great surgeon who told his patient's family their loved one's condition was so critical all they could do was pray. The wife of the patient responded: "Oh my God! Has it come to *that*?!"

Many professing believers share their perspective on prayer. I personally thank God for what during World War II they called *foxhole theology,* and I like the related remark that there are no atheists in foxholes. If we are honest, we will confess that without problems like downturns and recessions, we might not give God the time of day. It is an established reality in the Scriptures that our God does His most effective work in our lives when things are difficult, and not when we are experiencing prosperity. The man who was considered in his day to be the wisest man who ever lived wrote: *In the day of prosperity be joyful, but in the day of adversity consider: surely God has appointed the one as well as the other* (Ecclesiastes 7:14).

One of the greatest teachings on prayer in the Bible is recorded by Luke, who tells us that when Jesus had finished a long time in prayer, His disciples asked Him to teach them to pray. They not only meant that they wanted to learn the "how to" or the mechanics of prayer, but they also wanted Him to teach them what He knew that moved Him to spend so much time in prayer. He responded by giving them not only a prayer, but the greatest prescription for prayer this world has ever heard. We call it *The Lord's Prayer*, but it should more accurately be called *The Disciple's Prayer.* It is found in Luke's Gospel and right in the middle of the greatest discourse of Jesus, the Sermon on the Mount (Luke 11:1-4; Matthew 6:5-15). In principle and in profound depth, this prayer/prescription teaches us much about how to pray and why we should pray that way.

THE DISCIPLE'S PRAYER

Jesus begins His prescription for prayer by telling us to be sure to address our prayers to God and not to those who may be joining with us in corporate prayer. In His teaching, both preceding and following this Disciple's Prayer, Jesus clearly values private, or *closet* prayers, over public prayers. Jesus does not literally tell us to pray in a broom closet. He tells us to pray in private. This could be in our automobiles (one of the few places we are alone today). He teaches that when we pray in our prayer "closets," we are to "*pray to our Father Who* [really] *is in secret*," or in the secret, private place (Luke 11:1-4; Matthew 6:5-15).

There is nobody in our prayer closets to impress but God. Therefore, we are more likely to truly address God in our solitary, secret prayers than we are in our corporate prayers.

Jesus not only exhorts us to address our prayers to God, but He instructs us to address God as "*Our Father*." The Old Testament people of God were not invited to enter into the presence of God or converse with Him on intimate terms. A priest approached God for the people, but even the priest did not enter into the presence of God on a regular basis. Once every year, with all the people gathered around the Tabernacle in the Wilderness or the Temple of Solomon, the High Priest entered into the presence of God (the Holy of Holies) for all the people of God.

As His disciples, Jesus instructs us to enter directly into the presence of God and address God as "*Our Father!*" This was a radical concept for the disciples who heard Jesus give this teaching, because they were all Jews who had been taught throughout their lives to perceive and approach God in the manner I have just described.

THE THREE PROVIDENTIAL PETITIONS

"Hallowed be Your name"

Because prayer is so critical to effective ministry in the marketplace, we must understand the first concepts Jesus teaches us in *The Disciples' Prayer*. I call them providential petitions because they address God accurately as sovereign and also reflect our understanding of our position as children of the King in His kingdom.

The name of God represents the essence of Who and what God really is. In the marketplace, disciples will need to know God in all the ways these names of God suggest He can be known. The names attributed to God in the Bible tell us that our God is, was, and always will be (Jehovah). He is the God Who heals (Jehovah-Rapha), the God Who provides (Jehovah-Jireh), and the almighty, powerful God (El Shaddai). He is the God Who sees (El Roi), Who sanctifies (Jehovah-M'Haddesh), and the God Who is our Shepherd (Jehovah-Ra-ah). All these concepts, and many, many more like them, are represented by the names of God in the Bible.

When Jesus instructs us to pray "*Hallowed be Your name*," He instructs us to begin our prayer by asking that the essence of Who and what God really is might be known, respected and reverenced because we have offered the prayers we now bring before God.

I repeat, for emphasis, that the message of the Bible frequently sifts down to these words: "God first." In the Bible, from Genesis to Revelation, the bottom-line interpretation and application of the commandments, the character studies, allegories, parables, psalms, sermons, Gospels, Epistles and teachings is simply "God first." The prayer Jesus taught us begins with that "God-first" emphasis when He instructs us to begin our petitions by asking God that His name, the essence of Who and what He is, might be honored and reverenced because we are offering our prayer(s) to our perfect heavenly Father God.

"Your Kingdom Come."

The names of God in the Bible also tell us God is a King and has a kingdom. In the second providential petition of the prayer Jesus taught us, the God-first emphasis continues by telling us we should identify ourselves as subjects in the great kingdom of God – before we get to our personal petitions.

One of the many ways the Bible claims the deity of Jesus Christ is by describing Jesus as the "King of kings" and "Lord of lords." In the Gospel of Matthew, Jesus is a King and He is seeking subjects for His kingdom. When we pray, we are not to be building kingdoms of our own. This prayer of Jesus clearly teaches us that before we pray "*give us,*" we are to affirm our allegiance to the

Kingdom of God, and to the King of kings and the Lord of lords by praying, "*Your Kingdom come.*"

According to this inspired prescription prayer of Jesus, we are not only instructed to begin praying, "*Your Kingdom come,*" but we are also instructed to conclude our prayers by pledging to our heavenly Father, "*Yours is the kingdom.*" In this way, we begin and end our prayers with that God-first emphasis. Jesus teaches we should conclude by telling God that whatever results from all the answers to the prayers we place before God according to this prayer/prescription, will belong to our King – and to His kingdom.

"Your will be done on earth as it is in Heaven."

The third providential petition is actually a paraphrase of the second. When we pray "*Your kingdom come,*" we express the essence of the third providential petition – "*Your will be done.*" When God is our King, and we live as His loyal subjects, the purpose of our existence will be to do His will. Those of us who have always enjoyed the freedoms of democratic forms of government do not grasp these kingdom metaphors as quickly or as well as those who know what it means to have a totalitarian dictator, a king, or a queen ruling over them.

This third God-first petition has been called "the prayer that never fails." We don't have to know God's will to pray this petition. James writes that we don't have, because we don't ask, by which he means we don't have because we don't pray (James 4:2). The Apostle John assures us we will receive what we ask God for in our prayers if we ask according to the will of God (1 John 5:14-15).

Challenged by James and believing the promise of the Apostle John, our coming before God in closet or corporate prayers reveals that we do not know the will of God – and so we don't pray.

In another profound passage about prayer I have already referenced in chapter 7 of this book, the Apostle Paul writes we should not let the fact that we don't know the will of God keep us from praying:

"Likewise the Spirit also helps in our weaknesses. For we do not know what we should pray for as we ought, but the Spirit Himself makes intercession for us with groanings which cannot be uttered. Now He who searches the hearts knows what the mind of the Spirit is, because He makes intercession for the saints according to the will of God. And we know that all things work together for good to those who love God, to those who are the called according to His purpose" (Romans 8:26-28).

According to Paul, if our hearts are right when we pray, even if we ask God for the wrong thing, the Holy Spirit, Who does know the will of God, will make intercession for us according to the will of God. Paul tells us that when we pray, even if we ask God for the wrong thing, God will give us the right thing if our wills are aligned with the will of God. In chapter 7 we saw this illustrated in the lives of Moses, Elijah and Jonah. You can see why our Lord would teach us that we should always precede our personal petitions with this third God-first petition – "*Your will be done.*"

THE REAL LORD'S PRAYER

This Disciple's Prayer could be called, "The Prayer the Lord Never Prayed." However, there is a prayer the Lord did pray that could properly be called "The Lord's Prayer." In the three Synoptic Gospels (Matthew, Mark and Luke), when He is about to be arrested and crucified, Jesus sweats blood as He prays: "*O My Father, if it is possible, let this cup pass from Me; Nevertheless, not as I will, but as You will.*" (Matthew 26:39). Jesus not only taught we should pray after the manner of this third providential petition, He modeled this when He prayed before facing the greatest trial of His own earthly life.

James 4:3, as translated in the King James Version, informs us there are times when our prayers are not answered because we *ask amiss*. When James wrote that we ask amiss, he was telling us we sometimes forget to precede our personal petitions with these three providential petitions – "*Hallowed be Your name, Your kingdom come,*" and "*Your will be done on earth as it is in heaven.*" Most of our so-called unanswered prayers can be traced to one utilitarian cause. We pray more *misses* than *hits* because we fail to prioritize these providential petitions before we pray our personal petitions.

The Apostle Paul gave us a wonderful description of the essence of prayer when he shared this inspired metaphor with the Corinthians and with us – "*co-operators with God*" (2 Corinthians 6:1 J.B Phillips).

The King James Version uses the preposition "in" as it translates the petition, "your will be done." One of my favorite authors, Philip Keller, in his A *Layman Looks at the Lord's Prayer*, a book on this prayer/prescription of Jesus, relates this petition to a concept found in the writings of the Apostle Paul. Paul informs us that if we have the Treasure of the risen Christ living in our earthen vessels (our bodies), it might be obvious to everybody that the power source of our lives comes from God and not from us (2 Corinthians 4:7). Philip Keller believes that in this third providential petition, Jesus teaches we should ask our heavenly Father to do His will in our earthen vessels, just as His will is done in heaven. Obviously, if the will of the Father is done in us, then the will of the Father will be done on earth through us.

According to Paul, God delights in placing His risen, living Son in weak earthen vessels so it will be obvious to everyone who observes our lives and ministries that nothing comes from us, but everything comes from the great Treasure Who lives in us, "*Not that we are competent of ourselves to claim anything as coming from us; our competence is from God*" (2 Corinthians 3:5 RSV).

I once heard Dr. A.W. Tozer preach. He said, "The Bible says '*We have this Treasure in earthen vessels.*'" After an eloquent pause, he added, "And some of those vessels are a bit cracked!" He then went on to say he believed that sometimes the light of the Treasure shines out even more through the cracks in those earthen vessels. There are times when the cracks in the earthen vessels magnify the greatness of the Treasure and bring only greater glory to God (2 Corinthians 3 and 4).

The marketplace is not generally a welcoming place for men or women to exhibit weaknesses. But by way of application, perhaps Paul is exhorting Jesus' disciples to be willing to exhibit the true source of their competence. When Jesus' followers are honest about their cracks and how God can still work in and through their lives, people are often drawn to God by such encouragement, and He is glorified in their lives.

When you are discouraged because you believe the flaws in

your witness disqualify you from being salt and light for Christ there in the marketplace, think of these two realities: if you were without flaws you would be presenting an unrealistic and unattainable model. When you present a flawed model, God receives greater glory as His light shines through the cracks in your earthen vessel, and the model you present through your witness is realistic and attainable.

One of the greatest truths in the New Testament is: "*Christ in you, the hope of glory*" (Colossians 1:27). The Living Bible paraphrases this prayer petition of Paul for one of his churches to read, "*That they might learn this spiritual secret, that Christ in your hearts is your only hope of glory,*" by which he means of glorifying God.

When I compare this third providential prayer petition with the essence of the truth about prayer Jesus shared with the apostles in the Upper Room Discourse, I am persuaded to agree with Philip Keller when he writes that Jesus tells us to ask our heavenly Father to do His will <u>in</u> our earthen vessels, just as His will is done in heaven.

"Judas (not Iscariot) said to Him, 'Lord, how is it that You will manifest Yourself to us, and not to the world?' Jesus answered and said to him, 'If anyone loves Me, he will keep My word; and My Father will love him, and We will come to him and make Our home with him'" (John 14:22-23).

IN SUMMARY

When Jesus mandated that His three providential petitions must precede our personal petitions when we pray, He was teaching that prayer is not a matter of us persuading God to do our will. The very essence of prayer is an alignment between our wills and the will of God. Prayer is not a matter of us making God our partner and taking God into our plans. Prayer is a matter of God making us His partners and taking us into His plans.

In the fifties a man named O. Howlsby wrote a book with the simple title *Prayer*. The premise of his book was that Revelation 3:20 is a descriptive and prescriptive profile of what prayer should be. Prayer is for us to come before God and then open the door of our heart to whatever God may have for us at any given time for His glory. We surrender to His will and ask Him to come into our life and make us part of the answer to His prayer.

These three providential petitions prescribed in the prayer Jesus taught us, should send a message to every disciple of Jesus. We are not to come into our prayer closets, or into our corporate worship prayers, with a "shopping list" and send God on errands for us. When we pray, we should come into the presence of God with a blank sheet of paper and ask God to send us on errands for Him. In our closet and corporate prayers, we should be like soldiers reporting for duty to their King and Commander in Chief.

THE FOUR PERSONAL PETITIONS

"Give us this day our daily bread"

We must continue to look through the priority grid of God-first as we get to the *gimmie* part of this prayer Jesus taught us. The three *God-first* petitions should focus our motivation as we come before our heavenly Father with our personal petitions. Why do we want our heavenly Father God to give us our daily bread, one day at a time? We should ask our perfect heavenly Father to provide our bread daily because we earnestly desire to see the essence of Who and what God is, honored and reverenced on earth in and through us.

Most people don't even know they were created in the image and likeness of all that the names of God represent. We should want our heavenly Father to provide our daily needs because we want to see our Father's Kingdom come in our earthen vessels, and on earth through us. We should want our needs met because we want to be earthen vessels through which God's will is done, in earth and on earth, just as it is willed and done in heaven. In this way, the *three providential petitions* are designed to control the motives that drive all our personal petitions. These three God-first petitions should always be the grid we look through as we ask God to give us each day all that we need personally.

The Lord uses the symbol of bread here in this first personal petition to represent all our physical, emotional and creature comfort needs. We are a veritable network or intersection of creature needs. Our needs are spiritual, physical, emotional, and intellectual. This first personal petition should not be limited to our need for food but for all the needs we have as spiritual, physical, emotional, and intellectual creatures of God.

Observe that the concept of *one day at a time* is repeated twice in this petition of just seven words. Alcoholics and drug addicts with many years of sobriety tell me that when they took their first step toward sobriety, they could not even entertain the thought of being sober or straight for more than just one day. This prayer prescribes that we are to pray "*this day*" and "*daily*" when we present our creature needs to our heavenly Father. This principle of one day at a time has proven to be the difference between life and death for some of my closest friends who are celebrating many years of sobriety. Jesus concludes chapter 6 of Matthew with this same emphasis: "*So don't be anxious about tomorrow. God will take care of your tomorrow too. Live one day at a time*" (Matthew 6:34 TLB).

Your pressures and stresses in the marketplace may be so great that you can only grasp the thought of God providing for you one day at a time. In 2 Corinthians 12:9, God told Paul that His grace is sufficient. My experience is that His grace is measured out to us one day at a time as it is needed.

We read in the book of Numbers that when God miraculously provided bread from heaven (manna) in the wilderness for the children of Israel, they were only permitted to collect enough manna for one day. That story, recorded in chapter 11 of the book of Numbers, is obviously an allegory of this one-day-at-a-time principle Jesus prescribes in the prayer He taught us.

When we apply the story of that great miracle to our daily devotions, we should make the application that we cannot hoard our experiences with God. Receiving a word from God, or experiencing blessings of a time in God's presence, is meant to be a part of a daily spiritual diet. We must have our souls and spirits nourished and refreshed with heavenly manna every day, one day at a time, just as we must have our daily bread every day, one day at a time.

"Forgive us our debts as we forgive our debtors"

The next three personal petitions are designed for the spiritual needs we have every day. This second personal petition is for forgiveness, and the next two petitions are for guidance and deliverance. Forgiveness, guidance and deliverance are spiritual needs we have every day. The principle of that first personal petition for daily bread, one day at a time, should be applied to these petitions for our spiritual needs. The spirit of these four personal petitions could be: *Give us this day our daily bread, including our need for forgiveness, guidance and deliverance, every day, one day at a time.*

When I was an active pastor in a small town, the eight churches often had ecumenical services when the churches met together at special times of the year. We found it necessary when we prayed this prayer together to tell the people whether we were going to use the words *debts* and *debtors*, or *trespasses*. This was necessary because the Presbyterians pray *debts*, while most congregations pray "trespasses." Matthew uses the words "*debts*" and "*debtors*" as he records this second personal prayer petition of Jesus. Luke writes: "*and forgive us our sins; for we also forgive everyone who is indebted to us*" (Luke 11:4). The commentary of Jesus after He teaches this prayer/prescription makes it obvious He speaks here of sins or trespasses. That is why many people who pray this prayer, pray, "Forgive us our trespasses as we forgive those who trespass against us."

The concept of debts and debtors, as Jesus used those terms here, is illustrated in two parables Jesus taught about the forgiveness of sins. In Matthew 18, Jesus taught a parable, illustrating what He meant when He prescribed this petition about our forgiving our debtors, just as our debts have been forgiven. In chapter 7 of his Gospel, Luke describes the unusual setting in which Jesus taught another parable comparing the forgiveness of sins to the concept of debts and the forgiveness of debts.

Many people are disturbed by the commentary of Jesus on this second personal petition, when He had finished teaching this prayer. This petition for forgiveness is the only part of this prayer upon which Jesus comments when He has finished the teaching. According to Matthew, He supplements this second personal petition with the awesome commentary – if we do not forgive those who trespass against us, our heavenly Father will not forgive our own trespasses.

The only people who have no questions about the Bible are the people who never read the Bible. People who read the Bible have many questions about the Bible. This commentary of Jesus troubles many devout souls because it appears as if Jesus teaches God forgives us because we forgive others. This is a legitimate question that deserves an answer. That's why Jesus gave us His clear and profound answer to this question in these two parables.

Jesus told the story of a man who owed a great debt (Matthew 18:23-35). In those days, if you owed a large debt you couldn't pay, you were sent to debtor's prison and your wife and children were sold into slavery until your debt was paid in full. Since you certainly couldn't generate any income from prison, you would more than likely die in that prison and your family would be slaves for the rest of their lives. Those who heard this parable of Jesus were very much aware of that practice in their culture. (There was no such thing as *chapter eleven* or *chapter seven* bankruptcy.)

Relative to our currency, the debt in the story of Jesus was a multi-million dollar debt. When the man who owed this great debt was summoned to court, he begged for mercy because he could not bear the thought of prison and of his wife and family being sold into slavery. Miraculously, the one to whom he was indebted, out of compassion for him and his family, completely discharged the debt!

On the way home from his extraordinary day in court, this man, who had just been forgiven such a great debt, met a man who owed him twenty dollars and could not pay. He grabbed this poor man by the throat and shouted, *You pay me every cent you owe me or I will slam you in prison and sell your family into slavery!* (Matthew 18:28, paraphrase).

People who observed both these events reported what they witnessed to the merciful man who discharged the multi-million dollar debt. When the compassionate man heard their story, he summoned the ungrateful, forgiven man to another court hearing and reversed his merciful decision. He had the man sent to prison and sold his family into slavery. Having told that story, Jesus pronounced, "*So My heavenly Father also will do to you if each of you, **from his heart**, does not forgive his brother his trespasses*" (Matthew 18:35 NKJV).

The bottom line of the truth Jesus teaches is not that God forgives us because we forgive those who sin against us, but that if we see our salvation and forgiveness as the cancellation of a multi-million dollar debt, we will be forgiving because we have been forgiven so very much. If we are not forgiving, then we may not grasp that we have been forgiven a large debt. Our lack of faith in God's forgiveness at the heart of our salvation means we do not have the caliber of faith that can be called *saving faith*. If our faith is flawed because it falls far short of saving faith, our sins, in fact, are not forgiven!

We will never truly understand the second personal petition of the prayer Jesus taught us, especially His sobering commentary on that petition, without understanding His profound parable in Matthew 18 – and in another parable just like it. Jesus taught this same truth in a similar, though short, parable which Luke records for us in his Gospel:

"Then one of the Pharisees asked Him to eat with him. And He went to the Pharisee's house, and sat down to eat. And behold, a woman in the city who was a sinner, when she knew that Jesus sat at the table in the Pharisee's house, brought an alabaster flask of fragrant oil, and stood at His feet behind Him weeping; and she began to wash His feet with her tears, and wiped them with the hair of her head; and she kissed His feet and anointed them with the fragrant oil.

"Now when the Pharisee who had invited Him saw this, he spoke to himself, saying, 'This Man, if He were a prophet, would know who and what manner of woman this is who is touching Him, for she is a sinner. And Jesus answered and said to him, 'Simon, I have something to say to you.' So he said, 'Teacher, say it.'

"'There was a certain creditor who had two debtors. One owed five hundred denarii, and the other fifty. And when they had nothing with which to repay, he freely forgave them both. Tell Me, therefore, which of them will love him more?' Simon answered and said, 'I

suppose the one whom he forgave more.' And He said to him, 'You have rightly judged.' Then He turned to the woman and said to Simon, 'Do you see this woman? I entered your house; you gave Me no water for My feet, but she has washed My feet with her tears and wiped them with the hair of her head. You gave Me no kiss, but this woman has not ceased to kiss My feet since the time I came in. You did not anoint My head with oil, but this woman has anointed My feet with fragrant oil. Therefore I say to you, her sins, which are many, are forgiven, for she loved much. But to whom little is forgiven, the same loves little.'

"Then He said to her, 'Your sins are forgiven.' And those who sat at the table with Him began to say to themselves, 'Who is this who even forgives sins?' Then He said to the woman, 'Your faith has saved you. Go in peace'" (Luke 7:36-50).

Jesus was dining with a Pharisee who had apparently invited Jesus into his home to entrap and discredit Him. A woman, a known sinner who had experienced salvation through Jesus, began washing the feet of Jesus with her tears and drying them with her hair. The woman did this spontaneously because she observed that the Pharisee had not washed the feet of Jesus. In that culture, not washing the feet of an invited guest was like refusing to shake hands with someone you have invited to dinner. For this woman, who had likely been saved from a life of prostitution, it meant the Pharisee had not even extended common hospitality to her Lord and Savior, whom she loved so much.

While the Pharisee was thinking immoral thoughts about this gesture on the part of the woman, Jesus told him a parable. It was the story of two men who owed debts to the same wealthy lord. As the Living Bible paraphrases the story, one owed him five hundred dollars and the other owed him five thousand dollars. The wealthy man canceled both debts. After telling this story, Jesus asked the Pharisee which man would have loved their benefactor the most? The Pharisee answered, "*The one who owed him the greater debt.*"

Jesus agreed with the Pharisee. Then He asked him, "*Do you see this woman?*" The question was actually, ***How** do you see this woman?* Jesus was challenging the Pharisee to think about how he saw the sin of that woman relative to how he saw his own sin. He obviously saw her sin as the great debt, and he saw his own sin as the small debt in the parable Jesus had told him. Jesus then interpreted and applied His parable for the Pharisee by announcing, "*Her sins, which are many, are forgiven, for she loved much. But to whom little is forgiven, the same loves little.*"

Then Jesus said to the woman, "*Your faith has saved you.*" Those words of Jesus clearly affirmed the Gospel reality that loving much was not the reason she was saved. She loved much because she had saving faith. When the real sinner stood up from luncheon in the Pharisee's house, it was not that forgiven woman who loved much. It was a self-righteous Pharisee named Simon.

The parable Jesus told Simon the Pharisee illustrates that we cannot separate our personal forgiveness of sin from our attitude toward the sins of others. That is why Jesus wrapped His petition for the forgiveness of our sins in the same package with our forgiveness of those who have sinned against us.

These two parables that compare the forgiveness of our sins to debts that have been canceled show us why Jesus taught us to pray the forgiveness petition of His profound prayer/prescription this way: "*Forgive us our debts as we forgive our debtors.*" The scholars tell us this petition should be translated, "Forgive us our debts as we have already forgiven our debtors."

In this context of forgiveness, we should remember what God remembers and forget what God forgets. God tells us through the prophet Jeremiah: "*For I will forgive their wickedness and will remember their sins no more*" (Jeremiah 31:34 NIV). God remembers we are sinners and He forgets our sins when we confess them. We forget we are sinners and remember our sins long after we have confessed them.

The story is told of a monsignor who had a nun under his authority, who claimed she talked to Jesus every night. He called her in for a conference. When he confirmed she talked to Jesus every night, he asked her to do him a favor. He said when she next talked to Jesus, he wanted her to ask Him what sins he had committed in Paris before he became a priest. She was to report back to him when she had done that. She soon made an appointment. When he asked her if she had asked Jesus that question, her response was: "He told me to tell you He doesn't remember!"

"Lead us not into temptation"

Disciples who read the New Testament all the way through, encounter difficulty when they read the third personal petition of the prayer/prescription Jesus taught us. Their problem is that the earthly half-brother of Jesus writes, in the first chapter of his inspired New Testament letter, that when we are tempted to sin, we should never say we are tempted of God. According to James, God is not tempted with evil and He never tempts any man (James 1:13). In the light of that teaching, why would our Lord teach us to pray to our perfect, loving, heavenly Father God, Who never tempts any man, "*Lead us not into temptation?*"

I am persuaded that the spirit of this petition is based upon the collective teaching of Scripture that we are not pillars of strength when it comes to temptation. Jesus evaluated our human condition when He said, "*The spirit indeed is willing, but the flesh is weak*" (Matthew 26:41). According to biblical scholar William Barkley, when the Bible refers to our flesh, it often means "human nature, unaided by God."

One night, Jesus was having an all-night session of prayer. He had asked the apostles to pray with Him. He was grieved when they couldn't stay awake. Have you ever attended an all-night prayer meeting? If you have, did you find it hard to stay awake? The Lord said to the apostles on this occasion, "*You should be praying that you enter not into temptation*" (Luke 22:46).

His meaning seemed to be something like, "If you only knew the power of the evil one and the weakness of your flesh, you would be awake and praying that you enter not into temptation." When the Lord prescribed this third personal petition, "*Lead us not into temptation,*" He was being consistent with His evaluation of our human condition, our flesh, or our "human nature unaided by God."

I believe it would be a legitimate paraphrase of this third personal petition to pray it this way: *Lead us, and we will not find ourselves facing the confrontations of the temptation to commit sin.*

David tells us "*The steps of a good man are ordered by the Lord*" (Psalm 37:23). Do you agree with him? If you do, then answer this question: If you were following the leading of the Lord, step by step, do you think you would find yourself confronting the temptations to sin?

In His Sermon on the Mount, Jesus used some awesome metaphors. He taught that if our eye, even if it is our best eye, is leading us into sin, we should pluck it out; if our hand, even if it is our right hand, is causing us to sin, we should cut it off (Matthew 5:29-30). In another place in the Gospel of Matthew, Jesus included the foot in these metaphors (Matthew 18:8 Living Bible).

Jesus was obviously addressing sexual sin as He used these metaphors. Throughout the history of the church, devout men have actually made themselves eunuchs because they took this teaching of Jesus literally. The spirit of the truth Jesus was teaching through these awesome metaphors was actually something like this: If what you are looking at with your eye is causing you to sin, stop looking (Think how this applies to pornography in our culture.). If what you are doing with your hand is causing you to sin, stop doing it. If where your feet are taking you is causing you to sin, don't go there. Although it is a shame to read that men so sadly misapplied this teaching of Jesus, should we not marvel at God-passionate men who were that determined to live holy lives? If we stopped going where our feet could lead us into sin, would we not avoid many instances of temptation?

All this teaching is based on our Lord's assessment of our human nature, unaided by God. Since our flesh is so very weak, we must put rigid disciplines and structures in place to the end that we may not face the temptations which can lead us to commit sexual sin. The third personal petition in this prayer prescription is intensely realistic. We are not pillars of strength when it comes to the temptation to sin. We should, therefore, pray every day to our loving heavenly Father, *If You lead us, step by step, we will not have to confront the temptation to commit sexual sin.*

The Apostle Paul echoes the spirit of our Lord's prescription regarding the temptations to commit sin in the life of a believer. Paul writes "*but God is faithful, who will not allow you to be tempted beyond what you are able, but with the temptation will also make the way of escape, that you may be able to bear it*" (1 Corinthians 10:13). Many people memorize that verse, but they overlook the verses that precede and follow this great promise. The verse that precedes this promise warns us that the person who thinks they will continuously stand, or never fall, should take heed lest they fall. The very next verse tells us precisely what that way of escape from temptation is that God will always provide for us. That verse begins with the words, "*Therefore, flee!*"

In this third personal petition, Jesus teaches that even though our spirit may be willing to do the will of God, we are so weak in our flesh that we must pray every day, "*Lord, lead us, not into temptation.*"

"But deliver us from evil"

The better translations tell us this fourth personal petition is actually, "*but deliver us from the evil one.*" Martin Luther warned us:

"For still our ancient foe
Doth seek to work us woe.
His craft and power are great,
And armed with cruel hate,
On earth is not his equal.

Did we in our own strength confide,
Our striving would be losing,
Were not the right Man on our side,
The Man of God's own choosing.

You ask who that may be?
Christ Jesus, it is He!
The Lord of Hosts is His name,
From age to age the same,
And He must win the battle!"

Martin Luther understood we have an enemy who does not wish us well – and we must be delivered from him. Jesus obviously lived with that reality. He began His public ministry by having a marathon confrontation with the evil one in the wilderness. Jesus was more than a Conqueror in that wilderness where He defeated all the temptation strategies of the devil.

The Good News in this last personal petition in the prayer/prescription the Lord gave us is that we, also, can be delivered from the temptations of the evil one. The disciplines and structures against temptation I referenced above are part of the answer to our prayers for deliverance from the evil one. If we knew the power, craft and cruelty of our ancient foe, we would fervently pray these last two personal petitions together every single day, "*Lead us not into temptation, but deliver us from the evil one*."

There are so many attractive people in the marketplace today who have their moral sail set in such a way that they will come on to you. You simply must have your own sail set to be delivered from their temptations. This is such a great threat to a marketplace disciple that I am prioritizing much of chapter 12 to address this kind of challenge.

THE GOD-FIRST BENEDICTION

"Yours is the Kingdom, the Power and the glory forever, Amen."

In this prayer/prescription of Jesus, He teaches us to conclude our prayers the same way He taught us to begin our prayers. Jesus prescribed that we begin with three *providential petitions* before we pray our *personal petitions*. We are then to conclude by praying this profound providential benediction.

This means our Lord prescribes that we begin our prayers with a God-first mind-set and conclude with that same focus on *God-first*. We are to begin by looking through the grid of "*Your name be reverenced, Your kingdom come,* and *Your will be done* [in earth and] *on earth, just as it is willed and done in heaven.*" We are then instructed to conclude our prayers the same way.

"Yours is the Kingdom"

Jesus wants us to conclude our prayers by making this

commitment to our heavenly Father: "*Yours is the kingdom.*" By this confession, He means for us to pledge to God that the results of our heavenly Father's continuously answering our prayers will always belong to Him.

I have experienced the meaning of this providential, kingdom benediction in a special way twice in my nearly six decades as a pastor, serving two churches as a pastor for more than 20 years, and being involved in the founding of both churches. At one point, circumstances forced me to give up each of those churches after they had grown to be large. To start a church with about twenty people and watch it grow into a large one is a marvelous experience. However, it is difficult to step back and surrender that ministry to others once that church has become large, fruitful and an exciting place to pastor.

While serving those two churches, this prayer Jesus taught His disciples continuously guided my prayers. Therefore, when I was forced to give up those ministries, I said to the Lord, "As I have called upon You over the years for enabling grace to pastor this church, and You have consistently answered those prayers, the result (the church) belongs to You." It was in that context, on those two occasions, that I more fully learned the meaning of the words, "*Yours is the kingdom.*"

Yours is the power

As we face the challenges of life and ministry every day, we should be poor enough in spirit to confess we need the power of God. When I have gone through a challenging day of life and ministry, I have confessed, thousands of times in my journey of faith and ministry, *I can't, but He can.* By the way He closes this prayer, Jesus mandates that we confess to God that we have only been fruitful in ministry because He has answered our prayers. Over many years of life and ministry, when God has obviously blessed the church I have shepherded, I have practiced that part of the benediction prescribed in this prayer by confessing, *I didn't, but He did.* The power has come from my heavenly Father.

Yours is the glory

Finally, we are to conclude our prayers by confessing, *Yours is the glory.* When we apply this third providential benediction to our prayers, we are simply confessing, *Because I didn't but He did, all the glory goes to Him.* Along with our confessions about the kingdom and the power of God in the benediction with which we are to conclude our prayers, Jesus prescribes that we also make this solemn commitment to God: *The glory for everything that happens in my life because You have answered my prayer(s), will always go to You.*

The spirit of this benediction is, "Because the power will always come from You, the result will always belong to You, and the glory will always go to You. Amen." Amen simply means, *so be it*!

IN SUMMARY

The prayer Jesus taught His disciples challenges us to be sure to address our prayers to God. We are instructed to address God intimately as our perfect, loving heavenly Father. We are then to begin our prayers with three Providential, or God-first, petitions, which are: *Your name, Your kingdom, and Your will.* Those three providential petitions are to be followed by four personal petitions: *Give us, forgive us, lead us, and deliver us.* Finally, we are instructed to conclude our prayer by confessing, that *because the power to answer my prayer will always come from You, the result will always belong to You and the glory will always go to You. So be it!*

Chapter Ten
Faith and the Marketplace

Marketplace disciples have an intense need to understand faith. Just as there are different kinds of peace, there are also different kinds of faith. There is *saving faith.* We must have saving faith to understand and believe the Gospel of our salvation. There is also the kind of *faith that can move mountains*; that caliber of faith is a spiritual gift from God. Those who live and labor in the marketplace must often have *mountain-moving* faith.

Believers who follow Christ today need to have a deeper and more comprehensive understanding of this profound little five letter word, *faith.* As you read the Bible, you will find God has wrapped many important concepts like faith in the lives of people because He knows we learn from people. There are scores of character studies in the Word of God. God has given many examples of faith He wants us all to possess through stories of people in the Bible, particularly through a man, Abraham, who is called His friend.

Hebrews chapter 11, known as the Faith Chapter of the Bible, says this about faith: "*Now faith is the substance of things hoped for, the evidence of things not seen... Without faith it is impossible to please Him, for he who comes to God must believe that He is and that He rewards those who diligently seek Him*" (Hebrews 11:6). According to the faith chapter of the Bible, biblical faith always has an unseen object, yet there is evidence that tells us the unseen object is there. Most of the time that unseen object is God. A man or woman of faith diligently seeks that unseen Object because they have the conviction that God rewards those who diligently seek Him. The author of this chapter tells us we only have hope when there is no evidence of what we believe. Faith places a foundation of evidence under our hopes.

I once heard a rural pastor explain that verse to his congregation this way. He said when they invited him to their home for a meal after church, he was always hoping they would have a delicious fried chicken. Until he entered their home, he could only hope they would have chicken. However, when he entered their home and he smelled the aroma of chicken and saw from the parlor that chicken gravy was on the dining room table, that aroma and that chicken gravy were the *substance of things hoped for and the evidence of things not seen*! Now he could believe he would be eating chicken for dinner!

DEFINITION OF FAITH SUMMARIZED

We can glean from these verses in Hebrews 11 that faith is an act of belief in Someone or something we cannot see, based on evidence. If we study these opening verses carefully, we will see that the evidence of things not seen ***is*** the man or woman who believes. Since God is the Giver and the Author of faith, the man or woman of faith is the evidence of the unseen God who has given them their faith. The author of Hebrews presents what we might call *The Hall of Faith Heroes*, a list of those who demonstrated their faith by what they did.

This great faith chapter follows its opening remarks with example after example of people who demonstrated their faith by specific actions. Go through this chapter and underline all the action verbs. All of the people listed in this chapter are heroes of faith because they *did* something. That is why I say faith is an *act* of belief in Someone or something you cannot see, based on *evidence.*

Many people believe the metaphor the author presents in Hebrews 12:1-2 is that we are the athletes running in a race, while in the stadium watching us run our race is "*a great cloud of witnesses.*" They have already run their race. Do you believe it is possible that people who are deceased, those who have gone on before us, know what is happening in our lives today?

I heard a story about a young man who played football for a Big Ten University. His father died early in a week so he missed several days of practice. While he was putting on his uniform for the big game that Saturday, his coach came over to him and expressed his condolences. He also said to this young man who was not a starter, "If there is anything I can do for you, let me know." The young man said to the coach, "As a matter of fact there is something you can do for me. Let me start today." Since he had a game face on the coach let him start.

The young man played a tremendous ball game and was voted the MVP of the game. After the game the coach asked him, "Can you tell me the connection between the game you played and your father's death?" The player told the coach his father was blind and had never seen him play. He said that he played this game for his father because he believed his father could see him play for the first time.

As you serve the Lord by working in the marketplace, do you have anyone in that great cloud of witnesses, perhaps a parent or a mentor, who will be proud of you because of the way you do business for the Lord today? If that might motivate you, remember that God definitely sees everything we do. Does the way you do business please or glorify God? God challenged Abraham to "*walk before Me and be perfect*" (Genesis 17:1). Walk before God as you do business in the marketplace.

THE HALL OF FAITH BEGINS

When God commissioned Noah to build an ark, it had not yet rained on earth. This author describes that challenge to Noah's faith as, "*Things not seen as yet.*" Noah had never seen rain. The story of Noah, which covers four chapters in the book of Genesis, is described in one profound verse of this faith chapter: "*By faith Noah, being divinely warned of things not yet seen, moved with godly fear, prepared an ark for the saving of his household, by which he condemned the world and became heir of the righteousness which is according to faith*" (Hebrews 11:7).

A SUMMARY OF NOAH'S FAITH

Based on this seventh verse, we can summarize Noah's faith in this way: the foundation of faith, the Word of God, *is being warned of God.* The objective of faith unseen is *things not seen as yet* (Genesis 2:5-6). The inward evidence of faith is *moved with fear.* The outward evidence of faith is *prepared an ark.* The witness of faith is *he condemned the world.* The personal result of faith, salvation, is *became heir of the righteousness which is by faith.* The perpetual result of faith is *the saving of his house.*

Noah was a preacher of righteousness during the 120 years he spent building the ark. The only way you could be saved then was to be in that ark. That's what Peter meant when he writes that the ark is a picture of salvation. In the book of Genesis, we are told Noah is a picture of faith and of what faith can mean and of what faith can do.

THE CHARACTER OF MAN

"And the Lord said, 'My Spirit shall not strive with man forever, for he is indeed flesh; ... Then the Lord saw that the wickedness of man was great in the earth, and that every intention of the thoughts of his heart was only evil continually. And the Lord was sorry that He had made man on the earth, and He was grieved in His heart. So the Lord said, 'I will destroy man whom I have created from the face of the earth both man and beast creeping thing and birds of the air, for I am sorry that I have made them.' But Noah found grace in the eyes of the Lord" (Genesis 6:3, 5-8).

Here we have the beginning of the catastrophic judgment of God. The Bible describes a final judgment of God, which the prophets and apostles call "*The Day of the Lord.*" This is the first we hear of that side of the character of God. An important concept in this passage is the word *flesh.* This word is the diagnosis of God regarding the essence of the character of man. William Barclay, a professor of Bible at Edinburgh University in Scotland for 40 years, defined this word as "human nature unaided by God." According to what God has told us in the story of the flood in Genesis, the human nature of man, unaided by God, is a monstrous.

The Spirit of God had been restraining the character of the man He had created. When God stopped striving with man, there were terrible consequences. Consider verses 5, 11 and 12, where we see human nature unaided by God. The character of man is described in four ways: "*Great wickedness... only evil continually... all flesh had corrupted their way... filled with violence.*"

Imagine the President of the United States declaring a national week where everyone was to follow their impulses with no restrictions whatsoever placed upon them. What kind of a week would that be? When the Spirit of God stopped striving with the flesh of man, that was what happened on the earth.

In the Bible, the New Testament often presents a teaching and the Old Testament provides the illustration of that teaching. For example, in the New Testament, after Pentecost when the Spirit of God comes to live in man, we're taught that the Spirit of God is at war with the flesh of man (Galatians 5:16-17, 19-23). We read in Genesis 6 that the Spirit of God strives with man, but He will not <u>always</u> strive with man. When Paul writes of the Second Coming of Jesus Christ, he teaches that the Spirit of God is now striving with man, but one day the Spirit will cease to strive with the flesh of man again, as He did in the time of Noah. When that happens in the end times, the result will be great tribulation such as the world has never known (2 Thessalonians 2:7-8).

In the story of the flood, God decides He will wipe out the entire population of the earth and start over again with man. One definition of the wrath of God, by David Stuart Briscoe, is "the annihilating reaction of a holy, loving God toward that which is destroying His love objects." We see that dimension of the character of God illustrated here. In this account of the flood, we see a demonstration of the character of man and the character of God.

When the character of man is released to have its way and chaos is the result, you also see Noah, of whom you read, "*But Noah found grace in the eyes of the Lord*" (Genesis 6:8). "*I have seen that you are righteous before Me in this generation*" (Genesis 7:1 NKJ). We read that Noah was perfect "*in his generations*" (Genesis 6:9), meaning *in the eyes of his fellow man.* Later Scripture describes Noah as "*a preacher of righteousness*" (2 Peter 2:5). God is always looking for that one man who will be wholly committed to Him. When God finds such a man, He is willing to trade that man's life for a whole generation of people (Exodus 32:10). God nearly always seems to find one (Ezekiel 22:30).

However, when we meet Noah, we are also introduced to one of the most beautiful concepts in the Bible when we are informed that "*Noah found grace in the eyes of the Lord*" (Genesis 6:8). The reason God chose to save this man and his family was not because he was righteous in all his generations as we read here. God saved him because Noah received grace. Every sinner saved by God is saved because that sinner found grace in the eyes of the Lord – not because they deserved salvation.

THE CHARACTER OF GOD

The Bible presents the character of God as loving and merciful (Exodus 34:5-7a; Psalm 51:1; 100:5; 23:6). In the Old Testament, God personally loves us as a Shepherd and in the New Testament as a loving Father. However, the God of the Bible is also a just God

(Exodus 34:7b; Ecclesiastes 12:13-14; 1 Peter 1:15-16). God plays different roles. He is a loving Father and Shepherd but He is also a holy Judge. The story of the flood presents His justice and holiness. In Genesis chapters 6 through 9, God reveals His role as a just and holy Judge. If you survey the entire Bible, you will find that the Old Testament emphatically and consistently also presents a loving God – especially through the prophets.

After the judgment of this awful flood, God established a covenant with man. He committed to man, "*I will not again curse the ground... neither will I again smite anymore everything living as I have done.* [The order and balance of the universe] *shall not cease*" (Genesis 8:20-22 ASV). Additionally, man is given dominion over the animal world (Genesis 9:2), he is no longer commanded to be a vegetarian (Genesis 9:3), capital punishment is instituted (Genesis 9:5-6), and there will be no more floods that destroy "*all flesh*" (Genesis 9:11). God gives man the rainbow as a sign of His covenant.

The conditions of the Covenant are interesting. This covenant has no binding ifs. The one all-important condition is phrased in Genesis 8:22 (NKJV), "*While the earth remains.*" This immediately raises the question, "Is the earth going to remain forever?" Consult these Scriptures and then decide what you think: Psalm 46; Haggai 2:6, 21; Malachi 3:1-2; 4:1-3; Matthew 5:18; Luke 21:33; 2 Peter 3; and Hebrews 12:26-29.

Here is a thought-provoking quote from D. L. Moody, a famous evangelist of another century: "The earth is a sinking ship, and my job is not to save the ship, but to save as many people from the ship as I can before the ship goes down, because brother, that ship is going down!"

What is your response to this perspective of Moody? Are you trying to save as many people as you can from that ship before the ship goes down? Are you trying to save the ship or paint the ship? Are you trying to save the world, or do you want to see God save people out of this world?

I want to share some pictures with you that will give you a realistic concept of the ark God told Noah to build. Johan Huibers, a devout Dutch marketplace disciple, is a boat builder who studied the specifications God gave to Noah and built this replica of what the ark would have looked like. This shows us that the story of the flood is not a fairy tale or part of what some people refer to as T*he Folklore of the Old Testament*. He found a way to use his call to the marketplace, and his faith in the Word of God, to make a difference for God.

It is important for us to learn from this story the examples and warnings God wants to teach us (1 Corinthians 10:11). The character of God has not changed and the character of man is unchanged. God does strive with our flesh today and when God takes the breaks off that restraint next time, the result will be great tribulation such as the world has never seen. The concept of the Day of the Lord preached by the prophets is unfulfilled prophecy that will one day be fulfilled.

"But the day of the Lord will come as a thief in the night, in which the heavens will pass away with a great noise, and the elements will melt with fervent heat; both the earth and the works that are in it will be "burned up. Therefore, since all these things will be dissolved, what manner of persons ought you to be in holy conduct and godliness, looking for and hastening the coming of the day of God, because of which the heavens will be dissolved, being on fire, and the elements will melt with fervent heat? Nevertheless we, according to His promise, look for new heavens and a new earth in which righteousness dwells" (2 Peter 3:10-13).

In this awesome passage of Scripture, Peter describes something this world had not seen until we entered into the thermonuclear age. I remember my parents sharing this passage with my aunts and uncles when I was a small child. My relatives were secular people and I well remember them saying these things could not be. The earth could not be dissolved and the elements could not melt with fervent heat.

During the Cuban missile crisis, I was in a hospital in Florida after surgery for a ruptured appendix. For the first time in my life I was too weak to even raise my arms. A man who was a nuclear scientist and was on the Atomic Energy Commission visited me because he attended the church of which I was the pastor. I told him I felt so weak and helpless, being only ninety miles from Cuba, because I would not be able to escape the area if we had a nuclear war. He laughed and said we were all helpless and weak because if there were a nuclear war, there would be no hiding place and no place to go to escape a nuclear exchange.

I asked him if he could explain to me in lay terms precisely what a thermonuclear explosion was like. He touched his hands together and said, "It's a very, very intense heat that dissolves every material thing. Imagine a concrete wall a hundred yards long, fifty yards wide and fifty yards high. If a nuclear missile were exploded it would reduce that concrete wall to something like the vapor of smoke." I then read the passage written by Peter. He said that is almost a perfect description of a thermonuclear explosion. I told him those words were dictated by an illiterate fisherman 2,000 years ago. I am not implying the Day of the Lord will be a thermonuclear war. I am merely writing that man can now do what people thought even God couldn't do.

As you read this passage, observe that Peter proclaims, in the inspiration of the Holy Spirit, that the Day of the Lord will come. He compares the days before the Day of the Lord to be like the days of Noah. He also writes something that intrigues me. He exhorts us to live in such a way that we might hasten the coming of that Day of the Lord. That makes me think… *How can we hasten the coming of that day*?

In the Mount Olivet Discourse of Jesus (Matthew 24-25), where Jesus teaches about His Second Coming, He makes this statement: "*This gospel of the kingdom will be preached in all the world as a witness to all the nations, and then the end will come*"

(Matthew 24:14). This means one day the Gospel will be preached in one of the many nations of this world, and God the Father is going to decide it is time for the Day of the Lord to come. That should motivate all of the authentic disciples of Jesus Christ in the marketplaces of the world to make getting the Gospel out to the nations of the earth a magnificent obsession. By doing that, we are hastening the coming of the Day of the Lord.

When Billy Graham was in London preaching a great crusade, Winston Churchill invited him to Number 10 Downing Street with several members of his team. One of them told me this story. Churchill asked something of the young evangelist. He said, "I understand you have been telling the people in your crusade that Jesus Christ is coming back again. Will you tell me about that sir?" Billy was only too willing and he gave the Prime Minister a powerful presentation of the Second Coming of Jesus Christ.

When Billy finished, Churchill, who was a great student of history and feared the Communist threat in the Cold War more than he had feared the Nazis, shook his head emphatically and said, "Unless something like that is true then there is no hope, positively no hope!"

Churchill was right. The only hope of this world is the Second Coming of Jesus Christ. It is referred to in Scripture as the blessed hope of the Church and the only hope of the world. Those who follow Christ should want to hasten the coming of the Day of the Lord, because it is our blessed hope and the only hope of the world in which we live.

When I was in college, we studied the 25,000 suicides committed in 1952. Sociologists, psychiatrists, psychologists and social workers determined those people committed suicide because they lost hope. This means they lost the conviction that something good exists in this world, and that anything good could happen to them.

That reality was accentuated for me when a man jumped to his death from the top of my dormitory. That dormitory was adjacent to the public library of Los Angeles, California, located near the intersection of Sixth and Hope streets. After intersecting Sixth Street, Hope Street ended at the public library. When I checked the newspapers, I read that an unidentified man ended his life by jumping to his death from a tall building at the end of Hope Street. That newspaper reporter was more eloquent than they knew when they wrote their description of a man who committed suicide.

Believing in the only hope of this world and the blessed hope of the church, is it not criminal negligence for us to work in the marketplace next to people who have no hope, and not tell them about that hope?

THE WALKING DEFINITION OF FAITH

After telling us about the history of the universe and the many things He wanted to tell us in the first eleven chapters of the Bible, at the end of chapter 11, the Bible introduces us to a man named Abram. The life of this man is the most comprehensive way God wraps the concept of faith in the life of a person. God fervently wants us to understand, experience and apply the caliber of faith He has demonstrated for us in the life of Abram. This five letter word faith is one of the most important concepts our loving God wants us understand.

THE FATHER OF FAITH

In the Bible, the amount of space given to a subject reveals something about the importance of that subject. Faith is the subject of a whole section of Genesis that tells the story of this man Abram. As we study about a dozen chapters, God wants us to understand faith as it was and as it is to be now.

The way our loving heavenly Father profiles faith in the life of Abram is the most profound and prescriptive picture of faith presented in the Bible. That is why this man is mentioned more in the New Testament than any other Old Testament person. When the New Testament touches on the subject of faith, it isn't long before the author writes the name Abraham.

Since faith is so important, and God wants us to understand faith, He tells us the entire story of this man named Abram. If you want to deepen your understanding of faith, study the life of this man.

HIS NAME

When we meet him, his name is Abram. That name means "father of many sons." However, he is seventy-five years old and has no sons. They say the definition of an optimist is a seventy-five year old man who gets married and builds a house near a school. Imagine Abram introducing himself to someone at a camel watering stop. When he says his name is "father of many sons," people would undoubtedly say to him, "My, you must have a lot of sons." Then Abram would say, "No, I have no sons but as a matter of fact, if you can number the grains of sand on the earth and the number of stars in the heavens, you will have an idea of how many sons I will have one day!" When they asked him how he knew that, he would say, pointing up with his index finger, "God told me!"

Then later God changes his name to Abraham, which means "father of multitudes or nations of sons." But he still has no sons. So imagine him meeting those people to whom he had introduced himself earlier. If they said, "Hi, father of many sons," He would then say, "Oh, my name has been changed. It is now "father of multitudes or nations of sons!" And when they said, "Oh bless your heart you must have had a son" he would say, "No, as a matter of fact I don't have any sons yet." But then he would go into his description of his progeny being like the grains of sand and the stars in the heavens. And he would point up and say, "God told me!" Do you think that took faith?

THE TWO SIDED COIN

Like the two sides of a coin there are two sides to this story, as there are to every God story: the God-side, and the man-side. To see the God-side of the story of Abraham, study the appearances of God to Abraham. God appeared to Abraham eight times. Thus, God made Himself known to Abraham. It was God Who initiated the relationship. That is true of every relationship with God. Paul reminds us that no man seeks God – it is God Who seeks man (Romans 3:11). If a man looks as if he is seeking God, he is only responding to the God Who is seeking him. That is what it means when we read that God appeared to Abraham eight times, and that represents the *God-side* of the coin of a relationship with God.

The man-side of the relationship, or the response of Abraham to

God, comes in the form of four altars Abraham built. The first altar was erected in the plains of Moreh, where God appeared to Abram and told him, "*To your descendants I will give this land*" (Genesis 12:7). The word *Moreh* literally means "teaching" or "seeking." I call that first altar of Abraham *The Altar of Response*, because it was built in response to the God Who was making Himself known to this man and calling Abram into a wilderness. He went out not knowing where he was going. That describes his response to God at this point in his journey as he learns and gives us a definition of faith.

His second altar was built between Hai and Bethel. In Hebrew, *Bethel* means "the house of God." Since God did not have a house at this point, this word means "the place where God is." Hai means, "ruin", "misery" or "the pits." Romans 6:23 promises us that "*the wages of sin is death*," and that is what the name of this city represents. Further east beyond Hai are Sodom and Gomorrah. At his first altar, Abram was saying, "Teach me." At this second altar, he shows by its placement that he has not yet decided how to respond to what God is teaching him.

Abram leaves this second altar and goes south, geographically and spiritually. He tells his wife to say she is his sister so the Egyptian men will not kill him to take her. He gets into a lot of trouble with the political leader and seems to be *out of it* spiritually.

After this incident, Abraham returned to the site of his second altar and called on God more fervently there a second time. After that sincere worship, he suggested to Lot that they separate. It seems likely God reminded him that he was not supposed to bring Lot with him in the first place. And since later on we find Lot entrenched in the sin of Sodom and Gomorrah, we can see why God wanted that separation. I call this second altar, especially Abraham's second prayer at this altar, *The Altar of Repentance*. To repent means "to think again" or "to have a change of mind, heart, will and direction, plus being sorry for having gone the wrong way." At the beginning of chapter 12 we learn God had been appearing to Abram for some time: "*Now the LORD had said to Abram: 'Get out of your country, from your family and from your father's house, to a land that I will show you. I will make you a great nation; I will bless you and make your name great; and you shall be a blessing. I will bless those who bless you, and I will curse him who curses you; and in you all the families of the earth shall be blessed'* " (Genesis 12:1-3).

Actually, Abram was instructed by God to do three things. He was to leave his father, his family and his home country. We don't know how long God had been making Abram know these things. We do know that after some time had passed, Abram did one of the three. This means when we meet him, his faith was a fragment of what it should be, not unlike a mustard seed of faith. Just like yours and mine.

Bringing Lot with him was a violation of what God was making him know he was to do. It was, therefore, worked out at the altar of repentance that he must separate himself from Lot. When he did that, Lot went east while Abraham went west and built his third altar at a place called *Hebron*. The word *Hebron* means "communion" or "relationship" and I think this name too is symbolic. Where the first altar said, "Teach me," and the second altar said, "I need to repent of being Mr. In-between," this altar states, "God, I want to know You." I call this third altar the *Altar of*

Relationship.

In the first two chapters of Abraham's story, chapters 12 and 13, he built three altars. He does not build another altar until chapter 22. What happened between the third and the fourth altars?

When Abraham said, "God, I want to know You," I think God responded, "Abraham, if you want to have a relationship with Me, I want you to know something. If I am anything to you, I am everything to you, because until I am everything to you, I am not really anything to you." Before Abraham can establish a relationship with God, there are four other relationships God must address.

In Genesis chapter 16, we see Abraham and Sarah becoming concerned about how God is going to fulfill His promise to give Abram offspring – so they decide to help Him along. At his wife's suggestion, Abram has relations with her Egyptian maid, Hagar (Genesis 16:1-4). The child of that union was Ishmael, who fathered the Arabs. There would be no Middle East crisis if Abraham had not decided God needed his help and so listened to his wife.

The third altar, the Altar of Relationship, deals with the vertical and horizontal relationships, which are inseparable. For Abraham to know God, God had to have His rightful place in all of Abraham's relationships. God had to speak to Abraham about Lot and get Lot out of Abraham's life. Lot represents the people we put in our life, but who God does not want in our life. He also had to work Ishmael out of his life. Ishmael represents the reality that the greatest enemy of God's best is something good. God appeared to Abraham and told him to send Ishmael away. One by one, God roots out all these people who compete for first place in Abraham's life.

Sarah is a different kind of problem. Sarah is a picture of the people God does put in our life, but whom we do not recognize as coming from God. God had to appear to Abraham twice about Sarah. The second time, He said: "*As for Sarai your wife, you shall not call her name Sarai, but Sarah shall be her name. And I will bless her, and indeed I will give you a son by her*" (Genesis 17:15-16). When Abraham heard this, he fell on his face and laughed! When Sarah heard this news she also laughed!

A year later, a son was born to Abraham and Sarah, and God told them to call this son Isaac, which in Hebrew means "laughter." God never wanted these *heroes of faith* to forget they laughed at Him when He told them what He was going to do.

Finally, when Isaac is a young man, Abraham builds his fourth altar, and this is his most important altar. It was built on Mount Moriah. Moriah means "The Mountain of Jehovah." Up until now, Abraham had picked the location for his altars, but this time, God picks the place. This time, God also names the sacrifice – Isaac.

Isaac is not only the miracle son of Abraham and Sarah's old age, but also the fulfillment of 25 years of faith. And now God says, contrary to what makes sense, "I want him." And Abraham takes the boy up on the mountain with every trembling intention of following through with what God has asked. But at the last minute, when he has proven his obedience, God provides a ram as a substitution for Isaac's life (Genesis 20:1-19). Abraham calls that place Jehovah-Jireh, which means, "Jehovah will provide" (One suggested alternate reading is "Jehovah will prove.").

In summary, this allegory of faith teaches through the altars of Abraham that on the mountain of God's choosing, and at the altar of *God first,* God provides the fruition of 25 years of faith. To paraphrase the name Abraham gave to that fourth altar, we could say: *On the mountaintop of 'God first,' the man of faith provides faith in God and God provides for the man of faith.* Or we could say: *On the mountaintop of 'God first,' the man of faith proves God and God proves the man of faith.* Finally, for Abraham, God was first. At this fourth altar, Abraham did not offer up Isaac. At the altar of "God First," Abraham offered up Abraham.

So often the message of the Bible can be summarized in the words: *God first.* Now, that is not easy, but neither is it complicated. Either He is our God, or He is not our God.

THE COVENANT WALK

In chapter 15, Abram has a deep spiritual experience. In ancient Semitic cultures, they could not dial 9-1-1 when they had a problem. It was, therefore, part of their culture to enter into a covenant relationship with someone of similar wealth and power. When they made such a covenant, they had a ceremony. Their ceremony was to sacrifice an animal by splitting it in half. Standing on opposite sides of the sacrifice, they did a walk through the sacrifice, which was followed by a clockwise right turn in a circle and then into and through the sacrifice a second time. This was followed by a turn to their left in a counter-clockwise circle, which brought them back to where they started. The whole maneuver formed a figure eight movement around and through the sacrifice. Each covenant partner took their turn doing this.

Once they were in place again, facing each other on opposite sides of the sacrifice, they exchanged their top garment which represented the reality that they were swapping identities as a bride does when she is married in our culture. They took each other's name and made it part of their own name. This meant if anyone harmed one of them, they were harming the other.

They then exchanged their large belts which held their swords. This exchange of their weapons symbolized the reality that my strength is your strength anytime you need it. If anyone attacks you they attack me. All my fighting strength is yours when you need it.

Then they vowed the terms of their covenant. They pronounced a great many blessings on their covenant partner if they fulfilled the vows of this covenant. They also pronounced horrible curses upon them if they did not keep the commitments of this covenant.

All the time they were doing this a sword was glowing red hot nearby in a fire. The covenant was then sealed by branding each other on the inside of their wrist with that red hot sword. This was the covenant mark record of their covenant walk ceremony. From that time forward, when they greeted or said farewell to someone, they raised their arm and waved to them, exposing their covenant mark. The one they were addressing in this way knew they were in covenant with someone and they did not know who that was. They did know that if they attacked this person they were also attacking someone else and they did not know how powerful that other person might be.

In the Old Testament book of 1 Samuel, at the beginning of chapter 18, we read that David and Jonathan made this kind of covenant: "*Then Jonathan and David made a covenant, because he loved him as his own soul. And Jonathan took off the robe that was on him and gave it to David, with his armor, even to his sword and his bow and his belt*" (1 Samuel 18:3-4).

This brief dip into Semitic culture gives us the background to appreciate the experience Abram had, as recorded in chapter 15 of the book of Genesis. We read that God told Abram to split an animal as described above. Abram was then put in a deep sleep and when he awoke, a torch was doing the figure eight around and through that sacrifice. This was God's way of telling Abram that his God was in covenant with him. In response, we read: "*Abram believed God and it was counted to him as righteousness.*" This is a very significant spiritual dateline in the faith of Abram. It is a vital appearance of God to him. After this event he does not seem to doubt that God is in covenant with him.

A personal application of this experience is that we are in covenant with God today. The first half of our Bible is labeled the Old Testament and the second half is labeled the New Testament. The word *testament* means covenant. We are therefore being told there is an old covenant and a new covenant with God. The old covenant was that we should believe that Jesus is coming for our salvation. The new covenant is, *we should believe that Jesus came, made our salvation possible and lives in us and through us*. As the reality that God was in covenant with Abraham inspired his faith, so should we be inspired to know that God is in covenant with us.

Another important happening in Abram's journey of faith is when God changes his name to Abraham, in chapter 17. This name means "father of multitudes or nations of sons." This is right after Abraham listened to his wife and tried to help God. This is literally true today because all the Jews, Arabs, many Semitic peoples and authentic disciples of Jesus Christ consider Abraham to be their father. This event begins with God saying to Abram, "*Walk before Me and be blameless*" (Genesis 17:1).

WHAT DOES IT ALL MEAN?

The most important part of any study in the Bible is the application. The entire story of Abraham can be summed up as the meaning of the word *faith*. Faith is not a step in the dark or a leap in the light. Do we realize what we mean when we use the word *faith*? When I hear people say, "Keep the faith, baby," I wish we could have a Bible study on the life of Abraham so we could be sure we are talking about the same concept. Consider this entire story of Abraham. Add all these events and experiences as if they were a column of figures. Then realize that they all add up to the meaning of faith.

To many evangelicals faith is the initial decision to believe in response to an invitation by an evangelist. These believers remind me of the specialty teams in an American football game. They do the kickoff that gets the game started. Then they sit on the bench while others come in and actually play the game. The decision to believe is critically important because nothing happens until we decide to believe. But that decision is not the ballgame – it just gets the game started.

A good way to apply this study of Abraham is to ask ourselves, "How many altars have we built to our God who is giving us the gift of faith? Have we built the *Altar of Response*?" Nothing else is going to happen until we build the Altar of Response. This first altar is critically important but it is not the whole definition of the concept of faith.

Have we built the *Altar of Repentance*? Today I believe many believers are taking a bypass around the Altar of Repentance. When I spoke on these four altars of Abraham at a retreat for young couples, I was thrilled when a married daughter my wife and I had nurtured and mentored from birth responded to my invitation to build that altar. She was definitely a believer but she was not following the Lord at that time. There are many believers in our churches and spiritual communities who have great gaps in their spiritual lives because they have never built the Altar of Repentance.

Have we built the *Altar of Relationship*? I believe there is a serious lack of preaching on the subject of the pursuit of God today. As we learned in chapter 5, if we will confess the values of Christ in the marketplace, among other things, we will know we are to be God-passionate people. In two places, Jesus taught we are to ask continuously, and with perseverance we are to seek, which is intense asking, continuously and with perseverance. Then we are to knock, which is intense seeking, continuously and with perseverance, if we want to break through to an authentic relationship with God.

I quoted these passages in chapter 9 when I was writing about prayer in the marketplace. They are found in the middle of the greatest discourse of Jesus, His Sermon on the Mount and in chapter 11 of the Gospel of Luke.

Shakespeare, in *Hamlet*, wrote, "To be is to be in relations." There is no relationship as important as our relationship with

God. However, Abraham teaches us by example that vertical and horizontal relationships form a cross and they are inseparable. Our God is a jealous God and He demands first place in our life. If He means anything to us, He means everything to us, because until He is everything to us, He isn't really anything to us. He is either Lord *of* all, or He is not really Lord *at* all.

Our Lord Christ defined eternal life for us when He said: "*This is eternal life, that they may know You, the only true God, and Jesus Christ whom You have sent*" (John 17: 3). When we hear terms like eternal life, we believe this eternal life is the state in which we will exist throughout all eternity. We are correct in that assumption, but that is not all *eternal life* means. Technically the word *eternal* means that which was, which is, and which always shall be. When we say we have eternal life, it sounds as if we believe in reincarnation. We do not mean to say we are, we always have been and we always will be. What we really mean is that we are related to the God and His Son Who are, always have been and always will be, eternal. That quality of life is a relationship with our heavenly Father God and the One He has sent into the world to be our Savior, who are both eternal. According to Jesus, we have eternal life because we are related to those who are eternal. In addition to that, eternal life is a quality of life God and His Son want us to experience right now and until we are called home to be in fellowship with them forever. This is true because we have this on the authority, and out of the mouth, of Jesus Christ.

If you do not have a personal relationship with the risen, living Christ and God His Father, I challenge you to build that third altar of Abraham, the Altar of Relationship.

His third altar prepares us for his most important altar. I call it the *Altar of God First* or the *Altar of Reality*. I have spent most of my adult life teaching a survey of the entire Bible. When you continuously study and teach the Bible from Genesis to Revelation, you gain an appreciation of what the Bible emphasizes. This truth of *God first* is a primary emphasis all the way through the Bible.

The first commandment states we are to have no other gods before Him. The hard sayings of Jesus, which are so difficult for people to understand, consistently teach this truth of God first. In the New Testament Church, there was a simple doctrinal basis of fellowship. It was simply three words: *Jesus is Lord*! (1 Corinthians 12:3). Every year a Roman citizen had to throw a pinch of incense into a fire and confess, "Caesar is Lord!" Only God knows how many believers died because as Roman citizens they would not make that confession to Caesar. Their allegiance was expressed in that doctrinal statement of fellowship: *Jesus is Lord*!

The Apostle Paul wrote, "*No man can say that Jesus is Lord except by the Holy Spirit*" (1 Corinthians 12:3). Professing that Jesus is Lord is a byproduct of being born again. The purpose of being born again is that we might see and enter into the Kingdom of God, or enter into a relationship with God, whereby He is our King and we are His subjects. Another application could be that no man or woman could say in the face of martyrdom that Jesus is Lord, except by the Holy Spirit. I will discuss this vitally important concept of being 'born again' in chapter 13.

Our current spiritual culture in one word is characterized by *superficiality*. We can trace much of the cause for this lack of spiritual depth to the way believers define and apply their concept of the great Bible word, *faith*. It has never been more important for the Church of Jesus Christ to discover why God wrapped the concept of faith in the character and life experience of Abraham. If we apply Genesis chapters six through nine, which give us both a descriptive and prescriptive account of this great father of faith, it could revolutionize and bring a great revival to the Church of Jesus Christ in the 21st century. Invite the Holy Spirit into your personal and private study of this man who is the walking definition and application of one of the most important concepts in all the Word of God.

Chapter Eleven

Divine Guidance in the Marketplace

The question "How can I know the will of God?" is the question a pastor hears more than any other in the privacy of his study. Businessmen especially ask this question often because they frequently need to know the will of God. I have had marketplace disciples tell me the difference in a decision they must make could be $500 million. As I address marketplace disciples in this book I feel, therefore, that I should include a chapter on divine guidance.

In the Bible, the first time God speaks to fallen man, He asks man a question: "*Where are you*?" The second thing God says to fallen man is also a question: "*Who told you*?" The first question implies we are to be somewhere and we are not always there. The second question implies that if we want to know where we are relative to where we should be, God will make us know that difference. Divine guidance is one of the first truths God shares with us in the Bible. These two questions from Genesis 3 are the beginning of a prescription for divine guidance we will find in the Bible.

When we know where we are spiritually, and where we should be, we will realize we did not get that information from people. That is the time to let God ask us His second question, "*Who told you*?" In the Bible, the Hebrew translation of this second question is literally, "*Who made you know that*?"

When you realize God has told you where you should be and

where you are, you may not want to share that information with people. For example, if you told your family and friends that you were absolutely certain you were to make a career change, and they asked you how you knew you were to do that, you might feel more than awkward saying, "God told me!" (They may ask you if His voice was masculine or feminine.) You may be more comfortable referring to this second question more accurately, by saying, "God has made me know that I am not where I need to be at this point in my life."

When someone questions me, about the will of God, they might be referring to a *fork-in-the-road* decision. Sometimes the issue has been the broader question, "How can I know the will of God for my life?" While answering that question many times over many years, I have prescribed twelve steps I believe you should take when you seek divine guidance. These twelve steps are not a precise formula that will immediately and clearly lead you to the specific will of God, but they do focus some issues that should be visited, or bases you should touch, when you are trying to establish an alignment between your will and the will of God.

THE FIRST STEP

Believe there is such a thing as the will of God for your life.

There is a very real sense in which the will of God for all God-fearers, God seekers and disciples of Jesus Christ is simply applying the essence of The Ten Commandments and The Sermon on the Mount. The Apostle Paul focused on that dimension of the will of God when he wrote to the Thessalonians, "*For this is the will of God for you, even your sanctification*" (1 Thessalonians 4:3).

During his commencement speech, Ted Koppel, a well-known television journalist, reminded a class of university graduates that when Moses came down from Mount Sinai, he did not bring with him *The Ten Suggestions.* The Ten Commandments represent the will of God for the character of both the Old Testament and New Testament people of God. The Sermon on the Mount is the pinnacle revelation of God regarding the character of every disciple of Jesus Christ. There is a sense in which the whole Bible was written because it is the will of a Holy God that every man and woman of God might be perfect in character and thoroughly equipped for every good work God wants them to do (2 Timothy 3:16-17).

The teachings of The Ten Commandments and The Sermon on the Mount do not tell us to live out the character they profile for us that we might be saved. These teachings of Jesus and commandments of Moses are given to us from God that we might know how sanctified people (or saints) should live because they are the authentic people of God. In that sense, we can say the will of God for the character of all the people of God is the same.

We are told in the Word of God that the steps of a godly man or woman are ordered by the Lord (Psalm 37:23). The intellectually sophisticated neo-evangelical today likes to enlighten us by sharing the proposition that there is no such thing as the will of God for your life or regarding a difficult decision you must make.

In Psalm 139, verse 16, David tells us that before he existed, God had all David's days written in a book. The Living Bible Paraphrased paraphrases this verse to say God had every day of

David's life scheduled before David existed. David tells us God is with him, goes before him and pursues behind him in such a way that it is impossible for David to escape God's personal interest in every move he makes. This intimacy with God is obviously not only to be the experience of David, but can and should be the experience of every child of God.

Every time a tiny sparrow falls dead from a tree, God goes to the funeral. This is a paraphrase by an evangelist from another generation, referring to the teaching of Jesus that not one tiny sparrow falls dead from a tree apart from the Father's will. The application Jesus makes is that since two sparrows are sold for a penny and we are of far greater value to God than a sparrow, if God has a will regarding the details of the life and death of a sparrow, then we can be sure He has a will regarding every detail of our lives.

In this teaching about the sparrow, Jesus affirms David's revelation of a personal God Who cares about the minute details of our lives, schedules every day of our lives, and directs our steps. Jesus reinforces that emphasis when He tells us in the same passage that God knows the number of hairs on our heads (Matthew 10:30).

Paul exhorts us to "*prove in practice that the plan of God for you is good, meets all His demands and moves towards the goal of spiritual maturity*" (Romans 12:2 JB Phillips). The American Standard Version tells us we are to meet some specific conditions and then experience "*the good, acceptable and perfect will of God.*" Paul writes to the Ephesians that even though we are not saved by good works, we are saved *for* good works, which God has before ordained that we should do for Him. He also writes to the Philippians that his magnificent obsession as a disciple of Jesus

Christ was to grasp the purpose for which Jesus Christ grasped him when he was converted on the road to Damascus (Philippians 3:12).

I have observed above that in the first verses of the Bible, Moses told us there is a place where God wills us to be, and God will make us know when we are and when we are not in that place. When I consider these declared values of Jesus, Moses, David, and Paul, I find it difficult to understand how people can say God does not care who we marry, or whether we study law, medicine, education, or go to seminary and prepare for the ministry. Since these are the most important steps we take, how can we say that the God Who numbers the hairs on our heads, orders our steps and schedules our days is not interested in these vitally important life-altering decisions?

The Word of God teaches that God has a will for our *careers* as well as our *characters*. God desires to be personally involved in the steps we take as we live for Him in this world. A good place for you to begin to seek His will for your life is for you to believe there is a will of God for your life.

THE SECOND STEP

Be willing to do the will of God.

Jesus taught His disciples to pray, "*Your will be done.*" When Jesus modeled this, He sweated drops of blood as He prayed, "*Not My will, but Your will be done*" (Matthew 6:10; 26:39; Luke 22:42-44). In John 7:17, Jesus gives us a principle that shows us how we can know His teaching is the teaching of God. This principle also applies when we seek to know the will of God in the marketplace. The principle is simply this: *If any man wills to do, he will know.*

According to Jesus and Paul, knowing the will of God for our lives does not have to be difficult or complex. God does not deliberately complicate or obscure His will. The difficulty is not the will of God, but your will and my will. As Paul tells us how we can know "*the good, acceptable and perfect will of God*," he begins his prescription for knowing God's will by telling us to throw our hands up and offer an unconditional surrender of our wills to the will of God (Romans 12:1-2). Our unconditional surrender to God will significantly un-complicate our quest to know the will of God.

THE THIRD STEP

Spend much time in prayer.

When you must know the will of another human being, what is the first step you take? Our first thought is usually that we must meet with that person and have a conversation with them. When a man is in love and decides he wants to marry a woman, his first thought is that he must meet with her and have a conversation with her. When we seek to know the will of God, our first thought should be that we must meet with God and have a conversation with Him. Prayer is a conversation with God. If you do not know how to pray, think of prayer as simply meeting with and having a conversation with God.

The apostles, with honesty and some humility, asked Jesus to teach them to pray. In response to their candid confession and request, Jesus gave them the Disciple's Prayer (Luke 11; Matthew

6). I covered this teaching in-depth in chapter 9 of this book. That prayer was not as much a prayer as it was an instruction about how to pray. When you are alone, use that prayer as an outline for your conversation with God. As you do, you will find yourself applying the second and third steps I have just shared with you for knowing the will of God when Jesus instructs you to pray, "*Your kingdom come; Your will be done.*"

THE FOURTH STEP

Spend much time in the Word of God.

To maintain your spiritual equilibrium as you work in the marketplace and seek to know the will of God, it is imperative you have regular, structured and disciplined times of study in the Word. Let me show you why. In chapter 55 of his prophecy, Isaiah tells us there is as much difference between the thoughts and ways of God and the way we think and do things as the heavens are high above the earth (Isaiah 55:8-9). He then goes on to describe one of the many supernatural functions of the Word of God. The essential truth Isaiah shares with us in this great chapter is that the Word of God establishes an alignment between our thoughts, ways and wills, and the thoughts, ways and will of God.

Isaiah tells us he preached the Word of God because he believed it was the will of his God that His people think the thoughts, learn the ways and do the will of their God. If the people of God are to do the will of God, they must first know the will of God. If the people of God sincerely want to know the will of their God, Who does not think or act as they do, they simply must spend time in His Word.

There are two distinct dimensions to every good conversation. If you are considered to be a good *conversationalist*, that means you are a good *listener*. Every good conversationalist knows that the most important dimension of a conversation is when the other person is talking and he or she is listening. These two distinct dimensions of conversation must be in place when we pray and when we open God's Word. When we pray, the most important dimension of that conversation is not when we talk to God, but when God talks to us.

I once heard Billy Graham tell of boarding a plane before he was famous. He spoke to an old pastor friend who was sitting in an aisle seat, reading his Bible. The old pastor completely ignored Billy. When they had been in flight for about an hour, the pastor came back to where Billy was seated and greeted him enthusiastically. He apologized for ignoring Billy earlier. He said, "When I pray, I am talking to God, but when I open God's Word, He talks to me. He was talking to me when you spoke to me and I could not interrupt God just to talk to Billy Graham."

Thomas à Kempis opened his Bible every morning with this prayer: "Let all the voices be stopped. Speak to me Lord, Thou alone." If we sincerely want to know the will of God, we must be in relationship and in conversation with God. We should speak to our loving heavenly Father in prayer and expect God to speak to us as we open the Word of God. That is why two of the bases we must touch when we seek to know the will of God are prayer and the Word of God.

THE FIFTH STEP

Be completely open and unbiased as to what the will of God for your life might be.

A man who is paid huge sums of money as a consultant told me that much of the time when he is paid large fees, his clients do not want his consultation. They simply want him to affirm what they have already decided to do. A woman once said to her pastor during the heart of a counseling session, "Don't confuse me with Scriptures, Pastor. My mind is made up!" I have made the observation that knowing the will of God is complicated and made difficult by our *own* wills. The will of God is just out of our reach because we often have *our* agendas in place when we come to God seeking *His* will. If our minds are set like concrete before we converse with God regarding His will for our lives, we do not really seek His will when we pray or open His Word. We are actually asking God to bless *our* will, *our* agenda and the way *we* have decided to go.

James tells us that when we pray, we often ask and do not receive because our asking is flawed by our self-willed agendas (James 4:3). Therefore, we must be completely open to whatever the will of God may be. Our prayer and our commitment must be in the spirit of the familiar metaphor that prays, *Have your own way, Lord, have your own way. You are the Sculptor, I am the clay. Mold me and make me according to Your will. I am ready to accept Your will as passively as clay in the hands of a Sculptor.*

There are at least two reasons why you must be open and unbiased as you seek to know the will of God for your life. One reason is what we have learned from Isaiah: the ways and thoughts of God are as different from our ways and thoughts as the heavens are high above the earth. Another is that when we are born again, we become a totally new creation. The man who led me to Christ said, "As you make this commitment to Christ, if somebody could show you what you will be doing 20 years from now, you wouldn't believe it!" Nobody who knew me then would have believed that 20 years later I would be preaching an Easter Sunday sermon to a packed sanctuary in a church I started.

It is tragically possible for you to miss the will of God for your life because you do not have the faith to believe that God can make you a new creation in Christ. Your extraordinary potential as a new creation in Christ is one reason why you must be completely open and unbiased as to what the will of God for you may be. Seeking God with your mind already made up could rob you of the will of God for a life that is good, perfect and the only life acceptable to your God. God loves you too much to let you live a life that is only a fragment of the life He has planned for you.

THE SIXTH STEP

Examine the motives of your heart as you seek to know the will of God.

Why do you want to know the will of God as you work in the marketplace? Is it so you will make more money? We should ask that question because the Bible tells us the motives behind our actions are very important to God. It is only after God has exposed the hidden motives of our hearts that we will be judged for our works as believers (1 Corinthians 4:5 NIV).

The Word of God associates our motives with our hearts and the Bible tells us that *above all things* our hearts are deceitful. Jeremiah tells us our hearts are so deceitful that only God can know them (Jeremiah 17:9-10). Do you want to know the will of God for the glory of God, or for your own glory and personal gain? Your answer to that question will be important to God when your works are evaluated at the judgment seat of Christ. The motives of your heart then should be important to you today and every day that you live.

THE SEVENTH STEP

Evaluate your natural and spiritual gift patterns.

To know the will of God for your work in the marketplace, you must recognize both your genetic and spiritual heritage in terms of spiritual gifts. After the Apostle Paul gives us several specific conditions we must meet to find the good, acceptable and perfect will of God (Romans 12:1-2), he gives us some profound teaching about spiritual gifts. The sequence of his logic is this: if you sincerely seek to know the will of God, once you have surrendered unconditionally to the will of God, been transformed by the renewing of your mind and have determined that the world is not going to squeeze you into its mold, you should discover your natural and spiritual gift patterns. Then offer those gifts to God. This spiritual discipline will lead you into the heart of the will of God for your life. An old mentor of mine liked to say, "It should be obvious that God has not called a one-legged man to be an Olympic sprinter."

In chapter 3, I quoted what a mentor of mine called a *Spiritual Gift Inventory*. I strongly encourage you to consult that inventory because it can guide you into this seventh step for knowing the will of God. Once you get a good evaluation of your gift inventory, a principle application of your gift inventory to the will of God for your life is for you to accept the limits of your limitations and the responsibility for your abilities. John the Baptist is a good example of a man who implemented this application.

John knew who he was and he knew who he was not. He said, "*I am the voice of one crying in the wilderness, prepare the way of the Lord*" (John 1:19-34). That was who, what and where John was to be. He knew it was foolish to try to be more than he was called to be. He also knew that life was too precious to be anything less than that voice crying in the wilderness.

I have known parishioners who experienced a lot of needless pain because they would not accept the *limits of their limitations.* However, when we are evaluated at the judgment seat of Christ, most of us will suffer agonizing shortfall because we did not accept the responsibility for our abilities. Like the unprofitable servant in The Parable of the Talents, some of us believe we are not gifted and we bury our talents (Matthew 25:14-30).

John also told us he must decrease and Jesus must increase, because Jesus was the *Bridegroom*, the people were the *bride*, but he himself was just *the best man* at the wedding. All of this means John knew and accepted the limits of his limitations and the responsibility for his abilities. That is why Jesus said John the

Baptist was the greatest man and the greatest prophet ever born of woman (Luke 7:28, Matthew 11:11).

THE EIGHTH STEP

Look for a pattern in the way God reveals His will.

Since our God is a God of order and His "thumbprint" can be seen in the extraordinary design of His creation, we should expect to see order and design in the way God reveals His will for our lives.

In chapter 10 of the book of Acts, we read that the Apostle Peter had a vision of a sheet with animals on it, animals which the Law of Moses would not permit a devout Jew to eat. Peter was told three times to kill and eat those animals. He refused each time. Immediately after this vision, there was a knocking on the door of the home where he was staying. The Spirit told him to go with the men who were knocking, asking no questions about why they had come looking for him. Peter soon learned they were not only Gentiles, but the servants of his enemy, a Roman Centurion. When he arrived at the home of this officer in the Roman army, he was asked to speak to the entire household of the Centurion. The first thing Peter told them was that God had shown him not to call any man common or unclean.

Peter did not think this series of events was a coincidence, but saw these happenings as a pattern of divine guidance. These events are describing the way the Great Commission of Jesus, to preach the Gospel, crossed over a tremendous barrier of prejudice. Peter's experience ultimately revealed the glorious reality that the Gospel of Jesus Christ was not for the Jew only, but for every person in every nation on earth.

In chapter 2, I referred to a story recorded in the eighth chapter of the book of Acts. I called it a three-link chain because it describes how God reaches a lost secular person in this world. God works through the Holy Spirit who works through His Word and an available disciple-maker. Philip the Evangelist was having a fruitful evangelistic crusade among the Samaritan people when the Spirit led him out into the wilderness of Gaza, where the treasurer of Ethiopia just happened to be crossing that desert. He was reading the scroll of Isaiah and was waiting for someone to explain to him the meaning of what he was reading.

This is one of many, many Bible stories that show us what I like to call *Patterns of Providence.* We might also call these stories, *Patterns of Divine Guidance.* When you seek God's will, look for such patterns. They may not be as extraordinary or obviously supernatural, but they will be evidence of the great miracle that God leads in patterns.

THE NINTH STEP

There are times when you should look for a confirmation as you seek to know the will of God.

There are times on our journeys of faith into the marketplace of this world when we come to a fork in the road and we simply do not know the will of God. There is no verse of Scripture that tells us to go to the right or to the left. We have no prompting or leading of the Spirit. We do our best to make the proper choice, while acknowledging the hard reality that we simply do not know which direction is the will of the Lord. Having done everything we can to discern the will of God, we journey down one side or the other of that fork in the road.

Although there is no verse telling us which way to go, there is a verse of Scripture which can give us insight, and which we can apply as a helpful principle when finding ourselves at this kind of crossroad. The Berkeley translation of Psalm 37:23 reads, "*A person's steps are <u>confirmed</u> by the Lord.*" This means we should sometimes move forward into what we perceive to be the will of God, praying and looking for a confirmation.

That confirmation may be positive or negative. If everything works out and the direction we have chosen obviously has God's stamp of approval on it, we can say God has given us a confirmation of His will. We have the conviction of God saying to us, "*This is the way, walk in it*" (Isaiah 30:21). We see evidences of the reality Jesus described, that when He calls His sheep to follow Him, He goes before them (John 10:1-4). After we commit to a direction, we see evidences that the Living Christ has gone before us and prepared the way for us.

Sometimes, the confirmation is negative and the results are the opposite of those I have just described. When that happens, we should be humble enough to go back to that fork in the road and choose the other direction.

THE TENTH STEP

Wait on the Lord.

The marketplace challenges are so great we are often in a hurry. But God is not in a hurry. We often miss the leading of the Lord because we run far ahead, frantically directing the Lord to catch up with us and follow us as we lead Him into our good, acceptable and perfect will for our lives. That is why the expression, "*Wait on the Lord*" is frequently found in the inspired Word of God.

It takes more faith to wait than it takes to be active. God's guidance prescription for what we call Type A personalities like Jacob, is to *wait on the Lord.* Jacob was missing God's will for his life because he was always running ahead of God. He was a make-it-happen, Type A personality. Read the story of Jacob in Genesis chapters 25 through 32, and Paul's commentary on that story in chapter 9 of Romans. As you read how God crippled Jacob so he could crown him with His will for Jacob's life, you will see a great illustration of what it means to wait on the Lord.

Sometimes on our journeys of faith God puts us in a holding pattern. We are like commercial airplanes when they are directed by the control tower to circle the field while waiting their turn to land. In the book of Psalms, the word *Selah* is found in 73 places. The Amplified Bible's paraphrase for that word is, "Pause, and calmly think of that." (Scholars disagree about the meaning of this term. Many scholars believe the word means to be still, to be quiet, or to pause while the accompanying instruments play. Some tell us the word may represent the equivalent of the rest sign in our music today.)

God frequently places *Selahs* in our lives today as He leads us in the marketplace. God has His own good reasons for making us to be still and wait. Sometimes what God does in our life while we're waiting can be more important than what we're waiting for. He may want us to pause and calmly think about our priorities, our vision statement and mission objectives and other issues as we experience His will for our lives. When you encounter one of the Lord's *Selahs*, when He makes you be still, and when you find yourself in one of His holding patterns, ask yourself what God wants you to pause and calmly think about. And never put a question mark where God places a period in your walk of faith.

THE ELEVENTH STEP
Keep moving.

The Bible is filled with paradoxes. A paradox is something that appears to be a contradiction, but when you examine it closely, you discover there really is no contradiction. There are times when a paradox is not a contradiction because the two propositions stated by the paradox could both be true. It may be that the propositions that appear to be contradictory are resolved when you realize that it is not either/or but both/and.

When the Apostle Paul writes about how the Church functions, he uses the words diversity and oneness frequently. He brings these two opposite concepts together in his inspired metaphor of the body, which has a beautiful diversity yet functions with a oneness because it is under the control of one head (1 Corinthians 12). Sometimes, the paradox is resolved when you realize it is sometimes this way and sometimes another way.

The Scriptures tell us we can miss the will of God because we are in a hurry and God is not. When that is the case, we need to wait on the Lord (*Selah*). There are other times when we miss the will of God because we stay apathetic and indecisive, demonstrating our lack of faith and courage, and the Lord moves on without us. These two apparently opposite concepts are really not contradictory. It is not either/or, but both/and. The truth is we sometimes need to wait on the Lord and at other times need to keep moving.

We have an adversary who does not wish us well. His first strategy is to make us into lazy, indecisive, apathetic, spiritual wimps, who miss the will of God because we lack the faith and courage to follow the leading of the Lord. If that fails, he will turn us into obsessive, compulsive workaholic movers, shakers and doers who miss the will of God because we are out-reaching His will for our lives, running far ahead of the Lord. Obviously, we all need the balance between these two extremes that matures us into servants of the Lord who can discern and do the will of the Lord.

THE TWELFTH STEP

Seek wise spiritual counsel.

In his letter to the Romans, the Apostle Paul gives us the most profound and comprehensive statement of the Gospel ever written. After writing eleven chapters, which are a theological masterpiece, he begins the practical section of his letter by writing a great prescription for guidance. *The good, acceptable and perfect will of God* for you and me is the goal and the purpose, in this life, of the salvation about which Paul writes so magnificently in this masterpiece of all his Epistles.

It is not easy to discern the will of God for your life – the *present tense* purpose of your salvation. Therefore, as you work in the marketplace, it is wise for you to seek the counsel of older believers who have been seeking and finding the will of God in the marketplace for many years.

There is a statement found twice in the book of Proverbs (the Bible uses repetition for emphasis), which reads, "*In a multitude of counselors, there is safety*" (Proverbs 24:6; 11:14). This proverb of the wise does not mean you should consult a multitude of counselors when you come to that fork in the road I have described. That would could be confusing, because a multitude of counselors might give you a multitude of opinions regarding your difficult decision.

When the wise men who wrote the book of Proverbs made these two statements, they were teaching two basic truths. In the first one (Proverbs 24:6), they tell us that when two nations go to war with each other, the nation with the multitude of counselors will more than likely win that war. (That is what our Pentagon is all about.) In the other proverb (11:14), they tell us that when we come to that fork in the road, if we have had a multitude of good counselors in our lifetime (a good spiritual education), we will be safe as we make our difficult decision as to which side of that road we should choose to travel.

There is a beautiful, inspiring passage in the prophecy of Isaiah that describes what we call today *Christian Education*. This passage tells us that if we have had a multitude of good spiritual counselors in our lifetime, when we come to this fork in the road, we will hear the voices of those counselors: "*And though the Lord gives you the bread of adversity and the water of affliction, yet your teachers will not be moved into a corner anymore, but your eyes shall see your teachers. Your ears shall hear a word behind you, saying, 'This is the way, walk in it,' whenever you turn to the right hand or whenever you turn to the left*" (Isaiah 30: 20-21).

As I count my blessings today, I am so grateful that in my faith journey, which began in 1949, I have had extraordinary mentors who have given me very wise counsel at critically important junctures in my life and ministry.

A large convoy of ships was on elaborate maneuvers. The flagship at the center of the convoy signaled a hard right turn. Thus, the entire convoy was to make a synchronized hard right turn. The commanding officer of a large cruiser missed the signal from the flagship and his cruiser was not in line with that right turn. The cruiser thrashed around, hopelessly out of formation. There was chaos on the bridge of the cruiser when the standard Navy signal came from the flagship: "What are your intentions?" The skipper of that cruiser flashed this return signal: "My intentions are to buy a farm!" (In the Navy, there is a fast track that makes admirals out of captains and there is a slow track that sends captains into retirement. When a captain makes a mistake like that one, he might as well make his retirement plans.).

The cause of Christ is moving through this world like a convoy, in perfect formation, supernaturally synchronized by the Holy Spirit. The risen, living Christ is the Flagship at the heart of that convoy. Jesus Christ sends signals to that convoy all the time. If you have your eye on the Flagship and you get your signals from Him, you will be in formation and part of His great work in this world. If you do not have your eye on the Flagship and you miss His signals, the work of Christ will move on without you, while you thrash around, out of formation, never a synchronized part this magnificent convoy.

If you miss some signals, you do not have to *buy the farm*. The people who distinguish themselves as servants of Christ are not exceptional people because they never missed a signal. However, the great servants of Christ whom God uses today, and has used throughout the history of the church, have always been men and women who have not received their signals from their cultures. They are, and they always have been, servants of the Lord who have had their eye on the Flagship and have received their signals from the risen, living Christ.

I conclude this chapter on divine guidance in the marketplace the way I began, emphasizing this reality: there is a place we are to be in our walk with Christ, and God's will is for us to know that place. I pray these twelve steps will help you keep your eye on the Flagship, Who will guide you into His will for your life. His choice for you is good, perfect and the only life that is acceptable to the Him Who created, and recreated, you to live that life. This will make you a fruitful marketplace disciple, who will glorify God and impact many lives for Christ in the marketplace.

Chapter Twelve
Trials and Temptations in the Marketplace

The book of James is one of the most powerful books in the Bible, having much to say about temptation, sometimes using this word to refer to testing and sometimes using it to refer to the temptation to sin.

James' letter is intensely practical, referred to by some as *The Proverbs of the New Testament*. The letter of James is like a running commentary on the teachings of Jesus Christ, especially His Sermon on the Mount. You can find at least ten examples where specific teachings of Jesus from that discourse are amplified and applied by James.

Most scholars believe the James who wrote this letter was the earthly half-brother of Jesus Christ. James did not believe in Jesus while Jesus was living out His three years of public ministry. After the resurrection, we are told Jesus made a special appearance to Peter and James, this James, His earthly half-brother (1 Corinthians 15:7).

When James was converted, the New Testament Church was being formed in Jerusalem. He was almost immediately appointed to be one of the great leaders of the Church. This is the James who presided over the council at Jerusalem described in Acts 15. The apostle Paul refers to him in his letter to the Galatians when he writes that when he went up to Jerusalem, there were three men who seemed to be pillars in the Jerusalem Church – John, Peter and this James. There were two apostles with the name of James, but we should not confuse them with the author of this letter.

Tradition tells us James was thrown from the pinnacle of the Temple and then clubbed to death by the high priest. When this happened, tradition says the Jewish religious community revolted against the high priest and ran him out of office. When the Roman emperor, Titus, destroyed Jerusalem, in 70 A.D., many of the devout Jews, who did not become followers of Jesus, believed it was a judgment of God upon the city for the martyrdom of this godly man, James. This godly and great man had the high esteem of both the Jewish religious leaders and the New Testament Church as it was founded by the apostles.

THE MESSAGE OF JAMES

When you study the content of his letter, you will see why some believe James was trying to bring balance to the teaching of the Apostle Paul. Those who believe this feel that Paul emphasizes his *justification by faith through grace plus nothing*, meaning not by works. In chapter 2 of this letter, James tells us emphatically that we are not justified by faith alone, but also by works – to set the record straight.

I heard of a Christian school headmaster in the Philippines who was having chapel with his students when the Japanese invaded his village. Before the student body, a Japanese officer placed a pistol on his stomach and ordered him to tear down the American and the Filipino flag and spit on them. The headmaster was so frightened he could not even speak. He simply shook his head negatively from side to side. The officer then shot him in the stomach.

After the war, a war-correspondent heard this story. He was able to locate the headmaster who had been rescued by family and friends and survived the war in a prison camp. He asked the headmaster, "What thoughts went through your head that led you to take a bullet in the stomach rather than tear down those flags?" The man replied, "There comes a time in every man's life when he must show by his actions what he believes. That was my time."

James gives us a great statement about faith in the second chapter of his letter. He tells us there is not one time in our lives when we must show by our actions what we believe. That crisis of faith occurs all day long every day that we live. In his second chapter, James writes that faith alone can save but the faith that saves is never alone. Saving faith is always accompanied and validated by works which authenticate it.

Even though this letter of James comes at the end of the New Testament, his letter is one of the first letters written in the New Testament period of Church history. Paul's letters were written after the letter of James. So James was not having the last word and contradicting the emphasis of the Apostle Paul that we are not saved by good works. Many scholars believe James wrote before there were any Gentiles in the Church, and speculate that may be why the letter of James seems so Jewish and almost legalistic.

TWO KINDS OF TEMPTATION

Much of the teaching of Jesus could be labeled, *Two people in a pew; which one are you*? James follows that pattern throughout his letter. In the first chapter of this letter, we learn James is a man who is not so much concerned with the *superficial* (how things appear) but, rather, with the source (*where* things originate). James is very much like Jesus in this regard. Jesus emphasized the *inward man* and the *inward issues.* Jesus also emphasized our attitude toward things and the motive that drives our actions. The essence of the letter of James parallels these and other values Jesus emphasized in His teaching.

In chapter 1, James tells us about the sources and sequences of our trials. In some translations, these trials are described as temptations. He will make a distinction later between these two kinds of temptation, but in this case he refers to their trials of suffering. In his opening words, James writes: *"count it all joy" when you experience your trials.* James tells us we should rejoice in our trials because, *the **test** of faith is intended to lead us to the **trust** of faith. If we will allow the test of faith to lead us to the trust of faith, then we will experience the **triumph** of faith, which James calls 'the crown of life'* (James 1:1-12).

When you encounter a storm in your life, that trial will often bring you to the place where you just don't know what to do. You realize you need more wisdom than you have. James writes we must let the test of faith lead us to the trust of faith. When we lack wisdom, we must ask God, Who will be delighted to share His wisdom with us: "*If you need wisdom, ask our generous God, and he will give it to you* (James 1:5 NLT). To paraphrase the words of James, *God will <u>dump a truckload</u> of wisdom on you and me when we confess that we simply do not know what to do.*

In the Old Testament when the people of God were fighting

against overwhelming numbers, their frantic prayer of faith to God was, "*nor do we know what to do, but our eyes are on you!*" (2 Chronicles 20:12 NKJV). The earthly half-brother of Jesus exhorts us to pray that same way when we do not know what to do. We are to ask God for the wisdom we do not have, believing our loving heavenly Father wants to give us that wisdom. In humility and with faith, ask God for wisdom like a child asking his Father.

The JB Phillips translation writes that we should not treat our trials as intruders but welcome them as friends (James 1:2). The process of working through our trials to teach us that test of faith, which leads to the trust of faith and brings us to the triumph of faith, will lead us to a state of spiritual maturity or completeness many translations describe as perfection. In other words, the whole strategy of God in working us through our trials in this way is a process the New Testament calls *sanctification*.

In light of the current economic downturn and resulting hardships, we must address the trials marketplace disciples experience today. I have been in a wheelchair since 1984 and a bed-fast quadriplegic since the mid-nineties. I have, therefore, thought much about the suffering of disciples. God is not in denial about the hard reality that His people suffer. In addition to this first chapter of James, I have found many Scriptures that address the *why* of our suffering. Let me share just a few of them with you.

In the Bible, we are warned that God does not think as we think, nor does He do as we do, or as we *think* He should do (Isaiah 55:8-9). Consider this premise as you read the question Solomon asks: "*Man's goings are of the Lord; how can a man then understand his own way?*" (Proverbs 20:24 KJV). If the desire of my heart is to know God's will and to live my life in alignment with the will and the ways of God, wouldn't it logically follow that I should not always expect to understand the way I'm going? Obviously, that includes our suffering.

Moses shared an insight with us that we should add to the mix as we consider what God has said to us in His Word about the suffering of His people. He wrote: "*There are secrets the Lord your God has not revealed to us, but these words which he has revealed are for us and our children to obey forever*" (Deuteronomy 29:29 TLB).

According to Moses, there are secrets God has determined to keep secret. (Perhaps these secrets are on a need to know basis.) However, the things God wants us to do have been made plain through His Word, especially the Living Word, His beloved Son. But, if God has willed to remain silent about His secrets, then it would be pompous arrogance for us to say we can answer all of the why questions regarding the suffering of God's people.

Where did we ever get the idea we should expect to understand everything that happens to us? Where did we ever get the absurd notion that God owes us an explanation for everything He has done and is doing in our world and in our lives? If God gave us an explanation for everything and the answers to all of our *why* questions, the very essence of faith, and the need for faith, would be eliminated.

Almighty God has willed that without faith, we cannot please Him or come to Him (Hebrews 11:6). God is pleased when we echo those words of Job, "*Though He slay me, yet will I trust Him*" (Job 13:15 NKJV). God is pleased when we come to Him in our crucibles of suffering and cry, "If you heal me, that's all right. But, if you don't heal me, that's all right too, because <u>You</u> are all right!"

When God gave us the Scriptures, He had much to say about the why of suffering. An explanation that means a lot to me is found in chapter 5 of Paul's letter to the Romans. God's people sometimes suffer because there are times when God wants His people to learn how to access the grace He has made available to all His people:

Paul writes that God has given us access, by faith, to a quality of grace (charisma) that makes it possible for us to stand for Christ in this world, and live lives that glorify God. Then Paul writes we should rejoice in our tribulation, because it is our suffering that sometimes forces us to access the grace God has made available to us: "*We also rejoice in our sufferings, because we know that suffering produces perseverance; perseverance, character; and character, hope. And hope does not disappoint us, because God has poured out his love into our hearts by the Holy Spirit, whom he has given us*" (Romans 5:3-5 NET).

AMAZING GRACE

In another wonderful verse about grace from the pen of the Apostle Paul, we read: "*God is able to make all grace abound toward you, that you, always having all sufficiency in all things, might abound unto every good work*" (2 Corinthians 9:8 NKJV). This is the most emphatic verse in the Bible about the grace God has made available to His people.

I heard Dr. A.W. Tozer say, "When you read your New Testament and then look at our churches today, you cannot help but allow the thought that God oversold the product in the New

Testament." Since the superlatives Paul used in the verse above are true, how can we explain the pathetic lack of dynamic charisma in our churches today?

One pastor said, "When the Lord returns, my congregation will be the first to be resurrected, because the New Testament says, 'The dead in Christ will rise first!'" Another pastor, confronting the same lack of spiritual dynamic in his congregation, profiled the spiritual impotence of his people this way: "Ready, get set (in concrete), and never go."

God told the Apostle Paul, "*My grace is sufficient for you*" (2 Corinthians 12:9). The *spiritual anemia* in many of our churches today makes it seem we should follow that statement with the question, "True or false?" We must conclude that grace is available to us today, but we are not accessing the grace that is available (Romans 5:2). Perhaps we don't know how to access the grace of God today. Or, could it be that we don't believe in the grace of God today?

Another great biblical passage on the subject of suffering and the purpose of life is Isaiah's sermon about building a highway (Isaiah 40:3-5). Jesus told us John the Baptist was the greatest of all the prophets (Luke 7:28). Since we preachers often compile the sermons of other preachers, I have always been grateful that the greatest of all the prophets came preaching somebody else's sermons –the sermons of Isaiah.

This is the way Luke described John the Baptist preaching this sermon: "*As it is written in the book of the words* [sermons] *of Isaiah the prophet, saying: 'the voice of one crying in the wilderness: prepare the way of the Lord; make his paths straight. Every valley shall be filled and every mountain and hill brought low; the crooked places shall be made straight and the rough ways smooth; and all flesh shall see the salvation of God*'" (Luke 3:4-6 NKJV). Handel immortalized the great sermon of Isaiah in his famous oratorio.

HOW TO BUILD A HIGHWAY IN THE MARKETPLACE

Briefly summarized, Isaiah and John the Baptist preached that when you build a highway you do four things: you level mountains: you fill valleys, you straighten crooked places and you smooth out rough places. Basically, these two great prophets preached God will come into this world one day and He will need a highway on which to travel.

In ancient cultures, when a king wanted to visit a distant town or village in his kingdom, a highway was built on which he could travel. While it was under construction, that highway was referred to as *The King's Highway*. The prophet's prophet, Isaiah, undoubtedly had that cultural tradition in mind when he used this inspired metaphor in his profound sermon.

According to these two great prophets, the highway on which God was going to come into this world was the perfect life of the Messiah. The mountains of pride were going to be completely leveled in His perfect life; His valleys, or the empty places in His life, were going to be completely filled with the Holy Spirit all the time; the crooked ways of sin were going to be perfectly straight, and the Messiah was going to respond to the rough spots in His life, especially His cross, in such a way that the rough places were going to be made smooth.

When those four dimensions of the perfect life of the Messiah were in place, God would have a *highway* on which He could travel into this world. That is precisely what happened. I like to think of John the Baptist introducing Jesus by preaching, "Here He is! Here is the highway on which God is traveling into this world!"

After Jesus had been on earth for thirty-three years, He told His apostles who were celebrating the Passover with Him that He was going to leave this world, referring to His death on the cross and His resurrection. After His death and resurrection, He told these same apostles: "*As the Father has sent Me, I also send you*" (John 20:21 NKJV).

The original language in which these words of Jesus are recorded reveals that when Jesus spoke these words, He was saying to the apostles, "In exactly the same way I was sent into this world, I am sending you into the world." By application, Jesus was telling the apostles that just as He came into this world to be a highway for God, the apostles were to live their lives in this world as highways for God.

God wants our lives to be *highways* on which He can travel into our marketplaces. This is intensely true when we are suffering. How does that happen? Our lives can become highways for God when all of us pray this prayer every day: *Oh God, make my life a highway on which You can travel into this world and show Your salvation to the people I do business with today.*

Have you ever prayed that prayer? I dare you to pray that prayer! If you do, never pray lightly. When you sincerely offer that prayer, don't be surprised when God's *spiritual bulldozers* show up in your life.

CAUTION: GOD AT WORK!

When you pray that prayer, God will hang this sign over your life: "Caution: God at work!" As you pray that prayer, expect God's *bulldozers* to go to work leveling your mountains of pride, filling your valleys with His Holy Spirit, and straightening out your crooked places. Above all, expect God to give you the grace and strength to respond to your rough spots in such a way your life will be a smooth highway on which He can travel into marketplaces.

In chapter 15 of the Gospel of John, Jesus shared one of His greatest metaphors with the apostles while they were in a garden. Jesus and His apostles were apparently taking a break from the setting in which Jesus gave His longest recorded discourse, The Upper Room Discourse (John 13-16). In the Upper Room, Jesus challenged His apostles to be one with Him after His death and resurrection, so that His Word might be spoken on earth and His work might be accomplished on earth through them (John 13 and 14).

The apostles had been in awe of the profound teaching, preaching, and miracle-working ministry of Jesus. In the Upper Room, Jesus had told His apostles the key to His preaching, teaching, and supernatural ministry was that He and the Father were one. The Word of the Father was spoken on earth through Him and the work of the Father was accomplished on earth through Him because He was one with the Father.

While they were in the garden, Jesus pulled down a vine, which had many branches loaded with fruit. With His profound garden metaphor, Jesus was illustrating and applying the truth He had already taught the apostles in the Upper Room. He was saying, *I'm the Vine; you are the branches; the fruit is My work being accomplished and My Word being spoken on earth through you.* He also told them, *His Father is the Gardener* (John 15:1-16 paraphrased).

In this metaphor, the fruit does not grow on the vine. The fruit grows out on the branches because they are properly aligned with the Vine. The branches can bear no fruit without the Vine and the Vine can bear no fruit without the branches. By this metaphor, Jesus tells the apostles He is a Vine looking for branches. If the apostles want to be fruitful, they must be those branches and they must be in alignment with Him. If the Vine, Jesus, wants to see fruit produced, He must pass His life-giving power through the branches, the apostles.

Jesus the Vine wants to see this fruit produced far more than the apostles want to be fruitful. When our Lord gave the apostles this inspired metaphor, He was actually teaching two propositions: *Without Me, you can do nothing, and, I have decided that without you, I will do nothing.*

You may be wondering how all this relates to trials and testing in the marketplace. As Jesus taught this metaphor, He also told His apostles that when His heavenly Father sees a fruitful branch in alignment with Him, as the divine Gardener, the Father cuts it back (or prunes it) to increase the quality and the quantity of the fruit the branch will yield for Him. That pruning sometimes comes in the form of suffering.

In my lifetime I have personally known several men who lost everything and had a spiritual comeback that made them men of God. They confessed to me that the loss of everything led to a brokenness that was a pruning that profoundly influenced the quality and the quantity of the spiritual impact their life made in the marketplaces of this world. They were convinced that the discipline of their brokenness glorified God and became one of their most significant spiritual datelines.

A BIBLICAL EXAMPLE

What Paul calls his "*thorn in the flesh*" (2 Corinthians 12:7) was actually a cutback that forced the great Apostle to discover and implement the awesome strength and power of the risen Christ. I am convinced that his thorn was a physical illness that involved eyes that were running, sores and chronic fatigue. He wrote to the Galatians that his eyes were so terrible to look at they made them want to vomit. In Acts chapter 16, it is recorded that when Paul met these believers, his personal doctor, Luke, joined his missionary team because of Paul's illness. When he wrote his first chapters to the Corinthians, Paul mentioned severe weakness several times. I believe he lived with being chronically ill and fatigued all the days of his phenomenal ministry.

Another example of a cutback in Paul's life is his frequent imprisonments. Although he had a phenomenal ministry that put the Gospel and the Church of Jesus Christ on the world map, his greatest and most lasting influence was through his inspired writings. He wrote five of his inspired epistles while he was in prison. We might, therefore, consider the disabling *thorn* and the imprisonments of the Apostle Paul as *cutbacks* that looked like setbacks.

A PERSONAL EXAMPLE

For 40 years God had given me the burden and vision for what is now called *The Mini Bible College*. Like many busy pastors, I was an inch deep and many, many miles wide, operating as if activity was a substitute for productivity. There was no time to implement my vision until severe limitations provided the time and the discipline required to produce the material. The Lord knew that as a busy pastor, I would never in a million years have the wisdom or the discipline to prioritize the time to sit behind a desk long enough to put a four-year Bible study together, both in writing and broadcasts-around-the-world in over 30 languages.

It was as though the Lord looked on me and decided, "He's fruitful. But, I'm not satisfied with the quality or the quantity of the fruit his life is yielding for Me. So, I'm going to cut him back and make him more fruitful." It is incorrect to view my illness and limitations as a setback; rather, they demonstrate the cutback of a loving heavenly Father, Who would not permit me to go through life and miss my greatest opportunity to bring forth what Jesus called "*the fruit that lasts*" (John 15:16 NIV).

I love and thank the Lord for loving me enough to effect that intervention in my life and ministry. An old hymn asked the question in King James English, "Hast thou not seen how thy desires ere have been granted by what He ordaineth?" My desire and consuming passion throughout my adult life have been to teach *the whole Word to the whole world*. That desire has certainly been granted through my illness and limitations, which He has at the very least permitted, and may very well have directed.

I am by no means implying this is always the biblical

explanation for the suffering of God's people who have experienced limitations like mine. My claim of a biblical reason for my disability is an exception and not the rule. It may be worth considering, however, that a biblical explanation for your trials could be that your suffering is a cutback, even though it may appear to be a setback.

One of the most profound of the many passages of Scripture addressing the redemptive quality that can accompany suffering is found in 2 Corinthians 6, where Paul tells us that suffering is like a God-ordained *seminary* in which ministers of the Gospel are in training. There is a sense in which this *seminary* never ends. The apostle writes that by passing through this seminary of suffering, we can be proven to be the ministers of God. When Paul uses the word *minister*, he does not mean a clergyman; he means the minister that every believer is designed, created, and recreated by God to be.

How do we prove ourselves to be ministers in the way Paul uses that word? Paul tells us how God uses suffering to equip us for our ministries when he writes: "*In all things we approve ourselves as the ministers of God.* [And how are we approved as ministers of God?] *In afflictions, in necessities, in distresses, in stripes* [beatings], *in imprisonments, in tumults* [angry mobs], *in labors, in watchings, in fastings*" (2 Corinthians 6:3-5).

I call these adversities a *wringer*. (Old washing machines had a wringer, through which the wet soapy clothes were passed to squeeze the soapy water out of them. It was a very painful experience to get your hand caught in one of those wringers!) As we read about these challenging adversities, we read a description of the daily life experience of this great apostle. You can find some of the *wringers* of the Apostle Paul documented in the second half of the book of Acts and summarized in 2 Corinthians 11:23-27:

"I have worked much harder, been in prison more frequently, been flogged more severely, and been exposed to death again and again. Five times I received from the Jews the forty lashes minus one. Three times I was beaten with rods, once I was stoned, three times I was shipwrecked, I spent a night and a day in the open sea, I have been constantly on the move. I have been in danger from rivers, in danger from bandits, in danger from my own countrymen, in danger from Gentiles; in danger in the city, in danger in the country, in danger at sea; and in danger from false brothers. I have labored and toiled and have often gone without sleep; I have known hunger and thirst and have often gone without food; I have been cold and naked. ..." (NIV).

When we find ourselves in a wringer, the important thing is our response to that wringer. In verse 2 Corinthians 6:6, Paul tells us how to respond to our wringers when he writes: "*by pureness, by knowledge, by longsuffering, by kindness*" (KJV). In verses six and seven of this passage, Paul goes on to describe where we can find the spiritual resources to respond to our "wringers" as we should when he writes: "*by the Holy Ghost, by love unfeigned, by the Word of truth, by the power of God, by the armor of righteousness on the right hand and on the left.*"

At the end of the passage, in verses eight to ten, Paul describes the *results* when we respond to our wringers of life by drawing from the spiritual resources that are available to us when he writes: "*By honor and dishonor, by evil reputation and good reputation, as deceivers and yet true, as unknown and yet well known, as dying, and behold we live, as chastened and not killed, as sorrowful yet always rejoicing, as poor yet making many rich, as having nothing and yet possessing all things."*

These nine paradoxes profile the witness of the marketplace disciple who has been trained in God's seminary of suffering. Does what I am now writing mean you and I are not going to be qualified marketplace disciples unless or until we have suffered, or unless we know what it means to have a hurting heart? Not at all! We all know great servants of the Lord who have not suffered. However, I do believe we should agree with the Apostle Peter, who wrote we should not think it strange when challenging difficulties enter our lives:

"*Dear friends, don't be surprised at the fiery trials you are going through, as if something strange were happening to you. Instead, be very glad—for these trials make you partners with Christ in his suffering, so that you will have the wonderful joy of seeing his glory when it is revealed to all the world. So be happy when you are insulted for being a Christian, for then the glorious Spirit of God rests upon you*" (1 Peter 4:12-14 NLT).

This is especially true when trials enter the life of a believer whom God plans to use as a fruitful and effective marketplace disciple.

THE ANATOMY OF A SIN

To return to the book of James, after profiling the way God uses suffering in the lives of His faithful followers, this great leader of the New Testament Church then profiles a kind of testing in which we should not rejoice: the temptations to sins of sexual immorality. God is not the source of the temptation to sin. In the second half of chapter 1 of his letter, James gives us what we might call *The Anatomy of a Sin*. As he emphatically teaches that the temptation to sin does not come from God, he informs us that this kind of temptation does not even come from the devil. The temptation to sin in this way comes from within you and me.

It works this way: first, there is something you see. We might call it a <u>lure</u>. Then there is <u>lust</u>, or a strong desire for what you saw. It is as if the lure you saw is a piece of metal and your lust is like a powerful magnet. If you do not do something to break up that magnetic field between your lust and that lure, one day there will be the confrontation of <u>temptation</u>.

According to James, temptation is not sin. You have not sinned just because you have been tempted to sin. We are told our Lord was "*tempted in all points like as we are, yet without sin*" (Hebrews 4:15). An old church father said you cannot stop the birds from flying over your head, but you can keep them from building a nest in your hair. It is not a sin to be tempted, but temptation very often leads to overt acts of sin. When we yield to temptation and actually sin, the consequences of sin are always death (Romans 6:23).

Jesus taught this concept by illustrating how consequences differ. There is a broad way that leads to destruction and a narrow disciplined way that leads to life. Two houses are hit by storms. One stands, the other collapses. The one that stands pictures the person who knows and applies Jesus' teaching. The house that collapses pictures the person who knows yet does not apply His teaching. These arguments from consequences are found in His

Sermon on the Mount (Matthew 5-7). However, they can be found all the way through the teachings of Jesus.

As I have already observed, Jesus taught it is better to pluck out your right eye than to go to hell with two good eyes; He also used the same metaphor with *your right hand or your right foot*. The essence of the application in my opinion is that, if what you are looking at is causing you to sin, stop looking. This has great application today because of the curse of pornography. If what you are doing with your hand is leading you to sin, stop doing it. And if where your foot is taking you is causing you to sin don't go there anymore. The point is: do you or do you not want to commit sexual sin?

I have a good friend who graduated from a prestigious university and found an excellent position in the Los Angeles area of California. He did very well and was successful professionally. Women were hitting on him in ways he found difficult to resist. When he married a devout woman, they picked out Williamsburg, Virginia on the map and moved here because my friend did not want to live with the temptations of such an amoral culture. This can be an application for the metaphor Jesus used about cutting off your foot if it is causing you to sin.

If you do not want to commit sexual sin, you must win your battle with sin at the level of lust before you face the confrontations of temptation. Jesus taught us to pray every day: "*And don't let us yield to temptation, but rescue us from the evil one*" (Matthew 6:13 NLT).

One Monday night many years ago, my wife had to drive our youngest daughter back to her university. It meant that she would be gone for six or seven hours. At that point I was a paraplegic confined to a wheelchair. I was watching a football game on television. Every thirty minutes or so there was an advertisement promoting and selling pizza. I truly love pizza but I'm not supposed to have it because I am a diabetic. Each time the commercial was shown I developed a stronger desire for that pizza. They said they would deliver within thirty minutes or the pizza was free.

I had a telephone and some money so I eventually called and ordered a very small pizza. I told them I was in a wheelchair and so they were to walk in with the delivery. When that happened I told the man to place the pizza on the blanket that was on my lap and take the box with him (I was committing the perfect crime!). My wife returned and after some conversation, she picked up the blanket because she wanted to fold it. It was on the floor by this time. When she did, a small pizza crust dropped to the floor. The consequences were disastrous!

Those advertisements became like a metal lure for me. My strong desire for the pizza was lust, like a strong magnet. Since I did not break up the magnetic field between my lust and that lure, the pizza ended up in my lap. When I used this story one Sunday morning to teach the anatomy of a sin, I was surprised at the loud laughter I heard in response to my story. I then added the words "If it's pizza, it's funny. But if it were another woman it would be tragic!"

IN SUMMARY

James writes about how God can grow us spiritually in all

our trials. However, James also refers to this other matter, the temptation to sin. God is not the source of the sequence of temptation that leads to sin and to death. There is nothing good about sin, and that should be repeated for emphasis. There is really nothing good about sin. James has given us this anatomy of a sin because he does not want us to sin. A summary of what James has written could be this: tested to *life*, tempted to *death* and taught the *difference*!

DIFFERENT KINDS OF MARKETPLACE TEMPTATIONS

The temptation to commit sexual sin is not the only temptation a disciple faces in the marketplace. In this book, I have emphasized the proposition that disciples in the marketplace are to impact the lives of those they meet and do business with in the marketplace.

A hard reality is that those a disciple meets and does business with in the marketplace can also impact that marketplace disciple.

I've met missionaries who went to Hawaii to do good – and they made good, becoming very wealthy by getting involved in the import/export business. Unfortunately, their business success distracted them from the purpose for which they went to Hawaii. In the same way, marketplace disciples can be distracted and impacted with the temptation to succumb to the *love of money*, which can be the root of all kinds of evil. Money is not a root of all evil. The *love* of money is a root of all evil. When you do business with people who are wealthy and you discover ways you could make a lot of money, it is easy for you to forget why you have been called to the marketplace.

As we learned in the Parable of the Unjust Steward, we are to be good managers of the wealth we may accumulate in the marketplace. As faithful stewards we are to be successful business people. While it is not wrong to be wealthy, it is our responsibility to accumulate wealth for our Lord and then manage it for Him. But to be impacted by the love of money, the power that comes with wealth and all the things and pleasures money can buy, is something else. The Apostle Paul wrote: "*Those who want to get rich fall into temptation and a trap and into many foolish and harmful desires that plunge men into ruin and destruction. For the love of money is a root of all kinds of evil. Some people, eager for money, have wandered from the faith and pierced themselves with many griefs. But you, man of God, flee from all this*" (1Timothy 6:9-11 NIV).

We also considered the Parable of the Sower, where Jesus taught that the weeds which choke the plant God wants to use to make a person fruitful are things like the deceitfulness of riches and pleasures. The fundamental issue about wealth accumulation is stewardship. To whom does that wealth belong?

When I was in my early thirties, I had an elder who realized that I had a prejudice toward wealthy people. He was an older, white-haired godly man who loved me like a son. After lunch we were driving through a city in Florida. He remarked that he owned a particular high-rise building and then an entire neighborhood. I said to him, "John I don't know what I would do if I had that kind of wealth." He responded, "The Lord knows, and that's why He hasn't given it to you." He then confronted me with my attitude toward wealthy people. I actually did not believe a person could believe and accumulate great wealth with so much need in this world, especially the need of those who are spreading the Gospel to the ends of the earth.

My incorrect view was partly because I had never known a wealthy believer who was a faithful steward of their wealth. I was born into a family of six girls and five boys and our father worked as a mailman and a taxi driver in Pittsburgh. This dear elder was also from Pittsburgh and was the eldest of nine children. He promised his father on his father's deathbed that if his brothers and sisters were called to be missionaries, he would provide all the financial support they needed. At the time he made that promise, he was selling pots and pans door-to-door in Pittsburgh. Many years later, when he saw his youngest sibling off on a ship in New York City to the mission field, his accountant shook his hand abruptly. When he asked why he had done that the accountant said, "I just wanted to know what it feels like to shake hands with a millionaire!"

That was during the thirties when there were not many millionaires. At the time I knew him, he was supporting an extraordinary number of missionaries. Keeping track of all of them was like a full-time business. The way he expressed it to me was that the Lord knew He could trust him with money and so He did entrust him with a lot of wealth. He was the first wealthy man I met who was a faithful steward of what belonged to God.

My partner in ministry, Dois Rosser, is another wealthy-yet-faithful steward of what belongs to God. Dois is now in his early nineties and is very busy managing over 4,500 church buildings, schools and orphanages his ministry has built all over the world.

He also oversees the translation of the *Mini Bible College* into a growing number of languages all over this world. It is thrilling for me to be in harness with the most faithful steward I have ever known. His example is leading many to retire early and do nonprofit work. Several of them work with him daily, *nurturing believers and assisting Church growth around the world.*

Earlier you read how I have greatly benefited from the mentors who have invested themselves in me and my ministry. It is sadly possible you have never had anyone to mentor you in your faith journey. Please accept my encouragement to seek a mentor, but until you find one, let me offer a word of encouragement. God is our Mentor and He mentors us even before we come to faith, and especially after He brings us to faith. He uses everything we experience, both negative and positive experiences, to shape us into the people He wants us to be for His glory. We learn by action and reaction, even our reaction to what we are taught that may not be true.

Trust Him to be your Mentor. Claim these two verses from Paul's letter to the Philippians: "*being confident of this, that he who began a good work in you will carry it on to completion until the day of Christ Jesus. For it is God who works in you to will and to act in order to fulfill His good purpose*" (Philippians 1:6; 2:13).

The first verse declares that the God who began a good work in you will perform that good work until the day of Jesus Christ, the return of Jesus Christ in His Second Coming. The second verse declares that the reason for this hope is not in us but in the God who is at work in us. Trust God, Who always finishes what He begins because it is He who began the work of faith in us and it is

He who will finish that work according to His good pleasure, not yours or mine.

Chapter Thirteen
Born Again and the Marketplace

Although I have made several observations about the new birth, I now want to profile what the new birth looks like in the lives of people I have known. There is so much misunderstanding along with a superficiality and shallow interpretation of the new birth that I must address the subject in this way. I am also motivated because so much of what I am writing about the mission and ministry of the marketplace disciple is impossible if that disciple is not truly born again.

John Wesley preached so often on the text that you must be born again that some asked him, "Mr. Wesley, why do you always preach that you must be born again?" His response was always, "Because you *must* be born again!"

These words *born again* are used so often and in so many ways we must clarify what they mean and what they do not mean. In America when the Chrysler Corporation was going belly up and then a great leader named Lee Iacocca saved the company, people referred to Chrysler as being born again. When Jimmy Carter was in the White House he was perhaps the first president of the United States who publicly professed to be born again. Later when his administration was failing and then had a comeback, Time Magazine put his picture on the cover, over the words, *Born Again*!

It was Jesus who put these two words together, and in all the teachings of Jesus, there is only one place where He used these words. If you carefully read the Apostle John's Gospel prologue, however, you find him laying out what he is going to tell us (1:1-18). John informs us that his purpose is to show us how those who responded to Jesus properly were born again. He then gives us example after example of people who were born again when they related to Jesus in the right way. We can say the Gospel of John is really all about the new birth.

However, the only time Jesus used these words together is recorded for us in John 3:

"There was a man of the Pharisees named Nicodemus, a ruler of the Jews. This man came to Jesus by night and said to Him, 'Rabbi, we know that You are a teacher come from God; for no one can do these signs that You do unless God is with him.' Jesus answered and said to him, 'Most assuredly, I say to you, unless one is born again, he cannot see the kingdom of God.'

"Nicodemus said to Him, 'How can a man be born when he is old? Can he enter a second time into his mother's womb and be born?' Jesus answered, 'Most assuredly, I say to you, unless one is born of water and the Spirit, he cannot enter the kingdom of God. That which is born of the flesh is flesh, and that which is born of the Spirit is spirit. Do not marvel that I said to you, 'You must be born again.' The wind blows where it wishes, and you hear the sound of it, but cannot tell where it comes from and where it goes. So is everyone who is born of the Spirit.' Nicodemus answered and said to Him, 'How can these things be?'" (John 3:1-9).

This is one of the most familiar and most read passages in the four Gospels. Yet I submit to you it is one of the most misinterpreted and misapplied Scriptures in the Bible. The first observation I would like you to make as you study these nine verses is that the experience of being born again is not an end in itself but a means to an end. That end is the Kingdom of God.

The misinterpretation goes something like this: many believe Jesus was saying you will never see heaven nor enter heaven until you are born again. He clearly was not talking about heaven after we die when He spoke these words to Nicodemus. To understand the end to which the new birth is the means, we simply must know something about the Kingdom of God. Let me give you a short history lesson about the Kingdom of God.

GOD'S KINGDOM IN THE OLD TESTAMENT

Under Moses, the children of Israel had leadership according to God's will. The Lord wanted them to live in a theocracy, which means God ruling His people. All God needed for a theocracy was a prophet-priest like Moses (and others like Samuel). When Moses interceded with God on the people's behalf, he was a priest (see, for example, Numbers 11:1-2; 21:7). When Moses came down from Mount Sinai with words from God for the people, he was a prophet (Exodus 20-24). As long as God had someone like Moses, He could rule the people. This prophet-priest could be the conduit and vehicle of God's will, and God could govern His people. That theocracy was God's plan for the government of His chosen people.

In the book of First Samuel, we read Samuel was a prophet and a priest. But when Samuel grew old and the Israelites perceived his sons did not have the integrity of their father, they told Samuel they wanted to have a king like all the other nations (1 Samuel 8:1-5). Distraught, Samuel did a body slam and fervently prayed to the Lord. God told him not to take this rejection personally because

He, God, was the One the people were really rejecting. They preferred a human king, rather than having God as their King. In effect, God told Samuel, *If they want kings, Samuel, we will give them their kings!* (1 Samuel 8:6-22).

This parallels their experience in the desert when they wanted meat rather than manna and God gave them meat until it ran out their noses and they vomited meat. God will give us what we want even if it sends leanness to our souls. *"And He gave them their request, but sent leanness into their soul"* (Psalm 106: 15). In the kingdom literature of the Old Testament, we see God give them kings the way He gave them meat in the wilderness.

This introduces us to the concept of the Kingdom of God. The kingdom the people wanted was a national, earthly kingdom that governed a specific nation of people. To make that arrangement work, God needed a king who would obey Him and He needed priests who would come into His presence on behalf of the people. He also needed prophets to take a word from Him in His presence and then speak that word to the people and their leaders.

In summary, in the Old Testament, the kingdom God wanted was literal. It was a historical and geographical realm over which God was sovereign, with God Himself wanting to be the only Ruler over a specific people, in a specific place, at a specific time in history. The people, however, rejected God as their king and asked for human kings, which they got. What was the result? Tragedy!

I remember a lady who had never read the Bible before. She was a cultured, sophisticated person, who said of the kingdom books of the Old Testament: "I have never read anything so horrible in my life. If it were not for the Holy Spirit, I could never have gotten through these books. This is terrible!" Well, it is!

Remember that God never wanted His people to have these kings or the consequences of having those kings. The Lord was not responsible for all we read about in the kingdom literature – the kings were, because most of them were wicked. The people, too, were responsible because they wanted and chose those kings. As you read these Kingdom books, don't forget God never wanted them to have those kings. God put it this way through the Prophet Hosea: "*In my anger I gave you kings, and in my fury I took them away*" (Hosea 13:11 NLT).

GOD'S KINGDOM IN THE NEW TESTAMENT

The Kingdom Literature History Books provide a context that helps us understand the concept of The Kingdom of God in the New Testament. After the Jews returned from awful captivity to their land to rebuild their Temple and their city, they experienced 400 silent years after the prophet Malachi died. God did not speak in the sense of Special Revelation again until the New Testament period.

By that time the Jews had been conquered again, and this time their conqueror was the Roman Empire. The New Testament begins when John the Baptist and Jesus Christ the Messiah break a 400-year silence by preaching God's message. What was their message? The Good News of the Kingdom of God!

Jesus said that He was not preaching the geographical, national, or historical kingdom the people had rejected. Rather, He wanted the people to know God was willing to be their King again, but this time on an individual basis. This time the kingdom of God would be ***within*** them:

"Now when he was asked by the Pharisees when the kingdom of God would come, Jesus answered them and said, 'The kingdom of God does not come with observation, nor will they say, 'Here it is,' or 'There it is,' because the kingdom of God is within you'" (Luke 17:20-21 NKJV).

Do you realize what this means? Any man, woman, boy, or girl who surrenders to God and asks God to fly His flag in their heart, confessing, "I want You to be my King, and I want to be Your subject," has seen and entered into the Kingdom of God!

That is what Jesus was talking about when He told Nicodemus that we will neither see the kingdom of God nor enter into it unless we are born again. He was not speaking of heaven after we die. This is the concept He was sharing with Nicodemus and with the whole world.

AIMING FOR THE BULL'S-EYE

When I was a young pastor, I discovered my Elders had this misinterpretation of Jesus' teaching regarding the new birth. We had a retreat and I gave them an assignment, asking them to study Matthew 6:19-34 and answer two questions. My first question was, according to this passage of Scripture, what should your priorities be? I asked them to think of their priorities as a target with a bull's eye surrounded by 12 or 18 circles. Especially in light of verse 33, which tells us to seek first the Kingdom of God and what He shows us to be right, what should be the bull's eye of your priority target? Then, with that perspective established, how would you label those 18 circles that surround your bull's eye?

My second question was, "Based on how you spend your time, your energy, your gifts, your health, your talent, your money and all the things that measure the essence of your life, what actually are your priorities?" I urged them and challenged them to be honest in the way they answered my second question.

When they gathered together after about two hours of thinking privately about my assignment they were very honest in the way they answered my questions. The first man to share was the one who had been a believer and an Elder the longest. He said that for the first time in his life he understood that God was to be the first priority of his life. I was amazed because I had preached that for years yet he apparently did not hear what I was saying.

Then when it came to my second question he said, "To be perfectly honest, based on how I am spending the things that make up my life, the most important thing in my life is me, my wife and son and financial security in retirement. I wonder where Jesus fits into all of this?"

I asked him if he was born again. He answered enthusiastically that he surely was, so I asked if he could tell us about it. He told us he went to a tent meeting. "On Tuesday night the evangelist preached on hell and it was hell, brother! Then Wednesday night he preached on heaven and it was beautiful. The preacher then asked those to come forward who would rather go to heaven than hell. I went down that sawdust trail and I've been born again ever since!" When I asked how long it had been since he had that experience, he responded it had been 42 years.

When I asked him what had been happening in his life in the last 42 years he responded he had been working for the government on a large naval base. When I asked if he did that because he believed that was the candlestick on which the Lord placed him to be a witness for Him, he said, "I never thought about the Lord and my occupation. I mean, we have to make a living, don't we?"

Several of the other Elders shared in a similar way. Frankly, I have observed over many decades as a pastor that the perspective on being born again I discovered at that retreat is typical. After that time of sharing, I asked them to open their Bibles to John 3:1-9. I pointed out to them that in answer to my first question, most of them shared this misunderstanding about God being the bull's eye of their priority target. They had never realized that God is to be their King and that He and His Kingdom, along with what He shows us to be right, should govern their lives.

In answer to my second question, they confessed they had not entered into that kind of relationship with God. Then I challenged them with this: since Jesus clearly taught that seeing the Kingdom of God and entering into that relationship with God was the end to which the new birth was the means, did they really have a right to claim that they were born again?

Clearly, seeing and entering into a relationship with God, where He is our King and we are His subjects, is the purpose of the new birth. It follows that we know we have been born again when we join the spiritual AAA club and say to God: "Anything, Anywhere, Anytime!"

Since there is something to believe and Someone to receive when we are born again, another way we know we have been born again is what the Apostle Paul labeled the fruit of the Spirit: "*But the fruit of the Spirit is love, joy, peace, patience, kindness, goodness, faithfulness, gentleness and self-control*" (Galatians 5:22-23). By this expression, Paul means there will be evidence of the miraculous reality that we have received the risen, living Christ into our hearts and our lives. I have written about the nine fruit of the Spirit at some depth in chapter 2 and I will not repeat that here. You may want to review what I have written in chapter 2 at this point to repeat for emphasis something of the miracle work of God within us, our evidence of the new birth.

LEARNING FROM THE EXPERTS

Now that we have focused this critical issue of something to believe and Someone to receive, we can raise the question, how do we receive the Spirit of the living Christ into our heart or life? Here again I would like to address a need for some clarification.

In the sixties, I had the privilege of spending a week on the campus of Duke University with a man named Paul Little. He was an extraordinary evangelist to students all across America for Intervarsity Christian Fellowship, a ministry that reaches out effectively to college students. Paul Little was the most gifted evangelist to students I ever met.

Several decades later I had the privilege of attending a seminar that was led by Dr. Bill Bright, the founder of Campus Crusade for Christ. Bill Bright had been a businessman before he went to seminary and founded his worldwide miraculous ministry. His message to about 150 of us pastors was put in the terminology of the marketplace. If you were in sales and you wanted to make a lot of money, you had to get into sales management. To do that you had to train other people to sell. As a tool, you should have a sales manual that would insult your intelligence but would make it possible for others to be apprenticed into good sales people.

Bill said, "You pastors, take your Elders or leading laypeople with you when you visit new families. They may observe as you lead those people to Christ. However they cannot go out the next night and do what they watched you do unless you have a manual that would insult your intelligence, and which you do not need. But since they do not have your vast knowledge of Scripture and experience, they cannot do what you did unless you give them such a manual." Then he challenged us to use his little pamphlet which he called *Four Spiritual Laws*.

Both Bill Bright and Paul Little brought their Gospel presentation to a verdict by asking people to bow their heads and ask Jesus to come into their hearts. Between fraternity and sorority meetings at Duke University with Paul Little, I asked him if he could give me a verse of Scripture upon which he based his method of closure in his Gospel presentation.

At the pastor's retreat, each time we had our meals together at small tables, Bill Bright was at my table. I must say I held him and Paul Little in such high esteem I hesitated to ask them my questions about the way they led people to Christ, because they were the best in the world at doing so. Paul Little had an MBA and, as I mentioned earlier, Bill Bright was in business before he went to seminary. They knew from their marketplace experience the importance of bringing what they were presenting to a verdict of closure. I promised the Lord that if Bill Bright sat at my table for the last meal, since he was such a sweet and humble man of God, I would ask him what I had asked Paul Little. When we began the meal, he was not in the dining room but there was an empty chair beside me. He came late to the meal and sat right beside me.

When I asked these two great men of God for a verse of Scripture on which they based their invitation to ask people to bow their head and ask Christ to come into their hearts, they both referred to Revelation 3:20 where Jesus is standing at the door and knocking that He might gain entrance into our life: "*Behold, I stand at the door and knock. If anyone hears My voice and opens the door, I will come in to him and dine with him, and he with Me.*"

I responded that when you examine the context of this verse, you find that it was part of a letter the risen Christ wrote to an apathetic lukewarm church of uncommitted professing believers. He was asking shallow believers to let Him become part of the real areas of their lives. It was not a presentation of Christ as Savior that was made to secular people to receive Jesus Christ for the first time.

They also both referred to chapter 1 of the Gospel of John where we read: "*But as many as received Him, to them He gave the right to become children of God, to those who believe in His name: who were born, not of blood, nor of the will of the flesh, nor of the will of man, but of God*" (John 1:12-13).

My response was that these opening verses of the Gospel of John were describing the way people responded to Jesus when He was here in His earthly body. When they met Jesus, they certainly did not bow their heads and ask Him to come into their heart. For clarification, this verse adds, "*Even to those who believe in His name.*"

They also both referred to Colossians 1:27, where the Apostle Paul writes: "*Christ in you, the hope of glory.*" The Living Bible has

Paul sharing with us that he was raised up by God to share a secret with the Church, and that secret was that Christ in our hearts is our only hope of glorifying God. This phrase certainly establishes the reality that Christ is in us. But it does not describe how He gets there.

Again, the Apostle Peter gives us a beautiful description of how the new birth takes place in the life of a believer, describing the process in retrospect as he writes to people who have already been born again: "*Since you have purified your souls in obeying the truth through the Spirit in sincere love of the brethren, love one another fervently with a pure heart, having been born again, not of corruptible seed but incorruptible, through the word of God which lives and abides forever. Now this is the word which by the gospel was preached to you. Therefore, laying aside all malice, all deceit, hypocrisy, envy, and all evil speaking, as newborn babes, desire the pure milk of the word, that you may grow thereby, if indeed you have tasted that the Lord is gracious*" (1 Peter 1: 2-23, 25; 2:1-3).

Peter writes that they heard the Word of God when the Gospel was preached to them. They purified their souls by obeying the truth, which resulted in a sincere love of the brethren. They are exhorted by Peter to go on loving one another fervently. While this process was happening to them, they were being born again. The agent of their new birth was the Spirit working through the Word of God. This process was conceived in them by an incorruptible seed (the Greek word is *sperma*), which is the Word of God. Having been born again they are to "*desire the pure milk of the word*" that they may grow thereby.

When he exhorts them to "*desire the pure milk of the word,*" he uses Greek words which mean they are to go after the Word of God the way a newborn baby goes after the nipple because the baby knows their sustenance depends on what they are receiving from their mother's breast.

Observe here that the Word of God is the *prenatal* dynamic of the new birth experience from its conception, through the *gestation* period, to the crisis of the new birth, and on into the growth process. This is why it is critical that we get people into the Word of God and the Word of God into people. Likewise, it is critically important that you plan a structured regular time for getting into the Word of God before you begin your day in the busy and stressful marketplace.

MY HERO BILLY GRAHAM

Billy Graham has been a hero of mine since I was a freshman in college in 1949. The one time I met him privately was when he came to the area where I was a pastor in 1974. He called me and asked me if we could meet for lunch. I was mentoring a young navy dentist whose mother, a close friend of Billy's wife, Ruth, had asked him to call me for lunch.

As we were fellowshipping privately, I told him I was impressed the night before at the remarks he made while people were responding to his invitation. He had said something like, "For some of you, this is your new birth experience. For some of you, this is a matter of bringing your faith to a verdict. And for some of you, this is part of a gestation phase in your process of being born again."

I told him I almost jumped out of my seat when he said those last words because I had believed in that dimension of the new birth for some time, but I hesitated to preach it because it seemed to upset and confuse people. He very humbly said, "Don't quote me. I'm no authority!" I told him I thought people would be impressed if I told them Billy Graham agreed with me on this issue.

A CHRISTMAS CAROL SAYS IT WELL

Shortly after our Civil War, an extraordinary pastor in New York City named Phillips Brooks was depressed because two thirds of his congregation was dressed in black because they were widows. The church gave him a one year sabbatical and he spent that year in the Holy Land. That Christmas Eve, while sitting on a hill overlooking the little town of Bethlehem, he wrote my favorite Christmas carol.

In the first two verses of the carol, he reflected on the birth of the Christ child in that little town that first Christmas Eve. The second two verses are my favorite part of the carol because here he describes the way Christ is born in the heart of a human being today:

> "How silently, how silently God's wondrous gift is given.
> So, God imparts to human hearts the blessings of His heaven.
> No ear may hear His coming but in this world of sin
> Where meek souls will receive Him still the dear Christ enters in.
>
> Oh holy child of Bethlehem descend to us we pray.
> Cast out our sin and enter in be *born in us today.*

We hear the Christmas angels their great glad tidings tell.
Oh come to us, abide with us our Lord Emanuel."

In those words "be born in us today," Phillips Brooks agrees with Peter's profile and description of how the new birth takes place. The risen, living Christ is conceived, gestated and born in us today. That new birth experience is begun when we respond to the incorruptible seed of the Word of God. We might label that *spiritual conception.* As we continue to get into the Word and respond with obedience, our "prenatal" period of development continues until one day we experience the crisis of the new birth. The critical issue now becomes to sincerely, intentionally and aggressively desire the *sincere milk* of the Word that we may grow spiritually.

That is why I have devoted many decades, and as long as I have breath I will continue to devote my life, to *getting people into the Word of God and the Word of God into people.* One of the most critical factors in experiencing the new birth is how we respond to the Word of God. When Peter describes in retrospect how those people to whom he was writing were born again, he tells us it all began as they *obeyed* the Word, which was preached to them through the Gospel. Obedience makes the Word of God the powerful force it is meant to be in our life.

THE PARABLE OF THE SOWER

Jesus taught one of His most powerful and important parables about how we respond to the Word of God: *"A sower went out to sow his seed. And as he sowed, some fell by the wayside; and it was trampled down, and the birds of the air devoured it. Some fell on rock; and as soon as it sprang up, it withered away because it lacked moisture. And some fell among thorns, and the thorns sprang up with it and choked it. But others fell on good ground, sprang up, and yielded a crop a hundredfold. When He had said these things He cried, 'He who has ears to hear, let him hear!'*

"Now the parable is this: The seed is the word of God. Those by the wayside are the ones who hear; then the devil comes and takes away the word out of their hearts, lest they should believe and be saved. But the ones on the rock are those who, when they hear, receive the word with joy; and these have no root, who believe for a while and in time of temptation fall away. Now the ones that fell among thorns are those who, when they have heard, go out and are choked with cares, riches, and pleasures of life, and bring no fruit to maturity. But the ones that fell on the good ground are those who, having heard the word with a noble and good heart, keep it and bear fruit with patience" (Luke 8:5-8; 11-15).

When you visit the Holy Land today, you can still see farmers with a sack of seed under their left arm, reaching into the sack with their right hand and scattering seed as they walk back and forth across a hillside or a plot of ground. A summary of The Parable of the Sower could go like this:

A farmer goes out and sows seed in his field. The farmer takes the seed from his sack and scatters it. Some seed falls on hard soil, a path where people had been walking. That seed simply lies there on the surface. It never penetrates the soil, and the birds come and eat it.

Some of the farmer's seeds scatter where the earth was loose and those seeds start to put down roots, but under the surface of that soil there is rock. So the roots hit rock and turn back. When the sun came out, the plant produced by that seed scorches and does not bring forth any fruit.

Some of the seeds fall where the soil is much improved; it is deep, it is moist, and the seed takes root. But when the plants start to come up and grow, they encounter weeds, which choke off the plants so they, too, do not produce fruit. The last of the farmer's seed falls where the soil is good. There are no problems beneath or above the soil. That seed produces fruit – some thirty, some sixty and some a hundred times the seed that was planted.

Upon first reading this parable, we agree this parable should be called, *The Parable of the Sower.* When we study it carefully, however, we might think this parable should be called *The Parable of the Seeds*. Because *the seed is the Word*, this parable is a profound teaching about the Word of God and some of the issues involved when the Word of God is taught or preached. "*Take heed how you hear the Word of God*," is the way Luke applies the meaning of this parable (Luke 8:18). Still another good title for this parable could be *Four People in a Pew; Which One Are You*? This is because the parable is really all about how people respond to the Word of God when it is taught or preached.

Afterwards, when Jesus was alone with the apostles, they asked Him about the parable and He interpreted it for them. He told them the seed the farmer sowed is the Word of God and the four soils represent four ways people respond to the Word of God. When the Word is presented, the first person does not even understand the Word; their mind, or understanding, is not penetrated, and he brings forth no fruit.

The second person understands the Word. His mind is penetrated, but the rocky soil that prevents the seed from rooting deep into the earth represents what Jesus calls elsewhere *the hardened heart*. This suggests his will is not penetrated and his commitment is shallow. He believes the Word, and when tribulation or persecution comes, he quickly falls away or drops out, and brings forth no fruit.

The third person is not defeated by anything under the soil or within his life, like the understanding of his mind or the commitment of his will. He is defeated by forces above the soil or outside his life, like the deceitfulness of riches, and their accompanying pleasures. He may also be defeated by the "cares of this world," or by worrying about the riches he has or does not have. In the parable, these obstacles are weeds that choke the plant the Word would like to grow in the soil of that person's life. This third person is also unfruitful. We might say the first person is wearing a spiritual "hard hat." The second person has a hard heart, and the third is being distracted by hard choices.

The fourth person pictures the way Jesus would have all of us respond when we hear the Word of God. There is nothing under the soil or above the soil that prevents growth or fruit bearing from taking place. This pictures the person who determines that nothing within his life, like his understanding or his stubborn will, is going to keep him from being fruitful. He also determines that nothing in this world in the way of forces outside his life will keep him from fulfilling the purposes of God for giving him the Word of God.

As Luke describes this person, "*Having heard the Word with an honest and good heart*, [he] *keeps it*," and this makes him fruitful (Luke 8:15). Luke also describes the essence of this profound parable with these words: "*Be careful how you hear the Word of God*" (Luke 8:18).

Doing business in the marketplace teaches you to value highly what works and to under-value what does not work. Be just as pragmatic about what does and does not work when you teach or hear or read the Word of God. For example, determine what it means for you to be careful how you hear the Word of God. Be sure you are that fourth man Luke describes who receives the Word in an honest and good heart and keeps it.

The truth of this profound parable is obvious to anyone who teaches or preaches the Word of God. When the Word of God is taught or preached, these four people are always there and the discerning preacher or teacher can point them out to you.

All those who hear and teach the Scriptures should think much about this parable as they hear or teach the Word of God. First of all, we must look at our own soil. What kind of soil is God's seed finding in our life? Are we allowing God's Word to be productive? Are we very fruitful (100%) or just a little fruitful (30%)? Secondly, those who teach should be keenly aware of the hard reality that three-fourths of the time we teach and preach the Word of God, nothing happens. Unless those being taught understand the meaning of the Word they are hearing and surrender their will to obey what they hear and understand, nothing happens. Therefore, we must teach the Word simply enough to penetrate their understanding. We must also *prayerfully* bring our message to a verdict so the Holy Spirit might penetrate the wills of those who hear our teaching and preaching, leading to obedience, or nothing happens.

THE CRITICAL FACTOR OF PRAYER

We are not being challenged here in this great parable to produce "Bible experts" who know the Bible. Rather, Jesus calls us to nurture committed disciples of the Lord who practice the Word that has penetrated their understanding and their will. Thus, we must prayerfully hear, teach, and preach the Word. We also must pray the Holy Spirit will open the spiritual eyes and the wills of those who hear us, that they might understand and obey the Word of God – or nothing happens. We should pray He will give us, and those who hear us, the gift of faith, and the "will to do" the Word, so the Word will be fruitful (John 7:17; Philippians 2:13).

Although this great parable is not primarily about the new birth, it is about the way the Word of God is received. The planting of that Word is the key to the new birth happening to us and to those we lead. We must also rely on God to empower us, and those who hear us, to overcome all those forces in this world that work to ensure our hearing, teaching and preaching of the Word is unfruitful. Only God can overcome the forces that would prevent our effectiveness in planting His Word. That is why when we study, teach, or minister the Word, it must be "*prayer and the ministry of the Word;*" the two must go together (Acts 6:4).

When the apostles became distracted with a food services program, the first deacons were elected and charged with seeing to the business of the church so the apostles could give themselves continuously to prayer and the ministry of the Word. God greatly blessed their decision. Unless these issues are squarely and prayerfully faced, 75 percent of the time we teach and preach nothing will happen.

When Peter preached his powerful sermons following the Day of Pentecost, he bluntly stated that God gives His Holy Spirit to those who obey Him (Acts 5:32). When it comes to a relationship with God or the Holy Spirit, the operative word is *obey*. It is vitally important for us to remember it is obedience to the Word of God that makes the Scripture a powerful force in our lives, as well as in the lives of those we teach and mentor.

It is also important for us to remember that the objective of the new birth is the Kingdom of God; the reality that God wants to be our King and recruit us to be His subjects. In two very short parables, Jesus crisply and eloquently profiled what we might refer to as a total commitment to Jesus Christ: "*Again, the kingdom of heaven is like treasure hidden in a field, which a man found and hid; and for joy over it he goes and sells all that he has and buys that field. Again, the kingdom of heaven is like a merchant seeking beautiful pearls, who, when he had found one pearl of great price, went and sold all that he had and bought it*" (Matthew 13:44-46).

Here Jesus presents the Kingdom of God as a treasure hidden in a field. When a man finds this treasure for joy, not because it is a requirement, but for joy, he sells all that he has and buys the whole field that he might be sure to get that treasure. The same truth is repeated in the short parable about a man who is a connoisseur of valuable pearls. When he finds this pearl of great price, or the perfect pearl, he sells all that he has that he might buy that pearl. Jesus clearly states here that if you have not seen the Kingdom of

God to be the greatest treasure or pearl you have ever encountered, then you have really not seen the Kingdom of God or entered into the Kingdom of God. It would also follow that you are not born again.

FOCUSING THE ISSUE

In the privacy of my study, I have often had a conversation that went something like this. A man would say to me, "Pastor, I'm not sure I am Christian." I would respond by telling them the word *Christian* is only found three times in the Bible, and only once is it used by a believer. Sometimes it helps if we use the words the Bible uses to describe the followers of Jesus. I usually asked, "If you overheard us talking about you and we referred to you as an unbeliever would you be offended?" The answer was usually "Yes, that would offend me." Then you are a believer? The person I was interviewing usually confirmed they were a believer in Jesus Christ.

I would then ask them if they were born again. They might ask me what that really is. When I finished describing the new birth as it is described in the Bible like "*a new creation, old things passed away all things become new*" (2 Corinthians 5:17), they would often answer emphatically, "No." I would then ask, "Are you a disciple?" They often responded, "What's that?" And I would then respond, "That's the problem!" As I wrote in chapter 3 on the Great Commission, I agree with Dr. Dallas Willard that we are not obeying the Great Commission today because we are not making disciples. We are doing many wonderful things as His Church, but we are not making disciples.

We simply must get back to the basic charter of the Church,

the Great Commission. And we must have an authentic, correct perspective on what it means to be born again. If we return to these basics of Christianity, we will wake the sleeping giant of the Church and make it a dynamic force in our families, our culture and in our marketplaces.

PERSONAL APPLICATIONS

Now that I have reached the age of 82, I find myself looking back and reflecting on the journey of faith I have experienced with the Lord. I have been told that the Providence of God is like a Hebrew word; you have to read it backwards. Looking back, the Providence of God in my life is a no-brainer because it is so obvious. However, when I was living in the middle of many of the chapters in my journey of faith, I did not see the Providence of God at that time.

I am now thoroughly convinced of the beautiful reality that God has showed up in my life and that is the only explanation of my extraordinary journey. I have now removed from my vocabulary the words *fortunately* and *coincidentally*, because I no longer believe in luck. I believe in the Providence of God. Some spiritual heavyweight said that when we who are the followers of Jesus Christ think we have experienced a coincidence, we have merely discovered that God often prefers to remain anonymous. That's why I have eliminated the word *coincidentally* from my vocabulary.

It is my understanding that the famous evangelist Dwight L. Moody heard a devotional speaker say, "The world has yet to see what God can do with a man wholly yielded to him." When Moody heard that, he said in his heart, "By the grace of God, I'm going to be that man!"

At that time, Moody was a shoe salesman in Chicago. He became interested in reaching out to street children in what evolved into an extensive children's ministry. He then became an evangelist. Although he was not educated and could not even use good grammar when he preached, until Billy Graham, no evangelist ever spoke to more people face-to-face about the Gospel of their salvation than Dwight Moody. This was shortly after the Civil War in America. Moody did not use radio, television or the mass media and jet travel we have available to us today. On his death bed, the last words of Moody were, "The world has yet to see what God can do with a man wholly yielded to Him."

I reiterate that Dois Rosser is one of many examples I can share of business and professional people who are proving what God can do with *marketplace disciples* who are wholly surrendered to Him. Remember my earlier point, that our greatest ability is our availability.

A devout surgeon friend of mine told me that the word we use most in this life is the word, "Why?" and the word we are going to use most in the life to come is going to be the word, "Oh!". When he was in my home recently I told him that I'm not on the other side yet but I am already saying, "Oh!" When you accept the challenge of being an authentic marketplace disciple, get ready to say "Oh!" long before you are in the second dimension of your faith journey in Christ.

icm

INTERNATIONAL COOPERATING MINISTRIES

Mission Statement:
To nurture believers and assist church growth worldwide.

How do we do it? Two ways:

Mini Bible College: ICM-Partnered churches use Mini Bible College material by Pastor Dick Woodward, in their own language for teaching and nurturing believers in their congregation and Bible study groups as an outreach ministry of the local church.

ICM Church Building Program: provides a place and presence for believers in rural areas in over 65 nations around the globe.

ICM is a non-profit, trans-denominational parachurch ministry guided by our adherence to the Lausanne Covenant Statement of Faith. ICM is a ministry of the Rosser Foundation. 100% of every designated dollar goes to its purpose in the mission field.

www.icm.org
www.minibiblecollege.org

Mini Bible College Products

BOOKS	For a gift of...	Qty.	Total
Mini Bible College Old Testament Handbook	$10.00		
Mini Bible College New Testament Handbook	$10.00		
The God Who Hung on the Cross (PB)	$10.00		
The God Who Hung on the Cross (HC) 25th Anniversary Ed.	$15.00		
The 4 Spiritual Secrets	$10.00		
The First Christian Retreat - The Sermon on the Mount	$10.00		
God's Prescription for Marriage and Family	$10.00		
Thirty Biblical Reasons Why God's People Suffer	$5.00		
A Spiritual Compass: God's Eight Great Questions	$5.00		
Marketplace Disciples	$15.00		
BOOKLETS	**For a gift of...**		
How to be an Eagle Disciple	$5.00		
In Step with Eternal Values	$5.00		
A Prescription for Guidance	$5.00		
A Prescription for Peace	$5.00		
A Prescription for Self	$5.00		
A Prescription for Prayer	$5.00		
Communication: A Tool that Builds Marriages	$5.00		
Psalm 23: Sheep Talk	$5.00		
A Christmas Prescription	$5.00		
The Seven Spiritual Wonders of the World	$5.00		
Jonah: True Confessions of a Prophet	$5.00		
The 4 R's of Parenting	$5.00		
Ten Fingerprints of a Healthy Church	$5.00		
A Covenant for Small Groups	$5.00		
A Prescription for Love	$5.00		
Happiness that Doesn't Make Good Sense	$5.00		
AUDIO RESOURCES	**For a gift of...**		
Old and New Testament Teaching DVDs*	$150.00		
Old Testament Audio CDs*	$100.00		
New Testament Audio CDs*	$100.00		
Old and New Testament Audio CD*	$175.00		
The 4 Spiritual Secrets Audio Book	$10.00		
The God Who Hung on the Cross Audio Book	$10.00		
I'm In Him, He's In Me - Music CD	$10.00		

YOUR ORDER

Total Quantity / Gift Amount: $ ____________

Shipping: ____________

VA residents add 6% tax on products with *: ____________

Additional gift amount: ____________

TOTAL GIFT AMOUNT: $ ____________

Shipping Charges

$8.99 or less	$2.50
$9.00 - $25.99	$6.00
$26.00 - $50.99	$7.00
$51.00 - $100.99	$10.00
$101.00 - $25.00	$15.00
Above $250.00	Please call

Recipient

Name: ____________

Address: ____________

City, State, Zip: ____________

Phone: ____________

Email: ____________

To order via web visit www.icm.org/online_store

If paying by check, please make payable to ICM

Mail to: ICM, 1901 North Armistead Ave., Hampton, Virginia 23666-4311